Must Politics Be War?

Must Politics Be War?

Restoring Our Trust in the Open Society

KEVIN VALLIER

Oxford University Press is a department of the University of Oxford. It furthers
the University's objective of excellence in research, scholarship, and education
by publishing worldwide. Oxford is a registered trade mark of Oxford University
Press in the UK and certain other countries.

Published in the United States of America by Oxford University Press
198 Madison Avenue, New York, NY 10016, United States of America.

Library of Congress Cataloging-in-Publication Data
Names: Vallier, Kevin, author.
Title: Must politics be war? : restoring our trust in the open society / Kevin Vallier.
Description: New York, NY, United States of America : Oxford University Press, [2019] |
Includes bibliographical references and index.
Identifiers: LCCN 2018018341 (print) | LCCN 2018042421 (ebook) |
ISBN 9780190632847 (updf) | ISBN 9780190632854 (epub) |
ISBN 9780190632861 (online content) | ISBN 9780190632830 (cloth : alk. paper)
Subjects: LCSH: Political culture—United States. | Polarization (Social sciences)—
Political aspects—United States. | Liberalism—United States. | Civil society—United States.
Classification: LCC JK1726 (ebook) | LCC JK1726.V35 2018 (print) |
DDC 306.2—dc23 LC record available at https://lccn.loc.gov/2018018341

9 8 7 6 5 4 3 2 1

Printed by Sheridan Books, Inc., United States of America

To the partisans of all parties

CONTENTS

Introduction   1

PART ONE | Social Trust and Social Contract

CHAPTER 1   Moral Peace and Social Trust   17

CHAPTER 2   Trust and the Foundations of Public Justification   47

CHAPTER 3   Public Justification   79

PART TWO | A Liberal Constitutional Order

CHAPTER 4   Legal Systems   127

CHAPTER 5   Primary Rights   156

CHAPTER 6   Constitutional Choice   173

CHAPTER 7   Liberalism Justified   199

EPILOGUE   Liberal Politics Is Not War   220

Acknowledgments   223
Bibliography   227
Index   239

Must Politics Be War?

| Introduction

AMERICAN POLITICS IS MORE divided today than at any point since the Civil War.[1] There are fewer moderate politicians on either side of the political divide, and a spirit of hardened partisanship has made political compromise, even on issues where compromise is needed, all but impossible.[2] With the advent of internet politics and social media, and especially partisan cable news, Americans can insulate themselves from opposing points of view, reaffirming their own prejudices every minute of the day, and so grow more radical and intolerant over time.[3] Republicans largely inhabit a closed media circuit, with Fox News, Breitbart, and talk radio driving much of the political agenda of the Republican Party. And while the intellectual and media base of the Democratic Party is larger, the academy, where membership in the Democratic Party is increasingly ubiquitous, is becoming progressively hostile to alternative points of view.[4] Rising partisanship is perhaps part of the reason that many Americans, especially millennials, are losing their faith in liberal democracy.[5]

In light of our present predicament, one might reasonably wonder whether American politics isn't *invariably* a struggle for power between the righteous and the wicked. At present, American political life often looks like a brute contest for dominion, where the victors drag the country in their direction without concern or respect for the losers.

---

[1] Campbell 2016.
[2] Hetherington and Rudolph 2015.
[3] https://www.nber.org/papers/w23258.
[4] https://econjwatch.org/articles/faculty-voter-registration-in-economics-history-journalism-communications-law-and-psychology.
[5] For a review of some recent data, see http://www.washingtonpost.com/news/wonk/wp/2016/12/08/yes-millennials-really-are-surprisingly-approving-of-dictators/?utm_term=.b9272b63ede5.

Current American politics is war. Or is it that politics is always war, no matter the time or place? Can it ever be more than an out-an-out struggle? People have wondered this for centuries in times of strife and conflict. Whether the conflict is between the orthodox and the heretical, the rational and the superstitious, the racially pure and the impure, or the productive and the parasitic, the story is the same. Politics is an arena of strategic confrontation where parties struggle to defeat their opponents. Even democracy is a gladiatorial encounter. Philosopher David Enoch's remarks speak for many; with respect to politics, "there is no way out of the arena," and we are all mere players. We must "enter it, to fight, shoulder to shoulder . . . for what is just and good."[6] And, more famously, Michel Foucault argued that "politics is the continuation of war by other means."[7]

Indeed, many share this view, and the reason why is as simple as it is important. Many worry that they cannot *trust* people with different beliefs and interests. The presence of widespread disagreement on matters of fundamental importance makes it harder for us to understand one another, and so harder to see each other as persons of sincere and informed goodwill. We are therefore tempted to see our differences with others as irresolvable sources of conflict, and to assume that we must come to blows. Diverse societies cannot sustain social trust.

To believe such a thing would be to have a very dim worldview indeed. Fortunately, those that subscribe to it are mistaken. Diverse people exhibit social trust all the time, whenever they rely upon other persons to abide by the political, legal, and social rules that govern their day-to-day lives. A *moral peace* between persons is a state of society with a high degree of justified social trust in institutions constituted and governed by these rules, and it is within our grasp. Accordingly, this book explores the question of *which institutional structures can sustain moral peace between diverse persons*. Institutions that can sustain moral peace between diverse persons establish a political life that is not war.

The institutions that can sustain moral peace are those that can be jointly endorsed. Mutually justifiable institutions are ones that each person can follow from sincere moral conviction, and so help assure us that others can embrace these institutions on moral grounds despite their often foreign worldviews. When institutions are mutually justifiable, therefore, we can trust one another to abide by them despite our differences.

---

[6] Enoch 2013, p. 175.
[7] Foucault 1997, p. 48.

As this book will argue, liberal institutions and *only* liberal institutions are mutually justifiable, such that liberal institutions alone provide the conditions for moral peace between diverse persons. I understand liberal institutions as systems of equal civic, political, and economic rights that protect persons from control and domination by others. Liberal rights give each person or group the freedom to live their own lives their own way and so prevent persons from institutionalizing their own sectarian vision of the good or of justice.

Liberal rights thereby create an *open* society, where people are, as Karl Popper famously wrote, "faced with personal decisions," rather than living lives governed by rigid social rules that direct everyone to pursue a single vision of the social and common good.[8] A liberal society is open because it is governed by an abstract set of rules, often codified as constitutional rights, that do not specify a single social end that all must pursue, nor does an open society pursue a single, collective vision of justice.[9] Instead, each person and group is free to pursue their own values and visions of the best form of life.

While many will prefer regimes where their values are politically supreme, I argue that even nonliberals have adequate moral reason to endorse a regime of liberal rights as morally binding. On reflection, each person can see that liberal rights are the most she can respectfully demand of persons with incompatible ideologies. Liberal rights, therefore, lay the groundwork for sustaining social trust, since we can all see that others endorse liberal institutional arrangements from their own perspective. When each person is guaranteed a rights-protected life, she has adequate moral reason to ally herself with her political and economic institutions. Shared recognition of this fact encourages us to socially trust one another to abide by the institutional rules to which we are all subject. Liberal institutions thereby cultivate moral peace, and so are not mere cloaks for the will to power.

My argument that liberal politics is not war faces two related challenges. The first challenge is to establish the feasibility of moral peace in a diverse society; the second is to show that moral peace can be sustained in a way that treats everyone as free, equal, and worthy of respect. Moral peace is valuable, but it must be maintained for the right reasons.

These challenges are grounded in the recognition that our shared social institutions are sustained by rules that we use to direct one another's

---

[8] Popper 2013, p. 165.

[9] Gaus 2016, p. xvi. We explore the idea of an open society further in Thrasher and Vallier 2018.

behavior. We order one another to engage in or refrain from lines of conduct, from avoiding the smallest slight to sacrificing one's life for others, and those directives must be justified as essential for maintaining social trust through moral means. Without such a justification, these demands look like small-scale acts of war. They amount to domination and harassment. The moral order, not to mention the political order, becomes a mere contest for control, and even if social trust survives, it is not sustained in a way that treats each person with respect.

To show that moral peace can be sustained by moral means, we must identify a *test* that pinpoints which institutional rules can be justified to a wide range of evaluative perspectives and which ones cannot. The test must explain when each person has sufficient *moral* reason to endorse the institutional rules applied to her by others. If each person has sufficient moral reason to endorse the rules to which she is subject, then she (at least implicitly) authorizes the rules that her society applies to her; she imposes the rules *on herself* by means of her own conscientious convictions. Consequently, demands to follow these rules are not fundamental disruptions of her agency or a source of resentment or indignation. Institutional rules endorsed for moral reasons, therefore, give each person rational grounds for recognizing that diverse others have their own moral reason to follow shared moral and legal rules. This means that she can socially trust them to follow the rules because each person sees compliance as morally required. She can now expect others to be *trustworthy* by complying with the rules that can be justified to each person. And social trust is a rational response to observing the trustworthiness of others.

Further, since each person can tell that others are trustworthy and regards herself as morally bound to follow the same rules, she has her own reason to be trustworthy with respect to the rules. Her moral convictions require that she be trustworthy at least as long as others are trustworthy. In this way, social trust and trustworthiness should be mutually reinforcing. A joint endorsement test thus provides a foundation for relations of social trust by identifying the conditions under which social trust is justified; and from the soil of trust, peace can grow.

Readers are bound to be skeptical whether there is any such test, not to mention the claim that liberal institutions uniquely satisfy the test. Yet that is what I shall argue. The test is a *public justification principle*, which holds that the moral rules that we direct others to follow are legitimate and authoritative when and only when each person subject to our directives has sufficient reason of her own to comply with those directives. Legal and constitutional rules must be publicly justified in a similar fashion. And only a *liberal* constitution, one that protects a wide array of equal liberties for all, can be publicly justified.

The political theory that grounds liberal institutions in public justification is commonly known as *public reason liberalism*, a theory of political legitimacy and authority that emphasizes the importance of justifying coercive law to multiple reasonable points of view. As the inheritor of the social contract tradition in political philosophy, public reason liberalism attempts to create a social contract among citizens: a complex agreement on the terms of social life. But unlike the social contract tradition, which relies on the problematic notions of express and tacit consent, public reason relies on the idea of public justification.[10]

However, since this book shows that a liberal order is the best way to ensure moral peace between diverse persons, I only outline how specific liberal institutions can do so. The sequel to this book explains in detail how certain liberal institutions sustain social and political trust between diverse persons in the real world. There I defend five liberal institutional practices: freedom of association, the market economy, the welfare state, and democratic decision-making to both ratify legislation and select political officials. These constitutional rights give people the authority to live their own lives in their own way. Once we recognize the depth and breadth of reasonable disagreement among persons in free societies, we will see that only institutions that protect the freedom of diverse persons can be justified to each person, and so to form the basis of social trust in liberal institutions.

My approach to justifying liberal institutions draws inspiration from the influential public reason projects of John Rawls and Gerald Gaus. In *Political Liberalism,* Rawls advanced the most famous and one of the original accounts of public reason, in part motivated by his conviction that liberal theory must face the "fact of reasonable pluralism." Sincere and reflective people inevitably disagree about matters of ultimate import, such as the nature of the good and the truth or falsity of religion.[11] Consequently, a society governed by a single conception of the good life can only endure by oppressing its members; reasonable people will eventually reject that conception as incompatible with their fundamental convictions and so see no reason to give their allegiance to such an order.[12] This will undermine what Rawls called stability for the right reasons.

---

[10] For an analysis of the concept of public justification, see Vallier 2018b.
[11] Rawls 2005, pp. 54–58.
[12] Ibid., p. xvi.

In response to this challenge, Rawls argued that the theory of justice could reconcile reasonable persons with incompatible conceptions of the good, for these individuals could endorse a shared liberal conception of justice from different reasonable perspectives, thereby forming an overlapping consensus. Toward the end of his career, however, Rawls acknowledged that reasonable people could disagree about which liberal conception of justice is correct.[13] In my view, this late admission obscures the role of justice in reconciling persons with different conceptions of the good because now reasonable people can reject many conceptions of justice as well.

Anticipating this problem, Rawls argued that reasonable disagreement about justice was more limited than reasonable disagreement about the good. While reasonable people may affirm different religious views, they will all agree that the boundaries of a set of public conceptions of justice are narrow.[14] But Rawls said little in defense of this critical claim.

Since reasonable people disagree deeply about what justice requires, we must appeal to some *third* moral relationship to reconcile diverse persons. I claim that this third moral relationship is social trust. While reasonable people will disagree deeply about justice and the good, they should still be able to secure a rational basis for social trust if they can establish a series of agreements on a range of social rules, rules that will typically not be organized as parts of a single, or small set, of conceptions of the good or justice. Thus, the foundation for public justification lies in its capacity to promote social trust in the right way, for when our shared moral and legal rules are publicly justified, we can establish social trust and moral peace, and so live together on respectful, stable terms despite our disagreements.

My focus on moral relations, social rules, and dissensus about justice situates my project close to the account of public reason that Gaus develops in *The Order of Public Reason*. Gaus argues that a publicly justified moral and political order avoids authoritarian relations between persons and treats all as free, equal, and worthy of respect.[15] It does so because a publicly justified system of "social-moral rules" establishes an ongoing, stable practice of moral responsibility that is required to sustain

---

[13] Ibid., p. xxxvi. My interpretation is somewhat controversial, but no one model of political liberalism in *Political Liberalism* can do everything Rawlsians want. See Gaus and Van Schoelandt 2017. Weithman 2017 offers an explanation of how Rawls's project can survive acknowledging justice pluralism.

[14] Rawls 2005, p. xlvii.

[15] Gaus 2011, pp. xv–xvi.

profoundly valuable moral relations between persons.[16] So as I read Gaus, a central aim of the public reason project is to establish, maintain, and enliven moral relations between persons. However, while Gaus frequently discusses moral relations in *The Order of Public Reason*, he does not develop an account of the specific moral relations that members of liberal orders can have with one another.[17] I argue that social trust is the common denominator in almost all of the moral relations that we wish to have with others who are not our intimates, for there can be few moral relations without trust.[18] So while I follow Gaus in placing the value of moral relations at the heart of the public reason project, I find it more powerful and direct to ground a variant of public reason in an account of social trust. An additional advantage of focusing on social trust is the promise of defending public reason by appealing to the rich philosophical literature on trust, as well as the massive empirical literature on social trust in political science and economics. Such a synthesis allows us to draw on enormous and new resources to justify liberal order.

I also follow Gaus in developing an account of public reason for nonideal theory, where we try to determine whether liberal institutions can be justified to real-world persons by taking into account the serious possibility, even probability, that some moral, legal, and constitutional rules will be violated under normal conditions. I reject an assumption of strict compliance with publicly justified rules. This means that my account of public reason has a different purpose than accounts of public reason that are expressly developed as part of ideal theory, such as the recent account of public reason offered by Lori Watson and Christie Hartley.[19] Thus, in one way, my account of public reason doesn't conflict with approaches to public reason developed for an ideal, well-ordered society. I think public justification can sustain relations of social trust between real, diverse persons and so show that real liberal politics can be more than institutionalized aggression.

---

[16] Ibid., p. 8.

[17] Ibid., p. 315 mentions that publicly justified moral rules provide the basis for "relations of trust," though Gaus does not develop this point. Rawls also briefly mentions trust without much analysis. Rawls 2005, pp. 86, 163, 168. For discussion of how public justification sustains moral relations, see Gaus 2018, which draws on Stanley Benn's work on moral relationships, accountability, and moral personality. See Benn 1988, esp. pp. 98–99.

[18] Here I do not mean to say that some heretofore unexplored moral relation cannot ground public justification as well. I thank Alexander Motchoulski for raising this point.

[19] Watson and Hartley 2018.

1. Chapter Summary

I develop the argument of the book in two parts. In Part I, I develop an account of social trust and show how it grounds the mutual endorsement test—the public justification principle. This principle is grounded in duties of respect that we owe others within a profoundly valuable system of social trust, a system that gives rise to moral peace between persons over time. Part I thus explains how to justify a society's *moral* constitution, the order of justified social norms prior to government, politics, and coercive law.[20] This contrasts with a society's *political* constitution, the order of justified legal and constitutional rules that govern the structure of the law.

Part I has three chapters. Chapter 1 develops the ideas of social trust and moral peace that I use throughout the book, as well as explaining why so many of our moral, political, and religious disagreements are intractable and why we are so quick to assume that these disagreements indicate the moral failings of those who disagree with us. In doing so, chapter 1 offers a synthesis of the public reason literature in philosophy and political theory with the social trust literature in political science and economics. This synthesis is necessary to explain how public justification can establish a politics that is not war.

Chapter 2 defends my public justification principle by explaining the value of a system of social trust. We will see that social trust lays the foundation for the formation of social capital—knowledge that persons can use to form mutually beneficial social relations. Social capital is critical for making any large-scale political and economic institutions work well. Social trust also has value because it is a precondition for forming a wide array of social relations on which we place great value, such as romantic love and friendship. Since relations of love and friendship are among humanity's most cherished goods, a world without social trust has incredible costs. Social capital and social relations form what I call the *teleological* value of social trust and moral peace.

The book contains two arguments to establish the duties of respect we owe other members of a system of social trust. First, I argue that we should be trustworthy out of respect for those who trust us. If we fail to return trustworthy behavior in response to the trust that others have placed in us, then in most cases, we are manipulative and deceptive and show a general indifference to the worth of others. Second, when we trust others, we should

---

[20] Rawls 1980, p. 539 develops a related account of a society's moral constitution, as does Gaus 2013.

give them the benefit of the doubt, allowing them to choose to act in a trust-worthy fashion, and only reprimanding them for recognized, culpable moral mistakes. I call these two arguments the *argument from trustworthiness* and the *argument from accountability* respectively.

Our duties to be trustworthy and to treat others as trustworthy have limits. If the moral rules that are the object of social trust cannot be *publicly justified*, then respect for those we trust and who trust us does not require compliance with those rules. If others insist that we comply with a rule that is incompatible with our deep commitments and values, respect for them does not require that we respond in a trustworthy fashion. We do not owe others trustworthy behavior regarding a norm we have good moral reason to reject. Further, we should not hold others accountable to moral rules that cannot be publicly justified to *them*. If a moral rule cannot be publicly justified, then the person can see no good moral reason to obey it.

Consider a case. The Amish have very different attitudes toward the use of modern technology than almost everyone in American society. Americans generally travel by car, while the Amish use horse and buggy. But when I drive to Lancaster, Pennsylvania for Christmas, I don't *blame* the Amish for using a horse and buggy, though it invariably slows me down and would be blameworthy for almost anyone else given the inconveniences it causes. I know that they're acting in accord with their conscience, and so holding them accountable is inappropriate because they are not culpable for their actions. The Amish cannot reasonably be said to *know better* than to violate the rule.

In this way, the public justification principle figures into the two duties of respect that we owe others within a system of trust. Only publicly justified moral rules provide reasons to be trustworthy and treat others as trustworthy in a respectful fashion. Since a system of trust has great value, we have good, but not requiring, reason to enter one. But since we owe respect to those we trust and those who trust us, we are morally required both to comply with publicly justified rules and to insist only that others comply with publicly justified rules. Compliance and punishing noncompliance sustains the system of trust in the absence of nonrational countervailing factors.

Respect for persons helps explain how the standard of public justification determines how we should interact with those with whom we disagree. If we focus only on the teleological value of social trust, we cannot explain why other values cannot override public justification. But if public justification specifies a conception of respect for persons, it can inherit its moral priority from the priority of respect for persons. This priority is based on the fact that standards grounded in respect for persons lie at the center of what we owe to one another. In this way we identify the *deontological* value of a system social trust; respect for persons can be realized within such a system.

Chapter 3 develops a conception of public justification that can sustain a system of social trust. Unlike most approaches to public justification, I deny that coercive laws are the most fundamental social practice to be justified. Public justification applies not merely to laws but to moral rules that comprise what P. F. Strawson, Kurt Baier, Joseph Raz, and Gaus have called our *social morality*.[21] Social morality comprises *moral rules* that are a kind of *social norm*, an extant social practice backed by both empirical and normative expectations of compliance.[22] People expect all community members to follow social norms, and community members believe others think they *should* follow these norms. Sometimes violations of social norms are subject to social sanction; members of the community will often ostracize and penalize violators. Expressly *moral* rules refer to a type of social norm whose normative expectations are moral in nature, such that they ground judgments of moral responsibility and blame and engender the reactive attitudes of resentment and indignation in response to violations.[23] Moral rules must also meet the familiar conceptual restrictions, such that the rules are reversible, promote the common good, etc.

Public justification proceeds in terms of the *intelligible* reasons of each person, moral reasons that are rationally justified for the person who has the reason in accordance with her own evaluative standards. In other words, these moral reasons derive from her conscientious convictions, and not merely the reasons she happens to share with others. Since I am appealing to an account of the reasons that each person can be said to *have*, I endorse moderate idealization, where we ascribe reasons to persons based on the reasons they would affirm if they were adequately rational and informed. Respect requires treating persons in accord with our model of what their commitments are, not the reasons they claim to affirm

---

[21] Baier 1995, pp. 195–224; Strawson 1974, pp. 29–49; Raz 2009, pp. 41, 43; Gaus 2011, pp. 2–13.
[22] Bicchieri 2006, p. 11. To be more precise, a social norm can exist so long as most people *believe* that others have empirical and normative expectations of the right kind even when most people *in fact* lack these expectations. But since this state of social ignorance is not normally the case for most social norms, I set the possibility aside. I am grateful to Paul Billingham for this point.
[23] Bicchieri thinks moral norms are not social norms, but as we shall see below, Gaus provides a more attractive account of moral rules as social norms.

at the moment. Readers are often skeptical about idealization, so I address some common concerns about it.

The intelligibility requirement and moderate idealization are grounded in an account of which reasons we can reasonably expect others to consider in deciding whether to obey a moral rule, and so what reasons they have to be trustworthy with respect to that rule. Trustworthy behavior generates social trust, or at least the rational basis of social trust. Without it, social trust can be lost, along with the great goods it establishes.

In sum, my public justification principle is the correct test for determining which moral rules legitimately govern our shared moral life. Publicly justified moral rules alone secure the goods of social trust and respect for persons, telic and deontic value respectively. The principle will in this way help us identify political relations that are not war.

Part II justifies a *political* constitution, the system of legal and constitutional rules that comprise a society's laws and the processes for changing the law. In chapter 4, I explain why legal rules need public justification, how they can be justified, and how publicly justified legal rules generate a limited duty to obey the law. Legal rules *need* public justification because they involve the imposition of coercion, and legal rules *are* publicly justified when they are efficient means of helping the moral order perform its central functions. Members of the public are obliged to obey legal rules when they are publicly justified. This account of the public justification of law explains how we can derive a political constitution from the justification of a society's moral constitution. Legal rules are publicly justified as a means to supplementing the moral order because legal rules can perform tasks that the moral order cannot perform effectively.

Toward this end, I ask the reader to envision a state-of-nature scenario where social order is exclusively compromised of moral rules; in this *legal state of nature*, there is no law or formally recognized legal bodies. Members of such an order will want their system of moral rules to resolve disputes, but the moral order often lacks the ability to effectively resolve these disputes. The court of public opinion has its faults. Thus, moderately idealized members of the public will recognize that compliance with certain laws and the directives of formal legal institutions will efficiently improve upon their capacity to solve problems that arise in the moral order. In this way, laws can be publicly justified, for the legal coercion involved in enforcing them is necessary to perform functions that people want performed in the legal state of nature.

Once a moral order is properly constituted, members of the public do not seek to institutionalize a single conception of the good or even a single conception of justice. If we impose our sectarian conception of justice on others, there is an important sense in which we are at war with them. The theory of justice, then, plays a more restrained role in my theory than in other accounts of public reason. Contractors choose a set of political, economic, and civic rights and institutions to govern persons who disagree about justice and the good. I call these *primary rights*. Rawls denied that political philosophy was in the business of determining the nature of the authentic human good, so he developed a notion of primary goods, resources that anyone will want regardless of their rational conception of the good. Recognition of the value of these goods should be so widely shared that governmental provision of them will not be authoritarian or sectarian.[24] Primary rights have a similar basis: we identify a system of rights that all can converge on as necessary for each person or group to advance her good and her sense of justice on reciprocal terms with others. I develop an account of primary rights in chapter 5.

The third part of justifying political order involves choosing constitutional rules, rules that govern the formation, alteration, and repeal of laws. Constitutional rules come in two types: (1) rules that protect, define, harmonize, and enforce primary rights or *protective* rules and (2) rules that govern matters of political concern other than the protection of rights, such as the production of public goods and the regulation of negative externalities or *productive* rules. Few public reason liberals have developed accounts of constitutional choice, so I argue that we must appeal to other approaches to develop a substantive model. In particular, we should appeal to the public choice contractarianism advanced by James Buchanan and Gordon Tullock.[25] So chapter 6 is focused on the derivation of constitutional rules based on a new synthesis of public reason and public choice approaches.

Constitutional rules can be justified in a parallel way to legal rules. Legal systems sometimes lack law-changing institutions, and so we cannot easily change bad laws or improve upon good ones. Thus, members of the public will recognize that compliance with constitutional rules, even imperfect ones, will efficiently improve upon their ability to solve critical social problems that arise in the normal course of events in a legal order.

Chapter 6 also contains a new model of stability for the right reasons. Rawlsians agree that a just and legitimate political order must in some sense be self-stabilizing among moral persons. But the models of stability

---

[24] Rawls 1999a, pp. 78–81.
[25] Buchanan and Tullock 1962.

in the literature are, in my view, much too simple to be plausible. They do not recognize the complex dynamics of ensuring cooperative behavior in mass society. To avoid these problems, I have developed an agent-based computational model of stability appropriate for public reason views; I use the model here to distinguish between types of stability and argue that different constitutional structures can secure each type.

In chapter 7, I explain why only liberal institutions can be publicly justified. Liberal institutions recognize and secure an extensive scheme of equal civic, political, and economic rights. Nonliberal arrangements usually assign unequal rights and powers to a particular sectarian group, which the dominated sects have sufficient reason to reject. This implies, in turn, that the dominated sects lack moral reason to be trustworthy with respect to those social and political arrangements. So while each sect might prefer to be the moral and political hegemon, the only regimes they will assign moral authority are liberal because only liberal institutions protect all groups from the hegemony of their competitors.

2. Conclusion

The moral heart of this book is a plea that the reader not acquiesce in the view that politics is war. The liberal institutions of an open society can establish moral peace because they have the unique capacity to sustain social trust between persons with deeply divergent worldviews. Recognizing this can restore *our* trust in liberal order despite the many political challenges we face.

PART I | Social Trust and Social Contract

CHAPTER 1 | Moral Peace and Social Trust

TRUSTING THOSE WHO ARE different from us is a great social achievement. Our tendency to exhibit in-group bias, to favor our tribe, has been a part of human social life since *Homo sapiens* appeared on the earth.[1] And our in-group bias persists to the present day, arguably generating many of our pressing social ills.[2]

But the benefits of overcoming in-group bias are staggering. If we can truck, barter, and exchange with others, we can build a vastly more productive and prosperous society than if we only trust members of our family, tribe, or village.[3] By extending the division of labor across the world, we have become immeasurably richer, healthier, and more peaceful.[4] Attempting to suppress our in-group bias is usually in our self-interest.

Moreover, there is something *morally* attractive about being able to trust strangers; by coming to see others as worthy of our trust, we can better appreciate their dignity and form valuable relationships with them. Social trust is a precondition for valuable moral relations, including the great goods of love and friendship. We also use social trust to recognize persons as worthy of our respect and concern.

Despite recognizing these benefits, we nonetheless have trouble forming trusting relations with those who have competing worldviews and value systems. It is hard to see those whose values compete with our own as people of goodwill. And yet deep disagreement is the norm in large-scale social orders in the modern world, for people of goodwill in

[1] Brewer 1999; Hewstone et al. 2002.
[2] Tajfel 2010.
[3] Smith 1981; Ostrom and Walker 2003.
[4] Pinker 2011.

these societies disagree about what the good life consists in and what justice requires. At the least, they disagree about how to weigh shared moral values against one another. Forming a cooperative order that includes all these individuals, therefore, not only requires that we overcome prejudice based on race and gender, but to overcome *viewpoint prejudice*, prejudice based on another person's religious, moral, or political convictions. While free societies have made great strides in suppressing in-group bias against other races, genders, and religions, our political prejudices continue, and in the United States, they have considerably worsened since the end of the Second World War.[5]

This inability to trust those across the political aisle not only prevents government from working well, it constitutes a kind of moral loss. When we allow our political differences to cause us to devalue others, we not only lose the possibility of moral relations, we lose sight of their humanity, and so fail to fully appreciate the value and worth of those with whom we share our social lives.

We are led to a powerful and pressing question: is it possible for human beings to create and maintain a social order that overcomes in-group bias and establishes ongoing, rational, and morally valuable trust between strangers? Anyone steeped in contemporary American politics will be tempted to answer no. Those on the other side are mistaken, and often culpably so. That means there is no alternative to forcibly defeating them by capturing the coercive capacity of the nation-state at the ballot box. As Western European nations once thought religious difference could only be addressed by wars of conquest, so we today think that political differences can only be addressed by commanding the awesome powers of modern democratic nation-states. *Politics is war.*

The purpose of this chapter is to identify the social relationship that can maintain social cooperation while respecting the dignity and worth of others. The relationship I identify is *social trust*, trust held by society and placed in society. This form of social trust is *moral* because it involves the belief that members of society will generally comply with public moral rules, rules that are widely recognized and followed, and that are generally regarded as morally binding. It is *rational* when it is based on justified beliefs that others will be trustworthy by endorsing and complying with these rules. Societies with a high degree of justified social

---

[5] Campbell 2016, pp. 134–137.

trust have the capacity to avoid a politics of war, and instead engage in political contestation within the bonds of moral peace between persons.

I proceed in six parts. In section 1, I explain why even thoughtful people find viewpoint diversity hard to accept and respect. Sections 2 and 3 develop a conception of trust that involves the belief that others will comply with public moral rules. Section 4 defines social trust, and section 5 defines trustworthiness and explains how trustworthiness forms the basis of justified social trust. I end in section 6 by defining the idea of moral peace between persons as an order where justified social trust prevails. This sets the stage for chapter 2, where I explain the value of moral peace, and chapter 3, where I show that moral peace requires public justification.

1. Evaluative Pluralism and the Illusion of Culpable Dissent

In a wide range of contexts, persistent in-group bias leads us to distrust other people. Once we draw lines between our group and other groups, hostility to the out-group comes naturally.[6] In many cases, in-group bias is clearly irrational and so doesn't raise a significant philosophical problem; it clearly is misguided. But when in-group and out-group membership are determined by the side one takes in a reasonable dispute, as happens all too often, a puzzle arises in determining how to overcome putatively *rational* in-group bias. We may erroneously assume that the out-group is culpably and dangerously wrong, but our belief that they are culpably and dangerously wrong appears justified.

Of course, there are many cases in which our out-group *is* dangerously wrong, but we generally overestimate the prevalence of dangerous out-group error. That temptation, I believe, arises from our inability to understand how others could both reason well and yet come to different conclusions than we have. We have a hard time understanding how persons could have different reasons for action and belief. The atheist cannot understand how a Catholic could have good reason to believe and practice her faith. The Democrat cannot see how any good person could vote Republican. And the conservative cannot imagine how anyone could be a progressive of goodwill. And that's even after considering the arguments of the other side. Our viewpoint diversity is so great that what looks like

---

[6] Kramer 2017, p. 16 explains the conditions in which in-group contact builds trust.

a good argument to one group is regarded as a total nonstarter by another. And this experience leads us to suspect that others are cognitively and morally flawed, or at least more flawed than we are.

When people justifiably or reasonably affirm different reasons for action and belief, they face *evaluative pluralism*.[7] I use the term "evaluative" to convey that pluralism applies not merely to our goals and principles but also to our ways of reasoning toward those goals or principles.

Any adequate explanation of evaluative pluralism must include Rawls's "burdens of judgment," the factors that lead those who reason freely to adopt different and incompatible views about life's central questions.[8] Religious, moral, and political disagreements involve complex evidence, and when the matter is considered abstractly, it seems plain enough that people can look at the evidence and come to different conclusions. The same is true when weighing different arguments and values. Anyone who has taken an introductory ethics course knows that our moral concepts are vague and subject to hard cases; likewise for our political concepts. Most people will admit, when pressed, that our beliefs are based on our unique life experience. Reflecting on this fact helps us to see that diverse others might have good reason for believing and acting as they do.[9]

F. A. Hayek offers an account of the sources of disagreement that, while related to Rawls's version, is much richer. Disagreement about the relative weight of moral values will lead to evaluative pluralism; the "scales of value" of rational and moral persons "are inevitably different and often inconsistent with each other."[10] Hayek understands the mind as a system of rules that organize subjective percepts in cognitively unique ways. The mind itself is "a particular order of a set of events taking place in some organism and in some manner related to but not identical with, the physical order of events in the environment."[11] Consequently, different minds will map the world differently, such that their knowledge of the world is inevitably subjective, limited, and distinct from the knowledge of others. Much of Hayek's political project rests on these observations, since social scientific inquiry must recognize "that the concrete knowledge which

---

[7] I avoid describing pluralism as "reasonable" to avoid wedding pluralism to a term of art that Rawlsians often confuse with the intuitive idea of reasonableness. I speak to this point further in chapter 3, section 6.

[8] Rawls 2005, pp. 56–57.

[9] Or at least good *internal* or psychologically accessible reason to act as they do; there may be external reasons, reasons that are not, by nature, psychologically accessible to the agent, to act otherwise.

[10] Hayek 2007, p. 102.

[11] Hayek 1952, p. 16.

different individuals possess will differ in essential respects.[12] Solving social problems is also limited by insuperable complexity, given that "the number of separate variables which in any particular social phenomenon will determine the result of a given change will as a rule be far too large for any human mind to master and manipulate them effectively."[13] Each person possesses a tiny, *distinct* piece of knowledge about how to create a functioning social order in a vast complex of social understanding. Our *reasons* to accept the rules that comprise that order will, consequently, be radically situated and subjective.

Evaluative pluralism also assumes that disagreements about matters of ultimate import are largely *nonculpable*. If someone fails to believe the true religion, the fact that she has missed the truth is not cause to blame her for having false beliefs. Further, under conditions of evaluative pluralism, persons who reason well with respect to their evidence will come to dramatically different conclusions about what forms of life have ultimate value. In some weak sense, then, persons can be *epistemically entitled* to affirm their ends, as well as their reasons for pursuing them. That is not to say that all worldviews, or some restricted subset of them, will survive *all* rational, good-willed scrutiny. Instead, given their reasoning up to the time of most discussions, persons are rationally entitled to affirm entirely different views.[14] Additional reasoning and learning may lead persons to give up their fundamental doctrines, philosophies, etc. But this does not mean that persons have easily accessible and successful counterarguments for their divergent beliefs. Again, given our radical situatedness, reasoning well with respect to our evidence can easily lead to divergent views.

The peer disagreement literature presents a challenge to evaluative pluralism, however.[15] Those who affirm evaluative pluralism might be required to hold that epistemic peers, persons who share evidential bases and who reason with similar degrees of competency, *should not* suspend or reduce their confidence in their disputed beliefs when confronted with one another. Thus, affirming evaluative pluralism means rejecting this plausible form of "conciliationism," which claims that when "two peers

---

[12] Hayek 1979, p. 57.

[13] Ibid., p. 73.

[14] Pollock 2006, p. 6. We can understand the justification that applies to our reasoning up to the present time as *provisional* justification, which contrasts with nonprovisional justification, where we have completed all possibly relevant reasoning. We can hold that provisional justification is diverse while maintaining that nonprovisional justification will vindicate our particular approach to the right, the good, and the holy.

[15] Goldman and Blanchard 2015.

who disagree about p should subsequently become substantially less confident in their opinions regarding p." But this is a mistake; affirming evaluative pluralism has no implications about how epistemic *peers* should cognitively respond to one another. Instead, the burdens of judgment and our radical cognitive situatedness suggest that we rarely interact with epistemic peers, nor could we tell if we did. Even if people know all the same arguments, they could have easily encountered the arguments in a different order, or they could have nonculpably forgotten an argument they once knew, or perhaps they lack some hard-to-communicate insight due to life experience. Evaluative pluralism simply holds that people are rationally entitled to affirm different practical reasons for action and theoretical reasons for belief on matters of ultimate import. This does not amount to rejecting conciliationism.[16]

With a generic account of evaluative pluralism in hand, we can now ask which types of beliefs it applies to. Clearly evaluative pluralism applies to beliefs about the ultimate *good*. Sincere, informed people of goodwill disagree about what the good life consists in. But it also plainly applies to disagreement about what is right and wrong and about what is just and unjust. Thus, pluralism about the good and *justice pluralism* run deep and lead to sharp divergences between intelligent persons of goodwill. Some philosophers who admit pluralism about the good try to restrict the reach of justice pluralism, such as Rawls and Jonathan Quong.[17] I have argued elsewhere that the limitations they place on justice pluralism are either ad hoc, too vague, or based on contentious and unattractive conceptions of the public reason project.[18] I lack the space to review these arguments here, but Quong's more developed approach has been subjected to powerful challenge.[19] For now it is safe to say that, without some good reason to treat pluralism about the good and justice pluralism asymmetrically, the natural assumption is that evaluative pluralism applies to both the domain of the good and the domain of justice.

I argue that evaluative pluralism applies to beliefs about empirical facts.[20] This is plain if we allow that persons of informed goodwill can have considerably different religious beliefs, since some religious beliefs

---

[16] I take this point to explain the limited relevance of the peer disagreement literature to the public reason project, contra Enoch 2017.
[17] Rawls 2005, pp. xlvii–xlviii; Quong 2011, pp. 192–220.
[18] Vallier 2017b and Vallier 2019a.
[19] Billingham 2017 and Fowler and Stemplowska 2015.
[20] For some concerns about this approach, see Kappel 2017. I am not as concerned about indeterminacy in the justification of moral rules, laws, or public policies as Kappel is.

make claims about the world. A theist believes God exists; an atheist denies this. Given the fair assumption that informed, intelligent persons of goodwill could be theists or atheists, we here have an instance where evaluative pluralism applies to empirical facts, specifically the fact of God's existence (or nonexistence).[21]

A critic might wish to restrict evaluative pluralism to normative propositions; if evaluative pluralism applies to empirical facts, reasonable people can disagree about matters that are subject to direct scientific verification. This may mean that informed persons of goodwill can justifiably reject a number of scientific conclusions. While grossly antiscientific beliefs are irrational, such as skepticism about the benefits of childhood vaccination, people could in principle disagree about the extent to which climate change is a threat to humanity or about which macroeconomic policy is best during a recession. I suspect most readers will want to avoid a standard of rationally justified disagreement this permissive, as it legitimizes too many doubts about the verdicts of the scientific community. We can solve this problem by distinguishing between culpable and nonculpable errors in reasoning. Those who doubt the scientific consensus without good counterarguments have made a culpable error because their objections to trusting the consensus are frequently manifestly fallacious. Antivaxxers have strong counterevidence that derives from easily discoverable judgments of the relevant scientific experts.[22] But our panoply of engrained cognitive biases allows such beliefs to persist and spread.

Given the nature and sources of evaluative pluralism, one can see why it is hard to recognize. Our own perspectives on the world are sharply limited by our boundedly rational cognitive abilities and our highly situated and subjective experience. From our individual vantage points, viewpoint diversity is hard to respect, since we have trouble imagining how someone could think differently from ourselves, especially on issues close to the heart or that we see as related to our religious beliefs. But if evaluative pluralism holds, we should expect viewpoint prejudice, since our cognitive and environmental differences will make it hard for us to recognize when a disagreement is reasonable. This is why even many thoughtful people fail

---

[21] We can also have pluralism about social ontology. Muldoon 2017 explores what I call *social ontology pluralism* and the prospects for the contractarian project in light of such radical pluralism.
[22] This does not imply that we will be unable to establish relations of trust with antivaxxers, just that we lack reason to trust antivaxxers with regard to that particular issue.

to acknowledge and respect deep differences of opinion on fundamental matters.[23]

If we are to develop and sustain a diverse society rooted in social trust, we must acknowledge the fact of evaluative pluralism. Otherwise, we cannot see that others are people of goodwill who can be trusted to comply with our shared moral rules. Fortunately, reflection on evaluative pluralism quickly makes clear how pervasive the phenomenon is. And once we recognize it, we can fight our temptation to in-group bias against those with different religious, moral, and political viewpoints. We can begin to see those with different ideas as worthy of respect, rather than as irrational and dangerous enemies.

The pervasiveness of evaluative pluralism, coupled with our cognitive and in-group biases, means that recognizing evaluative pluralism is almost unnaturally difficult. This difficulty, among other factors, makes it very tempting to believe that politics in a pluralistic society is war, for we have great difficulty in seeing our political opponents as reflective and sincere. We are faced with what I call the *illusion of culpable dissent*, the false belief that others disagree with our moral, religious, and political viewpoints solely because of some cognitive or moral vice. We must find some way to cooperate with one another despite this illusion if we are to enjoy the benefits of shared social life and to treat others with adequate concern and respect. And cooperation begins with trust.

2. Trust

Broadly speaking, individuals trust one another to *do* something. As Russell Hardin puts it, A trusts B to Φ.[24] Typically, we trust someone to engage in certain lines of *conduct*. I can trust my wife to have the garage opened when I bike home, so I can place my bike in the garage. Reba trusts John to stop at a stop sign so that she can drive by without getting hit. To trust another person, then, involves some kind of expectation of trustee behavior by the truster.[25] This means that trusters must believe that trustees are *disposed* or *willing* to do what we trust them to do.[26] Trust also involves

---

[23] We needn't respect *all* views that people hold nonculpably and with some degree of reflection if we think at least modest additional reflection will undermine the view, but we should err on the side of caution in assuming that a bit more reasoning will lead someone to change her view.

[24] Hardin 2004, p. 9. Also see Kohn 2009, p. 8.

[25] Hardin 2004, p. 13. Also see Kohn 2009, p. 17.

[26] Castelfranchi and Falcone 2010, p. 16.

the belief that the trusted person is *competent* to perform the action we trust her to perform.[27] As Annette Baier writes in her seminal article on trust, "Trust . . . is reliance on others' competence and willingness to look after, rather than harm, things one cares about which are entrusted to their care."[28] If we do not believe that others are even able to do what we trust them to do, then we cannot be said to trust them. For Reba to trust John, then, Reba must have a "competence" belief.[29]

If Reba trusts John, she makes herself somehow *dependent* upon or *vulnerable* to him. We trust others not merely when we expect them to engage in a line of conduct, but when we in some way *need* or *want* them to do so. Sometimes we speak of trust loosely, saying that "I trust you're feeling well" or that "I trust that he will make the same mistake again." But when we appeal to paradigmatic cases of trust, we understand the truster as taking a risk in trusting others, since trust can be *betrayed*, as Baier also argued. Cristiano Castelfranchi and Rino Falcone argue that a truster only trusts when she has a goal that the trustee is required to facilitate.[30] We can call this as a kind of *reliance*.[31]

We can now offer some necessary conditions on trust:

A trusts B to Φ only if A has a goal and believes that B's Φing is necessary or helpful for achieving the goal and that B is willing and able to Φ.

So trust requires a goal and a belief that another agent is necessary or helpful for achieving the goal, and that the other agent will probably do her part in achieving the goal. I understand the idea of a "goal" as broadly as possible; one can have a goal of achieving a good or of following a rule such as an abstract moral requirement. Keeping the idea of a goal as open-ended will be critical for establishing how persons with diverse goals can trust one another.

The trust literature is nearly united in distinguishing *mere* reliance from trust.[32] As Karen Jones notes, "Trusting is not an attitude that we can adopt toward machinery. I can rely on my computer not to destroy important documents or on my old car to get me from A to B, but my old car is

---

[27] Hardin 2004, p. 8.

[28] Baier 1986, p. 259. Also see Jones 1996, p. 4 and Mullin 2005, p. 322.

[29] Castelfranchi and Falcone 2010, p. 16.

[30] Ibid., p. 39.

[31] Reliance can be weak. As Holton 1994, p. 8 suggests, "I do not need to have the belief that you will do what I rely on you to do, but I do need to lack the belief that you will fail."

[32] Annette Baier recognized the distinction from the outset. See Baier 1986, p. 234.

reliable rather than trustworthy."[33] Trust researchers agree so much on this point that Jeremy Wanderer and Leo Townsend simply take it "*for granted that there is a basic difference between reliance and trust.*"[34]

Philosophers have tended to distinguish between trust and mere reliance by appealing to P. F. Strawson's idea of the *participant* stance.[35] When I take the participant stance with respect to you, "I recognize that you are a creature that acts for reasons, and . . . I further allow your reasons to factor into my thinking and support my beliefs and decisions."[36] That means I do not see you as an obstacle, a nonagent to be conquered or avoided. Rather, I can hold you *responsible* for bad behavior. And bad behavior or expressing ill will can make negative *reactive attitudes* appropriate, like resentment. Margaret Walker argues that when we take the participant stance toward others, "we hold them responsible."[37] We expect them to act not simply as we assume they will, but as they should, and we blame, sanction, and punish those who are responsible.

Richard Holton claims that "the difference between trust and reliance is that trust involves something like a participant stance towards the person you are trusting."[38] Wanderer and Townsend argue that the "hallmark" of trust "is a propensity to feel resentment towards the one trusted when let down."[39] Bernd Lahno agrees: "trust involves a participant attitude toward the person being trusted."[40] Appealing to the familiar Strawsonian idea of the participant stance seems to me an excellent way to distinguish between trust and reliance. The participant stance helps to explain why John relies on his car and trusts his friend—John's friend is an agent capable of choice, and when John trusts his friend, he recognizes her agency; but John can only rely on his car because it is a machine, an object, and not an agent. We can in this way affirm "trust is *reliance from the participant stance.*"[41] I therefore expand my necessary conditions on trust:

---

[33] Jones 1996, p. 14.
[34] Wanderer and Townsend 2013, p. 3. Emphasis mine.
[35] Strawson 1974, p. 12. Strawson speaks of an "attitude" rather than a "stance"; I use the terms interchangeably.
[36] Hieronymi 2008, pp. 226–227.
[37] Walker 2006, p. 79.
[38] Holton 1994, p. 4.
[39] Wanderer and Townsend 2013, p. 3.
[40] Lahno 2001, p. 171.
[41] Hieronymi 2008, p. 216.

A trusts B to Φ only when A has a goal and believes that *participant* B's Φing is necessary or helpful for achieving the goal and that B is willing and able to Φ.

I define B as an agent toward whom the participant stance is appropriate.

The next condition on trust is that the truster must believe that the trustee Φs based on some kind of moral motive. Trust researchers differ on how this motive is to be understood. Some say that the truster must believe that the trustee bears her "goodwill," whereas others claim that the truster must believe the trustee acts from "moral integrity."[42] Some say that the appropriate motive is one of moral obligation.[43] And still others say that trusted persons should be motivated by a commitment to follow a particular social norm.[44] Sometimes people simply flesh out the idea as the claim that the trustee is responsive to her obligations.[45] And Jones, once one of the most prominent defenders of the goodwill condition, has changed her position based on her concern that goodwill is not something over and above one's being responsive to "another person's dependency."[46] Carolyn McLeod stresses that having moral integrity is often an appropriate motive for being trustworthy.

I think the goodwill condition is too vague to be helpful, and one can be trusted even if she lacks moral integrity in general. I also reject Hardin's "encapsulated-interest" account of trust, where trust involves the belief that the trustee has encapsulated the interest of the truster into her own interest. Hardin claims, "I trust you because your interests encapsulate mine to some extent—in particular, because you want our relationship to continue."[47] But we can trust people who do not know our interests. Hardin makes trust too intimate; he even says that "[t]rust as encapsulated-interest rules out the possibility or coherence not only of generalized trust but also of widespread trust by any individual."[48] That means social trust is *by definition* an incoherent idea, which seems clearly mistaken.

The proper motive for being trustworthy is instead that the trustee acts for *moral reasons* to comply with a *social norm*. In this way, I prefer elements of the trust theories advanced by Lahno and Amy Mullin. Lahno

---

[42] See Jones 1996, p. 4 for the former, McLeod 2000, p. 465 for the latter.
[43] Nickel 2007; Cohen and Dienhart 2013.
[44] Mullin 2005, p. 316.
[45] O'Neil 2012, p. 309.
[46] Jones 2012, pp. 68–69.
[47] Hardin 2004, p. xix.
[48] Ibid., pp. 179, 182.

claims "a situation of trust is perceived by a trusting person as one in which shared values or norms motivate both his own actions as well as those of the person being trusted."[49] Mullin argues that we sometimes trust persons we hardly know and cannot be said to have a relationship with, if we share with them "simply the assumption of a shared commitment to a particular social norm."[50]

One needs to act for moral reasons to trust because it is odd to say that Reba trusts John to Φ if she believes that the only reason that John Φs is that he is afraid of getting caught for not Φing or that, say, he is driven by the desire to gain Reba's trust only to betray it. Trust researchers commonly accept that trust involves a belief in the goodwill of another person. But we do not need to appeal to the idea of goodwill, only that the person sees the relevant norm as providing her with moral reasons to act, and not merely strategic or prudential reasons. This is why I think Mullin claims that trust "requires the assumption that the one trusted is *internally committed* to a particular social norm and considers that norm to be of significant importance in some arena of action."[51] A person is internally committed to a social norm when it is one that she follows at least in part because she believes it is normatively binding, or at least normatively expected of her, and not merely because of prudential reasons.

Critically, my definition of trust does *not* assume that the trustee *actually has* the moral reasons that the truster believes the trustee has. Trust simply requires that the truster believes that the trustee acts or is motivated to act for moral reasons. So in defining trust, I am not ascribing genuine moral reasons to the *trustee*; I am instead ascribing the belief that the trustee acts for moral reasons to the *truster*.[52]

We can update our necessary conditions on trust as follows:

> A trusts B to Φ only when A has a goal, believes that participant B's Φing is necessary or helpful for achieving the goal, and that B is willing and able to Φ by complying with social norm S where moral reasons are sufficient to motivate B to comply with S.

In this definition, we add the idea of a social norm, compliance with which facilitates the action Φ which A trusts B to execute. So Φ is not

[49] Lahno 2001, p. 171.
[50] Mullin 2005, p. 323.
[51] Ibid., p. 322.
[52] I thank Neera Badhwar and Harrison Frye for encouraging me to make this point explicit.

necessarily the act of complying with the social norm S. I have also added that moral reasons must be sufficient to motivate B to comply with the social norm, since otherwise I would have to allow that A can trust B even when A believes that B is motivated to comply by purely nonmoral reasons, which seems to move us away from trust and holding persons to the participant stance. That is why McLeod claims that "we expect trusted others, unlike those on whom we merely rely, to be motivated by a moral commitment."[53] Moral reasons should be enough to motivate the trustee to comply with the norm, even if her nonmoral reasons are also sufficient to motivate her to comply.

I do not think that a truster must believe that trustees typically act on moral reasons when they comply with social norms. Most people conform with social norms simply because doing so is easier than noncompliance given that noncompliance has social costs. Instead, trust implies that the truster believes that the trustee is not complying with social norms for immoral or nonmoral reasons alone, as this would indicate bad will on the part of the trustee. Rather, the truster must think, at least implicitly, that the trustee has psychologically accessible and adequately motivating moral reasons to act as she does, such that the truster can determine that the trustee is acting in a way that comports with her own moral commitments.[54]

Moral reasons are diverse. They can include concern and care for others, a desire to promote their well-being, a sense that one should respect the dignity of all, or that one has a personal duty derived from her faith or comprehensive doctrine to treat others in particular ways. Leaving the content of moral reasons open has two advantages. It allows social trust between persons with diverse conceptions of morality, and answers the concern that some moral reasons, such as those derived from one's comprehensive doctrine, may not look like moral reasons to everyone.

Sometimes a moral reason may look like a stable, strong nonmoral reason, such as a person's desire to be good at her job. In that case, we might think that John can trust Reba in the workplace if she acts on her desire to be good at her job, regardless of whether she has sufficient moral reason in her moral psychology to do what her job requires. While I recognize some may find trusting persons based on nonmoral reasons intuitive, I still think it is best to characterize persons in these cases as either having sufficient moral motivation to act or else to view their actions

---

[53] McLeod 2000, p. 474.
[54] I thank Jonathan Reibsamen and Harrison Frye for raising this concern.

and commitments as signs of reliability, not trustworthiness. Otherwise, we cannot appeal to moral considerations to distinguish between trusting someone to follow a moral rule and relying on them to do so. We thus fail to capture any moral motivation condition widely endorsed by trust theorists.[55] Second, we would have to acknowledge that we could trust persons who do not recognize moral reasons at all, like a psychopath, so long as they have a strong, stable motivation to act as we think they should. But it seems odd to say that we can knowingly trust a psychopath to do his job, rather than relying on or merely expecting him to do so.

Mullin and Lahno do not offer an account of social norms. Fortunately, Cristina Bicchieri's work on social norms provides us with a rich understanding of the idea. We will also see the need to specify which sort of social norm is necessary for trust, which I call a *moral rule*. I develop these ideas in the next section.

Before I do so, three brief points. First, I am only defining necessary conditions for trust, not sufficient conditions. I do this to remain neutral between doxastic and nondoxastic approaches to trust. Doxastic approaches hold that trust is a belief or a set of beliefs, whereas nondoxastic approaches understand trust as an attitude or stance.[56] Fortunately, I do not have to take a stand on this question, though I do want to claim, in contrast to some, that beliefs are necessary conditions on trust.[57] This is fairly obvious. As Arnon Keren argues, we often trust what persons *say*, and that invariably involves believing what they say.[58] If we do not believe that a speaker is trustworthy, then we will not form the relevant trust belief. Trust, therefore, seems to always involve at least some beliefs.

Second, some argue that trust necessarily involves the ascription of an obligation to the trustee.[59] As Nickel argues, "if one person trusts another to do something, then she takes him to be obligated to do that thing."[60] And the reason for this is that we think that blame and punishment are appropriate "upon nonperformance."[61] My position is that when A trusts B to Φ, B is not necessarily morally obligated to Φ, since B may recognize a countervailing reason to not-Φ. However, A will still usually *believe*

---

[55] I am grateful to Neera Badhwar, Hartmut Kliemt, and Stan Husi for encouraging me to elaborate on the moral motivation condition along these lines.

[56] For a defense of a doxastic account of trust, see Keren 2014, p. 2598.

[57] Jones 1996 and Holton 1994, for instance, think of trust as a kind of affective attitude or participant stance respectively, and not a belief.

[58] Keren 2014, p. 2599.

[59] Nickel 2007; Cohen and Dienhart 2013.

[60] Nickel 2007, p. 310.

[61] Ibid., p. 311.

that B is obligated to Φ, even if A is mistaken about this. That is because A's disposition to resent B can only be appropriate if A believes that B is obligated to Φ. Even so, there can be cases where one is trusted to act for reasons other than one's obligations, such as supererogatory compassion.

Third, a number of authors argue that when A trusts B to Φ, A will resist evidence that B is untrustworthy with respect to doing Φ. As Jones points out, "trust can give rise to beliefs that are abnormally resistant to evidence."[62] In contrast, I think evidence-resistance is characteristic only of certain kinds of trust, in particular interpersonal trust in someone with whom the truster has an ongoing relationship. To trust a friend means that one will be at least initially skeptical of evidence that the friend is not trustworthy. But our trust of *strangers* need not be resistant to evidence at all. Observing strangers' untrustworthy behavior typically justifies reducing our confidence in their trustworthiness.

3. Social Norms and Moral Rules

Trust depends on social norms, but what are social norms? Principally, of course, social norms are norms.[63] They typically involve regular patterns of social behavior that conform to a public standard or normative attitudes over time.[64] In contrast to conventions, which people follow because they believe they benefit in doing so, people follow norms less consciously and sometimes without seeing the benefits from social interactions based on the norms.

Following Bicchieri, we can understand some norms as based on *empirical* expectations that the norm is in effect and that we all expect others to comply with the norm. A *social norm* is one backed by empirical expectations *and* normative expectations.[65] Normative expectations imply that everyone believes that everyone thinks one *should* comply with the norm. And in many cases, violations of social norms will generate external

---

[62] Jones 1996, p. 15.

[63] Bicchieri and Muldoon 2011; Rescorla 2015. To define a social norm, I do not need to settle on a definition of norms *in general*. So I do not advance a social practice definition of norms in contrast to Brennan et al. 2016, pp. 20–21. I thank Steven Stich and Paul Billingham for this point.

[64] A descriptive norm implies that persons *conditionally prefer* to follow the norm so long as they believe others will follow the norm. See Bicchieri 2017, p. 19. Social norms add a second condition to the preference, namely that persons prefer to follow a norm so long as they believe that others believe that people generally *should* follow the norm. Ibid., p. 35.

[65] For Bicchieri, a social norm can exist so long as everyone believes there are shared empirical and normative expectations even when there are in fact no such expectations, but since this is an unusual case, I again set it aside.

sanction because other community members believe the norm ought to have been followed.[66] Bicchieri allows that normative expectations can be prudential, in that we find violators of the norm to be unwise. Yet many normative expectations have a moral character, such that violations render external sanction appropriate. That is, upon observing violations, people will blame or ostracize the violator based on their resentment or indignation, or at least violators will anticipate blame or ostracism. When someone refuses to allow us to merge onto the interstate, we think he is *wrong*, not imprudent.

I follow Gaus's extension of Bicchieri's analysis in developing the idea of a "social-moral rule." For Gaus, social rules are understood in terms of a "set/subset" analysis where rules identify "a certain set of actions" that may, must, or must not be performed.[67] Social rules do not identify particular actions but "issue directives for actions with these properties." Specifically, a social rule has four components:

(i)   a set of persons to whom the prescription is addressed;
(ii) a property of actions;
(iii) a deontic operator such that actions with that property may, must, or must not be performed, and,
(iv) a statement of the conditions under which the connection between (ii) and (iii) is relevant.

A social rule, then, is a publicly recognized prescription for a group of persons to engage, or to be allowed to engage, in certain lines of conduct according to the relevant context.

Like many social norms, social rules must somehow "exist."[68] Following H. L. A. Hart, Gaus argues that a rule is social under two conditions: some members of a group must view the behavior required by the rule as a general standard binding on everyone and that the rule is regularly followed by most members of the group.[69] On the first requirement, each group member must see the rule as having an "internal aspect" such that

---

[66] Bicchieri 2006, p. 11. Brennan et al. 2016, pp. 15, 36 acknowledge that norms primarily "serve the function . . . of making us accountable to one another," which is bound up with observed violations of normative expectations or beliefs.

[67] Gaus 2011, p. 123.

[68] Ibid., p. 165.

[69] Also see Hart 1961, pp. 54–56. Here I distinguish a social rule from what Brennan et al. 2016, p. 15 describe as a reductive account of norms, which characterizes norms in purely nonnormative terms. Rules are defined in part by the presence of normative expectations or normative attitudes. I thank Paul Billingham for this point.

members of the group think that they and others should follow the rule, and in fact, the rule may also be appropriately internalized as applying to one. We should regard the rules that apply to us as our rules, ones that we hold ourselves to. The rule must also be actually followed, for otherwise it is not a rule for the group at all. Unless the rule is followed, it cannot structure expectations or even be successfully agreed upon as applying to persons. In this way, social rules satisfy a kind of *publicity* condition, where they are the object of common recognition, where each person recognizes the rule and recognizes that others do as well. Traffic rules serve to illustrate; we insist that other drivers wait their turn, use their turn signals, and not speed because those rules are publicly recognized as in force and are widely followed. So Gausian social rules are similar to Bicchieri's idea of a social norm, though social rules must by definition exist.

Social rules also require that the rule establish a practice of "reciprocal obligation" where each person sees one another as responsible for following the rule out of a sense of reciprocity.[70] Just as I follow the rule, I expect others to do likewise, and they expect the same of me. Stop signs apply to me just as they apply to other drivers. Gaus understands reciprocal obligations in terms of establishing relations of mutual authority, where we can direct one another to comply with the rules. I develop a similar notion of authoritative rules in chapter 3.

Social rules are starting to look like moral requirements, and, indeed, Gaus understands moral rules as a type of social rule. He distinguishes moral rules with the following conditions:

1. Moral rules are emotionally infused with the moral emotions. Infractions of rules yield attitudes of resentment and indignation.
2. Moral rules are seen as nonconventional. Authority figures cannot waive moral rules at all.
3. Moral rules are also seen as categorical; we are to follow moral rules because doing so is the right thing to do, and not merely because we gain some benefit from doing so.
4. And yet moral rules are typically seen as promoting mutual benefit; genuinely *moral* rules should promote the interests of all, at least over the long run.

---

[70] Gaus 2011, p. 171.

5. Moral rules typically concern how we treat others, and must be distinguished therefore from mere rules of prudence that concern self-preservation or avoiding harm.
6. Moral rules are enforced with social ostracism, blame, and even violence; infractions of moral rules are seen as warranting punishment and not mere disappointment or criticism.[71]

Moral rules, as social rules, must also be reciprocal or universalizable. Moral rules must apply equally to those who demand compliance with them: when Reba demands that John not violate a moral rule, she must also regard herself as subject to the rule were she in John's circumstances. Strawson argued that moral rules cannot exist without "reciprocal acknowledgment of rights and duties."[72] A universal feature of morality is "the necessary acceptance of reciprocity of claim." Kurt Baier also claims that moral rules are "universally teachable and therefore universalizable" in virtue of the fact that they license claims against all members of the moral community.[73]

One important difference between Bicchieri's analysis and Gaus's is that Bicchieri claims that people follow social norms solely due to a conditional preference; they only want to follow the norm so long as others do likewise. This is why a "social norm is different from a shared prudential or moral norm because it involves (socially) conditional preferences."[74] For Bicchieri, a moral norm is one that is not influenced by social expectations, since the person would prefer to follow the moral norm (say a norm that prohibits harming others) "no matter what." Moral norms lack social conditionality because "one's personal moral convictions are the primary motivator of one's actions and such convictions overwhelm any social considerations."[75] So moral norms are not social norms.

This is true of the account of social and moral norms found in Geoffrey Brennan, Lina Eriksson, Robert Goodin, and Nicholas Southwood's account of social and moral norms, where "moral norms are clusters of unconditional normative judgments, whereas social norms are clusters

[71] Ibid., pp. 172–173. Gaus's position allows us to provide an account of the moral-conventional distinction. See ibid., p. 124, n. 51. For recent work on the distinction, see Fessler et. al 2015, Quintelier and Fessler 2015, and Curry, Chesters, and Lissa 2017.
[72] Strawson 1974, p. 40.
[73] K. Baier 1954, p. 108. Also see pp. 111–112.
[74] Bicchieri 2017, p. 72.
[75] Ibid., p. 31.

of conditional normative judgments."[76] Moral norms are "practice-independent," whereas social norms are "practice-dependent."

These accounts of moral norms pose a problem for my argument, since I claim that moral rules are a type of social norm. Fortunately, Gaus shows that one can interpret the conditional preference for following a rule in a different way:

> The core of social rules is to identify reciprocal obligations. . . . Given this, if there is low expectation that others perform as the rule instructs, this undermines the belief that a reciprocal structure of obligation is in fact recognized in the group.[77]

So the reason that a moral rule is conditionally followed is that, were the rule not to exist, no one would believe in the reciprocal obligations established by the moral rule. We can, along the same lines, answer the skepticism of Brennan et al. by identifying a category of what we might call a "social moral" norm, since for Brennan et al. moral norms are strictly personal norms, whereas social norms are interpersonal, but not moral. This leaves room for a category of interpersonal moral norms that they do not acknowledge but that is critical for my purposes.[78]

For this reason, then, I take a *moral rule* to be type of social norm where the rule is an extant practice backed by (*a*) empirical expectations that persons generally comply with the rule and (*b*) normative expectations that people believe that others think they *should* follow the rules.[79] The normative expectations appeal to (*c*) a moral (rather than a prudential) "ought" that (*d*) establishes a practice of reciprocal obligation, and (*e*) the rule, when violated, typically evokes, and is widely expected to evoke, the negative reactive attitudes of resentment and indignation, as well as blame and punishment.

4. Social Trust

We can now expand my account of trust to define trust that is mass and mutual—social trust. In mass society, few goals are shared among all

---

[76] Brennan et al. 2016, p. 61.
[77] Gaus 2011, p. 171.
[78] Bicchieri could answer the criticisms of her view found in Brennan et al., pp. 23–26 if she would allow for conditional moral norms.
[79] That is, it is commonly believed that everyone should follow the rule.

citizens. So social trust does not require some substantive shared goal like realizing the common good. Instead, social trust requires the belief that others are necessary or helpful for achieving each person's or small group's ends and that people are generally willing and able to do so by following publicly recognized rules of conduct—moral rules, in our case. It is also important to recognize that social trust is not confined to compliance with any one moral rule, but rather a wide array of such rules. Social trust, then, involves the general expectation that all members of society will comply with moral rules. It requires beliefs, and not just a generic feeling of security in the appropriate behavior of others. So in contrast to Lawrence Becker, I do not employ a noncognitive form of trust, but rather a complex belief that most people will follow most moral rules most of the time, where the agent can detect when persons violate specific moral rules.[80] In this way, then, we can define trust as involving the belief that "the other person or persons will abide by ordinary ethical rules that are involved in the situation."[81] And when we trust, we expect others to engage in "ethically justifiable behavior—that is, morally correct decisions and actions based upon ethical principles of analysis."[82] In this way, then, we can define necessary conditions for when one individual has social trust:

> *Personal Social Trust*: A socially trusts participant members of the public
> $[P_1, P_2 \ldots P_n]$ to follow moral rules $[R_1, R_2 \ldots R_n]$ only if A believes that
> participant members of the public are necessary or helpful for achieving her
> goals and that they are generally willing and able to do their part, knowingly or unknowingly, to achieve those goals by complying with moral rules
> where moral reasons are sufficient to motivate compliance.

John must expect others to act in concert with public expectations for him to formulate his projects and plans.

Social trust appears, therefore, when all or nearly all members of the public have these beliefs and expectations, that is, when all persons have personal social trust.

---

[80] Becker 1996, p. 44.
[81] Messick and Kramer 2001, p. 91.
[82] Hosner 1995, p. 399.

Social Trust: a public exhibits social trust to the extent that its participant members generally believe that other participants are necessary or helpful for achieving one another's goals and that (most or all) members are generally willing and able to do their part to achieve those goals, knowingly or unknowingly, by following moral rules where moral reasons are sufficient to motivate compliance.

Large societies largely lack shared goals and, due to their size, they are unable to explicitly communicate the beliefs upon which trust is based. Therefore societies establish social trust through *mass compliance with moral rules*. As long as each person believes that most or all others will comply with moral rules based on observing compliance, she can socially trust others. It is also critical to stress the centrality of normative expectations that are backed by punishment, since punishment is required to stabilize some moral rules.[83]

The social trust literature supports the notion of social trust outlined here. In a recent survey of conceptions of social trust, Marc Cohen develops an account of generalized trust where "social order depends on moral relationships between the persons involved."[84] He denies that we can understand social trust purely in terms of expectations by insisting that trust involves some sort of dependence relation between the truster and the trustee. Further, social trust involves reference to moral obligations; with respect to generalized trust, "A trusts B to act in accordance with some (specified) general or background moral obligation, where A can assume that B is committed to acting in that way because of the character of the obligation."[85] Social trust can also be understood in terms of the "fundamental constitutive practices that make a social order possible." And moral rules are clearly constitutive practices that make a social order possible. Accordingly, my account of social trust, which requires morally normative expectations, lines up with Cohen's survey, such that my account of social trust is compatible with many conceptions of social trust in the literature (though not all).[86]

In a famous study of social trust, Eric Uslaner argues that generalized trust is tied to "moralistic trust," which is the belief that "others share your

---

[83] Social trust may require punishing those who fail to punish; see Boyd and Richerson 2005, pp. 193–203.
[84] Cohen 2015, p. 465.
[85] Ibid., p. 475.
[86] Accordingly, I think my conception of social trust is operationalizable for empirical research in social trust. I defend this point in the sequel to this book.

fundamental moral values and therefore should be treated as you would wish to be treated by them."[87] Broadly speaking, then, moralistic trust involves a "fundamental ethical assumption: that other people share your fundamental values."[88] Similarly, moralistic trust is based upon belief in "the goodwill of the others."[89] Generalized trust is connected to moralistic trust, as "generalized trusters see the world as a benign place with limitless opportunities. They believe that most people share the same fundamental values."[90] Following Uslaner, one could argue that we should understand social trust in terms of a person's beliefs about the world in general and about whether humans are fundamentally good or trustworthy, rather than a belief that others will comply with moral rules when one needs them to do so, as I argue.

However, there are some difficulties with Uslaner's view, especially given his acknowledgment that moralistic and generalized trust does not presume deep agreement on fundamental moral matters like politics or religion: moralistic trusters "don't necessarily agree with you politically or religiously," and "placing trust in others does *not* require agreement on specific issues or even philosophies."[91] Further, Uslaner's view oscillates between defining moralistic and social trust in terms of "values," "worldview," or "goodwill." So social trust allows for widespread disagreement and the belief that others reject one another's deepest commitments. I suggest that we replace the idea of shared values and worldviews with a shared willingness to comply with moral rules. Social norms can represent shared values, as compliance with these norms can be seen as grounded in those shared values. We can also share moral norms while allowing our religious, political, and moral views to differ considerably. So given the ambiguities in Uslaner's theory, my account of social trust need not be opposed to his, but could instead be understood as a specification of his position.

Uslaner presents a second challenge to the kind of account of social trust I defend. Moralistic trust, for Uslaner, is a fundamental attitude toward others that is *not* based primarily in personal experience, but is drawn more from one's own worldview. Moralistic trust, then, "is not a prediction of how others will behave. Even if other people turn out not to be trustworthy, moral values require *you* to behave *as if they could be trusted.*"[92]

---

[87] Uslaner 2002, p. 18.
[88] Ibid., p. 2.
[89] Ibid., p. 18.
[90] Ibid., p. 79.
[91] Ibid., pp. 2, 18.
[92] Ibid., p. 19.

Moralistic trust grounds social trust. Uslaner then presents evidence that measures of social trust are remarkably stable over time, and so social trust does not seem responsive to personal experience. But on my view, social trust involves believing that others are able and willing to comply with the moral rules of their society, and this suggests that if persons observe that moral rules are disobeyed, social trust should fall because those beliefs will change. Observing defection will affect the strength of the social norm and so reduce trust in others to follow the norm.[93]

In reply, notice that Uslaner thinks moralistic trust can be learned from one's parents and that some significant experiences can shape trust.[94] He also admits that social trust is somewhat more conditional than moralistic trust.[95] Uslaner claims, for instance, that the scope of social trust is more limited and less stable than moralistic trust.[96] So his view does not contrast as sharply with the position I defend as one might think. We can further answer Uslaner's challenge if we recall that empirical measures of social trust are based on whether persons generally believe that others can be trusted. Such a belief is sufficiently general that we shouldn't expect it to change based on the observance or collapse of some *particular* moral rule. Instead, social trust can be based on an overall assessment of whether most people can be expected to follow moral rules over time.

My view only requires that observed violations of a particular moral rule will reduce social trust that persons will comply with that particular rule.[97] So these empirical measures of social trust are not targeted enough to contradict my conception of social trust. My definition of social trust, therefore, should be compatible with Uslaner's empirical work.

5. Trustworthiness and Justifying Social Trust

A liberal order worthy of our allegiance helps to sustain social trust of a particular kind, trust that others will comply with moral rules for moral reasons. However, if persons do not regard social trust as rationally justified, then the order of social trust may destabilize, since people will see themselves as having sufficient reason to disobey their society's moral

---

[93] There's considerable empirical evidence that social trust is deeply affected by a society's cultural norms. See Helliwell et al. 2014 and Dinesen and Sønderskov 2017, p. 26.
[94] Uslaner 2002, pp. 77.
[95] Ibid., p. 85. Also see p. 112: our experience can affect our "basic sense of optimism and control."
[96] Ibid., p. 27.
[97] Though observed violations of one rule may lead people to think others are not trustworthy with respect to other rules.

rules, and may do so when they can get away with it. That means we need an account of when social trust is rationally justified, epistemically speaking. We need to know when others will find that social trust is a rationally appropriate response to their experience, such that social trust can survive sustained rational scrutiny.

The critical source of any cognitive form of trust is *trustworthiness*. For Hardin, "a full account of rational trust must be grounded in reasons for expecting another to fulfill a trust and in reasons for holding general beliefs about trustworthiness."[98] Thus, to rationally trust another person, we must believe that she is trustworthy, that the person can be counted on.[99] As McLeod notes, trust "is an attitude that we have toward people whom we hope will be trustworthy, where trustworthiness is a property, not an attitude."[100] Persons have the property of trustworthiness when they are disposed to act in the way we expect them to.

To begin defining trustworthiness, let us review Jones's account:

> B is trustworthy with respect to A in domain of interaction D, if and only if she is competent with respect to that domain, and she would take the fact that A is counting on her, were A to do so in this domain, to be a compelling reason for acting as counted on.[101]

It is certainly true that A can only be trustworthy if she is thought to be competent with respect to the domain of action that others might trust her to engage in. Moreover, A must be willing and able to comply with the relevant moral rules that she is trusted to follow. But I do not think that trustworthiness requires that the trustee take the fact that A is counting on her as a compelling reason for acting as counted upon.[102] For a person to be trustworthy, she need only be psychologically constituted such that her moral reasons alone are sufficient to motivate her to comply with the relevant set of moral rules. That is, moral reasons must be sufficient to motivate her compliance even if she is presently motivated by other reasons. We can therefore define trustworthiness as follows:

---

[98] Hardin 2004, p. 130. Even Uslaner agrees that to have social trust "we must have positive views of strangers, of people who are different from ourselves and presume that they are trustworthy." Uslaner 2002, p. 2.

[99] Jones 2012, p. 83.

[100] McLeod 2015, p. 3.

[101] Jones 2012, p. 70.

[102] Though recognizing the fact that A is counting on B is *one* of the considerations that should lead B to be trustworthy *out of respect* for A.

Trustworthiness: A is trustworthy with respect to Φ-type behavior only if A is generally willing and able to engage in Φ-type behavior where A's moral reasons are sufficient to motivate Φ-type behavior.[103]

And we can now define social trustworthiness by bringing in the ideas of moral rules and a much broader domain of behavior.

Social Trustworthiness: A is socially trustworthy only if A is generally willing and able to comply with moral rules where A's moral reasons are sufficient to motivate compliance.

Social trustworthiness is required to justify social trust. If persons do not believe that others are socially trustworthy, then their social trust is not rationally sustainable over time. This means that a sufficient number of violations of moral rules may gradually undermine perceived social trustworthiness, and so will gradually drag down a society's level of social trust. Or it will at least undermine the rational basis of social trust such that reflection on social trust will tend to undermine it.

The kind of justification at work here is a kind of epistemic justification, as it applies to the rational justification of beliefs that are constitutive of social trust. The form of epistemic justification involved is *internalist*, meaning that the reasons that justify belief are broadly psychologically accessible to the agent.[104] As Wanderer and Townsend argue, an internalist conception of epistemic justification is most appropriate for justifying the rationality of trust since trust invariably involves subjective beliefs about the dispositions of other persons.[105] The beliefs that justify trust must be based on internally accessible psychological factors if these beliefs are to determine that trusting makes sense for the agent.

Another reason that epistemic justification for moral rules should be understood in an internalist fashion is that persons need to be able to see the reasons for their beliefs if they are to trust on the basis of those reasons. The notion that a belief could be justified based, say, on whether it was formed by an objectively reliable process renders obscure the idea of a

---

[103] I assume that A is a participant in the Strawsonian sense and that B will generally take the participant stance concerning A upon encountering him.
[104] Keren 2014, p. 2612.
[105] Wanderer and Townsend 2013, pp. 9–10.

rational expectation based on observation and evidence, so the factors that externally justify belief cannot justify trust.[106]

Based on the foregoing, we can define justified social trust as based on an observation that most persons are socially trustworthy, so long as that belief is at least somewhat sensitive to the evidence one has that others are trustworthy. I think it is safe to say that social trust is justified so long as someone does not observe mass failures of trustworthiness or hear as much from an otherwise reliable testifier. So we can allow Reba to default to an attitude of social trust so long as she has only weak evidence that others are not socially trustworthy. In this way, social trust can justifiably survive observing others occasionally violating particular moral rules. So it will take a lot of evidence of moral rule violations to undermine justified social trust. On the flip side, in a low-trust society, it will take many observations of trustworthy behavior in order to rationally justify social trust. In this way, social trust is hard to rationally undermine and hard to rationally build.

We can now define justified social trust:

> *Justified Social Trust*: social trust is rationally justified only if the beliefs constitutive of social trust are appropriately sensitive to the evidence that others are socially trustworthy.

Evidence-sensitivity means that the belief that others are socially trustworthy is appropriately reflective of both one's own observations and the testimony provided by others, so long as the truster regards the testifiers as reliable or has good reason to regard them as such. I also allow that each person may only be somewhat evidence-sensitive; for such persons, confirming or disconfirming social trust will require a great deal of evidence. Observing individual violations of social trust may provide them with at best weak evidence that people are not socially trustworthy in general.

---

[106] I adopt a form of access internalism about justified belief where S is justified in believing P just when she can make herself aware of her justifiers for P. This notion of epistemic justification provides some degree of precision about what makes social trust rational and so justified. Pappas 2005 discusses access internalism in more detail. I have elaborated on using access internalist accounts of epistemic justification to defend public reason liberalism in Vallier 2014, pp. 104–105.

6. Moral Peace

If a society has a high degree of social trust, and this degree of social trust is sensitive to the perceived social trustworthiness of most members of the public, then we have the basis for what I shall call *moral peace between persons*. Such a peace can be contrasted with a mere *modus vivendi* truce, where hostilities cease solely because the parties at war cannot conquer the other.[107] Rather, as Rawls notes about peace between nations, "There is true peace among [nations] because all societies are satisfied with the status quo for the right reasons."[108] In a society with high social trust based on perceived trustworthiness, people will recognize that society is bound by moral rules that ground reciprocal obligations and that people are generally willing and able to comply with these rules based on their own moral reasons. So we have an order where members of society are all satisfied with the status quo for moral reasons.

We can see how justified social trust yields a state of moral peace by analyzing the state of war in classical social contract theory. Social contract theories, including contemporary ones, begin their justification of political power by describing a state of nature, identifying its flaws, and suggesting government as a remedy for those flaws. The challenges of life in the state of nature engender considerable conflict, as we see in the states of nature described by Thomas Hobbes and John Locke.[109] In contrast, I contend that we can identify an attractive foundation for public reason if we focus on the less familiar analysis of the state of *war*. The significance of the state of war for our purposes is that characterizing it appropriately will help us identify its opposite—a state of moral peace.

Of course, analyses of the state of nature often appeal to the threat of the state of war, on the grounds that the former leads to the latter. Hobbes's theory postulates a particularly tight connection between the two. However, even for Hobbes, the state of nature and the state of war are conceptually distinct.[110] And for both Hobbes and Locke, states of nature are established merely by the absence of a public arbiter of disputes about the interpretation of natural law. In this way, states of nature can

---

[107] Fiala 2014.
[108] Rawls 2002, p. 47.
[109] Hobbes 1994, pp. 74–79; Locke [1690] 1988, pp. 269–278.
[110] Hobbes 1994, pp. 74–76. See Rousseau 1997, p. 46 and Locke [1690] 1988, p. 280.

lead to states of war, but they are not the same. Consider Locke's account of the state of war:

> The state of war is a state of enmity and destruction: and therefore declaring by word or action, not a passionate and hasty, but a sedate settled design upon another man's life, puts him in a *state of war* with him against whom he has declared such an intention, and so has exposed his life to the other's power to be taken away by him, or any one that joins with him in his defense, and espouses his quarrel.[111]

A society whose members use violent force against one another is in a state of war. However, persons can enter a state of war merely by one person developing a "declared design" upon another's life.[112] This means that the state of war can arise even if the attacks have yet to occur. In principle, a society could enter a state of war even if *everyone* were biding her time, waiting for the right moment to strike.

We can extend Locke's account of the state of war to a society in which a group mistakenly perceives a declared design upon its members' person and property. That misperception may be enough for the group to develop designs upon the person and property of others, if only to protect themselves. So we can establish a state of war simply by responding to the public expectation of aggression against person and property even if the purported aggressors in fact have no such plans. States of war can arise, therefore, merely from a change in public expectations about the dispositions of groups to use force. And this expectation can lead other groups to properly perceive a declared design upon themselves. Accordingly, we can imagine an entire society of peace lovers willing to submit to a common authority but who nonetheless lack assurance that others are so willing; such a society can thereby enter a state of war through false expectations alone.[113] In this way, a state of war can arise from a collapse in social trust since social trust depends upon empirical expectations that others will comply with recognized rules of peaceful conduct.

Critically for our purposes, the conditions for establishing Locke's state of war are not obviated by leaving the state of nature, since Locke claims that society enters a state of war if its ruler abuses his power.[114] A state of

---

[111] Locke [1690] 1988, p. 278. Emphasis mine.
[112] Ibid., p. 280.
[113] There are elements of this point in Hobbes's account, since most people want peace.
[114] At the least, society enters into a state of war with the ruler.

war is established by "he who attempts to get another man into his absolute power" since absolute power embodies a "declaration of design upon his life" or, less dangerously, an attempt to "take away the freedom that belongs to any one in the state [of nature]" or the freedom "belonging to those of society or commonwealth."[115] So even the existence of a nation-state with a constitution is not sufficient to exit the state of war. Improper uses of political power can create a state of war, just like improper uses of force in the state of nature. Therefore, a government creates a state of war between itself and its citizens just by *claiming* more power than the people delegated to it. The government need not even exercise that power. Combining this point with that of the previous paragraph, we can say that a government can create a state of war even when people mistakenly perceive that it has claimed more power than it has been given. That is, we can enter a state of war due to failures of social trust, in or out of the state of nature.[116]

We can begin to see how one might use the idea of social trust to distinguish between a politics of war and a politics of peace. When a society has justified social trust, it imposes a significant social restraint on our tendency to engage in nonmoral political conflict, even violent conflict, and so social trust helps to establish a condition of peace between persons. Consequently, institutions, practices, and commitments that create and sustain social trustworthiness can establish moral peace between persons, and so give us a social and political order that is not a state of war.

Recall the illusion of culpable dissent. Due to our own cognitive biases combined with the fact of evaluative pluralism, we will tend to regard deep evaluative disagreement as evidence that others are culpably mistaken in holding the views that they do. We can now see that the illusion of culpable dissent can undermine social trust because we often see the actions of others as driven by normative beliefs that they *know better* or *should have known better* than to act upon. That means we will be inclined to view their behavior as driven by nonmoral considerations, and perhaps as not capable of being motivated by moral considerations. How could

---

[115] Locke [1690] 1988, p. 279.
[116] John Dunn has made clear that Locke's social contract is concerned with trust, arguing that for Locke "the duty to be trustworthy simply is more fundamental than the moral rules or positive laws of any society," for without trust, "human society would not be possible at all." See Dunn 1984, p. 280. In one of his political essays, Locke claims that trust is the "bond of society." See Locke 1997, p. 132. So I believe my analysis of Locke's position is consistent with his thought. Simmons 1993, pp. 156–160 argues that breaches of trust and a return to the state of war are not always the same thing for Locke on the grounds that when a government fails to be trustworthy in protecting natural rights, it loses only the authority to enforce those particular rights. For our purposes, however, this refinement of Locke's position need not undermine my main point.

anyone vote to restrict abortion unless he wants to control women? How could *anyone* support the separation of church and state without secretly harboring a hatred of God? How could *anyone* oppose universal healthcare without being in the pay of the rich and powerful? How could *anyone* favor the redistribution of wealth without being in the grips of envy? The illusion of culpable dissent is powerful, but in these cases, we should acknowledge that many people support the policies they do conscientiously and after reflection. In a state of moral peace, where social trust exists, we observe that others largely comply with the moral rules of our order, even at cost to themselves, and that their compliance is driven at least in part by moral considerations. Social trust is therefore the fruit of observed trustworthiness, which becomes evidence of goodwill. In this way, a morally peaceful order full of moral behavior helps to overcome the illusion of culpable dissent. Most people, despite their deep disagreements, conduct themselves in a trustworthy fashion. Thus, we will no longer be so tempted to regard the fact of evaluative pluralism as ground for judging others to be mistaken. And this means there is hope that we will not regard our political differences as creating a state of mere conflict between the forces of light and the forces of darkness.

This chapter has developed the idea of justified social trust and moral peace between persons. That means justified social trust is central for demonstrating that politics need not be war. But before we can use justified social trust to defend liberal institutions, I have to explain the value of social trust and what respect requires of persons who trust one another. I turn to that task in chapter 2.

CHAPTER 2 | Trust and the Foundations of Public Justification

HOWEVER MUCH WE MAY disagree about politics, all of us can agree that love and friendship matter. Our relationships with our partners, friends, and families are, for most of us, what matter most of all. And regardless of whether we disagree about who should be president or which party should be in power, we have something else in common: these relationships which we value so dearly are founded on trust. There can be no moral relations of any kind, and certainly no love or friendship, without it.

The foundation of public justification is the value of moral relationships between persons, such as love and friendship. Without these moral relations, our social lives will be greatly impoverished, and so we have reason to act in ways that preserve them.[1] When our shared moral rules are publicly justified, they help to establish and preserve these relations by preserving social trust. Moral peace is a happy byproduct.

This way of connecting relationships, trust, and peace undergirds the recent attempt to ground public reason in the value of civic friendship.[2] I am skeptical that relations of friendship are general enough to characterize the relationship between citizens in a polity.[3] But if this line of defense is going to succeed, we must be able to root the

---

[1] Gaus 2011, p. 282.

[2] Ebels-Duggan 2010, Lister 2013, and Leland and Wietmarschen 2017 pursue this line of argument, though Leland and Wietmarschen expressly focus on grounding a principle of deliberative restraint, not an account of public justification.

[3] This skepticism is due in part to the observation in Muldoon 2016 that evaluative pluralism applies to the ways in which citizens conceive of themselves, such that some reasonable persons might see citizenship as involving civic friendship, but others might reasonably accept a thinner notion.

idea of public justification in the value of trust because trust is a precondition for civic friendship, for social trust is a precondition for friendship with strangers.

The need for moral relations with strangers points to an additional, and equally crucial, reason that social trust is valuable: social trust makes cooperation with strangers possible despite our deep disagreements. In a social order with high social trust, many of the great goods of social cooperation are more readily secured, such as economic growth and economic equality. So social trust not only sustains our most valuable relationships, it makes a productive, mass society possible.

We will also see that social trust helps to create a social context within which respect for other persons is possible. Within a system of trust, we can treat others with respect when we demonstrate our trustworthiness by following shared moral rules; we will also confine holding others accountable for violating moral rules to cases where we have ground for regarding their violations as culpable. This deontological value combines with the teleological values of social trust to yield a complex set of normative goods that only social trust can establish.

My emphasis on respect for persons will remind some readers of Charles Larmore's defense of public reason, where respect for persons is to ground public justification.[4] I think attempts to show that respect for persons *as such* requires the public justification of coercion have been subjected to powerful challenges by Christopher Eberle, Chad Van Schoelandt, and Gaus, but I do not need to repeat those challenges here because I do not need to reject the claim that respect for persons requires public justification.[5] I am simply offering an account of why respect for persons *within a system of trust* requires the public justification of moral rules, and legal and constitutional rules as supplements to moral rules. So I agree that respect requires public justification conditional on relations of trust, but I take no stand on whether respect for persons requires public justification unconditionally. View my arguments as trying to establish specific conditions under which respect for persons requires public justification, while allowing that respect could require public justification under other conditions.

The chapter unfolds in eight parts. In the first two sections, I explain the teleological value of a system of trust. Section 3 then explains why

---

[4] Larmore 2008, pp. 139–167 recapitulates Larmore's famous respect argument.
[5] For criticisms of the generic respect argument for public justification, see Eberle 2002, pp. 84–108, Van Schoelandt 2015, and Gaus 2018.

appealing to the teleological value of a system of trust is insufficient to motivate persons to sustain such a system. I examine the conditions required to justify and rationally sustain a system of trust by connecting the ideas of respect, social trust, and moral accountability in section 4. Sections 5 and 6 develop my two arguments from respect, the first based on the respect that trustees owe trusters, and the second based on the respect that trusters owe trustees. These are the argument from trustworthiness and the argument from accountability respectively. To transition into the next chapter, section 7 addresses concerns about obligations that may conflict with the trust-based obligations I identify. In section 8, I explore the interrelated teleological and deontic values found in a system of trust and the roles these two kinds of value play in the argument of the book.

1. The Social Value of a System of Trust

A *system of social trust* exists in any public that exhibits a high degree of social trust in a wide array of moral rules.[6] Thus, in a system of trust, persons are confident that others will be trustworthy with respect to moral rules that apply in a variety of social contexts. In such a system, people have a high degree of trust in the political system, the legal system, the economic system, and civic society.

Economists, sociologists, psychologists, and many others have argued that social trust is critical for maintaining well-functioning political and economic institutions. If members of a society do not trust one another, then they have little reason to take the risks required to create, build, and sustain good institutional structures. So it stands to reason that social trust contributes greatly to the goods that are reported in the social scientific literature. This is the *social* value of social trust—its contribution to the formation and maintenance of effective economic and political institutions.

Many researchers believe that social trust is critical for the creation of *social capital*, which Edward Glaeser, David Laibson, and Bruce Sacerdote define as "a person's social characteristics—including his social skills, charisma, and the size of his Rolodex—which enable him to reap market and non-market returns from interactions with others."[7] Social capital is built in part by being trustworthy in the eyes of others, and being trustworthy requires acting in concert with public expectations of norm

---

[6] I will use the terms "system of social trust" and "system of trust" interchangeably.

[7] Glaeser et al. 2002, p. 48. For further discussion and several related definitions, see Dasgupta and Serageldin 2000.

compliance. When we trust one another over a long period of time, we are able to establish social networks and other relationships that we can rely upon in taking the risks required to build social institutions. Social capital accumulates only within a system of social trust.

The World Bank has made a significant effort to measure social capital in various populations, making comparisons not merely between nations but between intranational organizations, regions, communities, and households.[8] The Social Capital Assessment Tool (SCAT) and the Social Capital Integrated Questionnaire (SC-IQ) are now used to measure social capital around the world.[9] The SCAT collects data on social capital at the household, community, and civic organizational level, providing information about how social capital is linked to the welfare and outcomes of families. The SC-IQ focuses on the degree of social capital found in developing nations. The World Bank keeps hundreds of studies using SCAT and SC-IQ measures in a database—the Social Capital Library.[10]

The metrics used to measure social trust are answers to one to three national and international survey questions. The most common question is this: "Generally speaking, would you say that most people can be trusted or that you can't be too careful in dealing with people?"[11] In more recent surveys, the following two questions have often been included: "Would you say that most of the time people try to be helpful or that they are mostly looking out for themselves?" And: "Do you think most people would try to take advantage of you if they got a chance or would they try to be fair?" In many cases, an overall social trust index is formed. Many readers will immediately worry that these questions are too vague. How could such simplistic survey questions form the basis for hundreds of studies and dozens of books? Perhaps surprisingly, it turns out that generalized trust is a stable measure across a wide variety of contexts, both across cultures[12] and within different radii of groups trusted.[13] Trust researchers often think that these measures of generalized trust really are getting at some stable, society-wide attitude[14] that other persons can be relied upon to engage in basic ethical behavior, which I would argue

---

[8] Grootaert et al. 2004.
[9] Grootaert and van Bastelaer 2001.
[10] When this book went to press, the database was inaccessible through the World Bank's website.
[11] Jennings and Stoker 2004, p. 350.
[12] Reeskens and Hooghe 2008, p. 530 find that "Generalized trust . . . seems to refer to the same latent structure across Europe."
[13] Delhey et al. 2011, p. 786.
[14] Nannestad 2008, p. 418.

is sustained by public compliance with moral rules, rather than broad assessments of personal character.

These studies largely conclude that social capital and economic performance measures are positively correlated. As Paul Whiteley has argued, "social capital . . . plays an important role in explaining the efficiency of political institutions, and in the economic performance of contemporary societies."[15] He focuses on a study of the relationship between social capital and economic growth in thirty-four countries between 1970 and 1992, and argues that the impact of social capital on growth "is at least as strong as that of human capital or education," both of which are themselves positively correlated with growth. Social capital has a similar impact on the ability of poorer nations to adopt technological innovations introduced by richer countries and to "catch up" with rich countries in terms of their level of development. Social capital is thought to reduce transaction costs in markets and reduce the burdens of enforcing agreements. It also limits fraud and theft. Recent work by Fabio Sabatini has helped to quantitatively substantiate Robert Putnam's famous comparison of northern Italian and southern Italian institutions, with the former exhibiting higher functioning and higher levels of social capital than the latter.[16] Sabatini finds that "strong ties," such as familial ties, do not promote economic development, but "weak ties" do, as weak ties act to diffuse knowledge and trust among strangers.[17] Vidmantas Jankauskas and Janina Seputiene have found that social capital, understood as a form of social trust and the maintenance of wide social networks, is positively correlated with economic performance in twenty-three European countries.[18] Reino Hjerppe, in a survey of the relationship between social capital and economic growth, argues that social/generalized trust positively correlates with many measures of economic performance.[19] Robert Hall and Charles Jones find that in 130 countries, differences in "social infrastructure" lead to considerable social differences in the accumulation of capital, in economic productivity, and even in educational attainment, which impacts income across countries.[20] And Bo Rothstein and Dietlind Stolle argue that a survey of the social

---

[15] Whiteley 2002, p. 443 equates social trust and social capital, but his point still stands if these ideas are distinguished in the way I have proposed.

[16] Putnam 1994.

[17] Sabatini 2007, pp. 19–20. We will see in the next book that social trust does seem to cause economic growth and probably not the other way around.

[18] They find no correlation, however, between the degree of civic involvement in these societies and economic performance. See Jankauskas and Seputiene 2007.

[19] Hjerppe 1998. The term "generalized trust" derives from Fukuyama 1995, p. 29.

[20] Hall and Jones 1999, p. 84.

trust literature finds that social capital produces "well-performing democratic institutions, personal happiness, optimism and tolerance, economic growth, and democratic stability."[21] The literature demonstrates the great value of social trust, since social trust facilitates the effective functioning of vital social institutions.

Many researchers are keen on distinguishing between trust *in society* and trust *in government*, and they worry that trust in society may not transfer to trust in government.[22] Rothstein and Stolle find that "citizens make distinctions between various types of institutions," though they do "make strong connections between the impartiality of institutions and generalized trust at the micro and macro levels."[23] They also argue that generalized trust is connected to *order* institutions, the legal institutions of police and the courts: "there is a rather strong relationship between aggregate levels of confidence in order institutions and generalized trust."[24] Generalized trust is weakened when people "experienced widespread corruption, inefficient institutions, unreliable police, and arbitrariness and bias of courts."[25]

Let's understand *political trust* specifically as trust in government, trust in democracy, or trust in more specific political institutions and groups, such as the civil service, parliament, and particular elected officials, but not trust in the legal system, such as the police and the courts.[26] Political trust itself probably has various positive effects, though the empirical evidence here is weaker than for the benefits of social trust. Marc Hetherington argues that political trust is important to give leaders the confidence they need to enact programs that improve lives.[27] Rothstein argues that countries with higher political trust have higher-quality government, which leads government to spend more on social policies and improve other outcomes.[28] Political trust may, therefore, make it easier for governments to function and so to give engaged citizens what they want in terms of better policy.[29] However, political trust might have drawbacks, as Hardin could be right that distrusting politicians can be useful.[30]

---

[21] Rothstein and Stolle 2008, p. 441.
[22] Hardin 2004, p. 151 stresses this distinction and doubts a connection between the two. See Cook 2001 and Braithwaite and Levi 1998 respectively.
[23] Rothstein and Stolle 2002, p. 27.
[24] Rothstein and Stolle 2008, p. 450. Emphasis mine.
[25] Ibid., p. 451.
[26] Norris 2017.
[27] Hetherington 2005.
[28] Rothstein 2011.
[29] I will discuss political trust in much more detail in the next book.
[30] Hardin 2004, p. 107.

The connection between social and political trust is less clear. While Rothstein and Stolle find that "there is no relationship between *political* institutions with elected office and generalized trust at the aggregate level," Sonja Zmerli and Ken Newton find "robust and statistically significant correlations between generalized trust, on the one hand, and confidence in political institutions and satisfaction with democracy, on the other" in twenty-three European countries and the United States.[31] So there is some evidence that generalized trust is connected to trust in political institutions.

A significant worry about much of the empirical literature derives from laboratory work on trustworthy behavior. Trust game experiments suggest a "lack of close correlation between behavior and questionnaire responses," such that those who say they are high trusters are not more likely to cooperate in micro-level trust games.[32] It should worry us that "the three questions most often used in survey research to measure general trust were not predictive of the likelihood that subjects will trust each other even in a repeated setting," such that the subjects may be "responding in a glib manner to this survey instrument." This is a serious concern, since it suggests that people may say that they trust, while acting as though they do not trust. However, the authors who made this discovery did find that "specific questions about past experiences of being trusted or extending trust in the past" were tied to trusting behavior and that the survey questions "were positively correlated with trustworthy, if not trusting, behavior." And since trust is arguably produced by the perception of trustworthy behavior, the fact that the authors find that high trusters behave in a trustworthy fashion in experimental settings provides a basis for social trust to form. Moreover, recent work has found a correlation between self-report measures of trust and trusting behavior in trust games with high financial payoffs; Sapienza et al. found that higher payoffs in the trust game draw trusting behavior closer to the survey measures.[33] And Rick Wilson found that "when the appropriate controls are put into place (at least among students in the lab), it appears that the first mover's behavior and the GSS item [the main trust question] are correlated."[34] So it looks like the trust game data need not be taken to undermine the survey data.

---

[31] Zmerli and Newton 2008, p. 706.
[32] Ahn et al. 2003, p. 345.
[33] Sapienza et al. 2013
[34] Wilson 2017, p. 8.

2. The Relational Value of a System of Trust

Social trust's connection to intrinsically valuable moral relations—romantic love and friendship-love in particular—provides a powerful second argument for its value.[35] When I speak of romantic love and friendship here, I am talking about what we might call, following Immanuel Kant, "moral" love and friendship, specifically love that is based not merely on emotional affect or passion, but that involves a sustained, rational commitment to maintaining a relationship with others.[36] Moral love excludes mere affective loves, such as a "crush" or finding interaction with another person pleasurable. Moral love can be understood as a rational commitment to satisfying two desires. To love is to desire the good of the beloved and union with the beloved—a willed connection that involves both the feeling of intimacy and the commitment to living life together, sharing burdens, celebrating each other's accomplishments, serving as confidants, and so on.[37]

Some philosophers deny that love includes a desire for union with the beloved. David Velleman has famously argued that "love is an arresting awareness of value in a person" where our motivation "is to suspend our emotional self-protection from the person rather than our self-interested designs on him."[38] If love is partly a desire for union, then Velleman would argue that, like any other theory on which love is a desire, the desire makes the beloved "instrumental . . . in which he is involved."[39] Instead, Velleman argues that the person who is loved is in an important sense *revered*: "he is a proper object for reverence, an attitude that stands back in appreciation of the rational creature he is, without inclining toward any particular results to be produced."[40] I agree with Velleman that the lover must regard the beloved as valuable simply in virtue of her personhood, but while love per se might be an appreciation of the beloved's value, romantic love and friendship essentially involve a desire for union. Lovers and friends want to be together; they may grow tired of one another, they may come to believe that their love is unhealthy and so avoid one another, but in the

---

[35] Adams 2018, p. 11 argues that "relations of trust enable and partially constitute some of the most valuable aspects of our lives," but does not connect valuable relationships to social trust in particular.

[36] Gaus 1990, pp. 287. Also see Kant [1797] 2009, pp. 217–278.

[37] Stump 2012, p. 91. See Aquinas, *Summa Theologica*, I-II q.26, a.4.

[38] Velleman 1999, p. 362.

[39] Ibid., p. 354.

[40] Ibid., p. 358.

normal case, these loves mean a desire to be in each other's presence. And I see nothing about the desire for togetherness that implies a failure to recognize the inherent worth and dignity of the beloved; for we may desire to be with the beloved because we value her. As Niko Kolodny argues, love involves valuing some kind of relationship with the beloved, however distant, such that love involves striving for some kind of union, and that this relationship is not valued instrumentally, but as a final end.[41]

Both kinds of moral love require responding to the reasons the beloved takes herself to have. If John loves Reba, he does not merely will Reba's good, but wills Reba's good as she understands it from her own perspective. As Rawls claimed, "Love clearly has among its main elements the desire to advance the other person's good as this person's rational self-love would require."[42] Kyla Ebels-Duggan argues that if we care merely for the interests of the beloved, and not her own understanding of her interests, we fail to "take the beloved's agency seriously enough."[43] Instead, given that "achieving her aims is what she takes herself to have most reason to do," it will seem to the beloved that "she should be able to count on her intimates to help her enact these choices." The problem with characterizing love in terms of desiring the objective best for a person is that "it refuses to acknowledge the beloved's competence and right to make the decisions that significantly affect her life."[44] Similarly, Melissa Seymour Fahmy argues that Kant believes that, with respect to those we love, our duties of love mean that "we are not simply obliged to promote others' happiness: we are obliged to promote their happiness *unselfishly* and in accordance with *their* conception of happiness."[45] Dean Cocking and Jeannette Kennett agree that "we shall miss much of the good of friends, and of what we think we have reason to do on account of friendship, if we focus exclusively on our pursuit of the well-being of the other."[46] Though Velleman disagrees with this view of love, he describes the common view as holding that all loves "necessarily [entail] a desire to 'care and share,' or to 'benefit and be with.' "[47]

This account of love raises a critical question: what if we come to believe that what our lover or friend desires is, in fact, bad for her? Ebels-Duggan

---

[41] Kolodny 2003, p. 151.
[42] Rawls 1999a, p. 166.
[43] Ebels-Duggan 2008, p. 151.
[44] Ibid., p. 153.
[45] Fahmy 2010, p. 327.
[46] Cocking and Kennett 2000, p. 284.
[47] Velleman 1999, p. 353.

argues that love essentially involves what she calls "authority in judgment" by treating the lover's "choice of an end as if it were evidence that the end is worthwhile," and while this does not require treating the lover's judgment as infallible, the lover "must operate under the presumption that [the beloved's] choices are good ones."[48] But then, what happens when you are justified in thinking the beloved's choice is not good? Do you still have reason to pursue your partner's ends, or at least help her advance her own? What "if you think your beloved's ends are not worthwhile—or worse, impermissible?"[49] Ebels-Duggan answers that we typically find it "uncomfortable to attribute confusion about what is worthwhile to our intimates." And yet, suppose our lover, or adult child, falls into drug addiction and she comes to affirm her addiction as good for her. In that case, does love require valuing drug use? Most people will say no, but that is likely because we think our beloved knows that she is fooling herself and that, even if she has formed a contrary judgment, she has done so under the duress of physical or mental addiction to the drug.

With a working conception of love, we can now identify three connections between love and social trust. A system of trust strengthens our capacity to sustain relations of love and friendship, allows for the establishment of relations of love and friendship beyond members of our in-group, and helps maintain relations of love and friendship among persons who leave the in-group.[50]

As shown, love requires that we see others as moral persons with a will of their own and that we take their desires and projects to give us reason to act. True love requires taking the perspective of the beloved into account in shaping almost all of our choices, from remembering to take out the trash to deciding how many children to have. Without trust, there is no basis for advancing the beloved's good as she understands it because we cannot make ourselves vulnerable to each other and so we cannot devote ourselves to one another's projects. Trust creates the conditions for the central activities that constitute and sustain love. So while we can love those who have betrayed our trust, love can only be sustained when lovers trust each other.

If we want love to endure, as most people do, we need *a lot* of trust, enough to ensure that the love will survive "changing interests and periods

---

[48] Ebels-Duggan 2008, p. 159.

[49] Ibid., p. 161.

[50] Preston-Roedder 2017, p. 7 argues that when a person is untrustworthy, "she forms a gulf between herself and people around her, and being cut off from others in this way is, by itself, undesirable."

of intense commitment to various projects."[51] If, for instance, one partner works to put another through medical school, then she has to trust that her partner will stay in the relationship once she completes her medical degree. During long nights alone, while the beloved is studying and working, the lover must trust that eventually she and the beloved will have a more intimate union. There is also a sense of entitlement at work, where the lover will resent the beloved if her sacrifice is not appreciated. Trustful love often invokes a sense of justice and reciprocity.

Many who write on social trust distinguish sharply between social trust and particularized trust, with particularized trust understood as trust in members of our immediate social circle.[52] So a critic might object that forming these loving relations with others only requires particularized trust, not social trust. But particularized trust is a less effective basis for love and friendship than generalized trust. Uslaner argues that persons formed and driven primarily by particularized trust have moral defects. They are frequently self-centered, have difficulties in establishing personal relationships, feel threatened by the outside world, tend toward paranoia, and lean toward authoritarianism.[53] Arguably, then, mere particularized trusters will be less able to love even members of their in-group because they are less likely to have the array of attitudes required to take the lover to be sources of reasons for them to act. So love rooted in justified social trust may make for a better sort of love because persons generally disposed to trust others will be better lovers.[54]

Love grounded in particularized trust is harder to sustain. If we see our friends and lovers as generally moral persons who respond to strangers with care and respect, this can strengthen our conviction that our friends and lovers are valuable social partners. So if romantic bonds and friendship loves are rooted in social trust, rather than particularized trust, they will be stronger and more stable. Persons will see that they have additional reason to love their partners and friends, for their partners and friends have generally good character, as exhibited by their treatment of strangers.

Second, in a system of trust, people not only trust members of their in-group, but most strangers as well. Since we cannot sustain relations of moral love and friendship without trust, then when we cannot trust

---

[51] Gaus 1990, p. 291.

[52] Some argue that social trust and particularized trust are not only poorly correlated, but may move in opposite directions. Uslaner 2002, pp. 31–35. Also see Fukuyama 1999, p. 241.

[53] Uslaner 2002, p. 123.

[54] High-trust persons can be good lovers, but experience of betrayal is bound to undermine one's trusting behavior over time.

strangers, we cannot form relations of love and friendship with them. That is a considerable cost; probably every reader of this book has formed valuable relations of love and friendship outside of her immediate in-group. In a low-trust order, forming and maintaining these relations would be impossible or risky. For a society without social trust is one that is likely to be in a kind of cold (or hot) civil war, with persons constantly pitted against one another and living in persistent fear that conflict can break out at any time. Justified social trust allows people to rationally let their guard down in order to form loving relations with others.

To see the third connection between social trust and love and friendship, suppose that we could be content with forming relations of love and friendship with members of our in-group. Even then social trust can help. People leave and enter social networks all the time, and not only by birth or death. Often marriage leads to joining a new group, say another religion. People often move to a new geographical location, and that involves an in-group shift as well. And all sorts of social and environmental challenges can lead to in-group cleavages, separations, and schisms. If we wish to maintain relations of love and friendship with people who were once members of our in-group but no longer are, then we have strong reason to value a system of trust. For without social trust, if someone leaves the in-group, retaining relations of love and friendship with that person will be exceedingly difficult. There may even be penalties for continuing to associate with those individuals, both from one's in-group and the in-group of the former friend or lover.

3. The Value of Trust Cannot Justify Trust

If we want to sustain a system of trust, however, we cannot simply point to the value of such a system.[55] There are two main reasons for this. First, we will encounter a familiar kind of social dilemma, since the social and relational value of trust can be enjoyed even if we individually decide to be untrustworthy, which creates an incentive to free ride on the trustworthy behavior and trusting attitudes of others. It is true that public failures of trustworthiness will tend to be punished, but there are other ways to undermine the system. For when people see themselves as having overall moral reason to comply with moral rules when others aren't watching, they will avoid socially destructive *opportunism*.

---

[55] I thank Jerry Gaus and Charles Larmore for encouraging me to reflect on this point.

David Rose defines opportunism as "acting to promote one's welfare by taking advantage of a trust extended by an individual, group, or society as a whole."[56] A critical feature of opportunism is that it does not always cause perceptible harm, or even any harm at all. If a society is sufficiently large, small acts of opportunism are not in themselves harmful. For example, taking a single bribe as a public official may not do perceptible harm, but it is opportunistic. We can understand bribe-taking and similar kinds of defection as *first-degree opportunism*, which involves taking advantage of the imperfect enforceability of contracts by reneging on them.[57] Taking a bribe or offering one is a case of first-order opportunism. Importantly, opportunism need not be driven by the desire to engage in immoral behavior. Instead, one might find greater *moral* value in being untrustworthy, such that the value of complying with a system of trust is overridden by the desire to achieve other sorts of value.[58]

Opportunism chips away at social trust because people cannot trust that community members will follow moral rules when their violations cannot be detected. This means that people may be tempted to believe that the social norms that we trust one another to follow are in fact disliked and ignored by other members of the public, such that our belief in the empirical and normative expectations of the rule is threatened. People might violate the norm in private, and their willingness to violate it may suggest that they do not think the norm is one they or anyone ought to follow. So we need norms to be seen as morally binding across social contexts, including in some cases where violations cannot be detected. The norm must be seen as prescribing the right thing to do in general, and guilt should be seen as the appropriate response to the observation that one has violated the norm. Guilt alone cannot prevent all cases of opportunism, but it can discourage violations to a significant enough degree to sustain compliance with moral rules in private and so to sustain social trust generally.

A second problem with appealing solely to the teleological value of a system of trust to sustain the system is that social trust is primarily a cognitive response to perceived trustworthiness.[59] We usually cannot trust others just because we think it will be beneficial for us to trust, just as we find it hard to believe a proposition because belief is beneficial and not

---

[56] Rose 2014, p. 21.
[57] Ibid., p. 30.
[58] I thank David Estlund for this point.
[59] For discussion of this point, see Simpson 2018.

because the belief is based on good evidence.[60] So to sustain a system of trust, we must engage in behaviors or recognize considerations that incentivize trustworthiness such that trust is an appropriate and motivating response. Thus, the reasons that sustain the system of trust must be reasons to be trustworthy and to respond appropriately to trustworthiness, and not merely that maintaining the system of trust confers benefits on all of us.

To sustain a system of trust for moral reasons, we must instead establish that members of the system of trust have *motivating, moral reasons to be trustworthy*. The reasons must be motivational if they are to drive people to engage in the desired lines of conduct, so we are looking for reasons that frequently lead people to act. They must also be motivating in order to override the temptation to realize greater value through moral rule violations. The reasons must be moral reasons to sustain social trust, both because social trust must be able to be motivated solely by moral reasons, and because when we believe that an action is morally required, we usually take it to override the temptation to pursue other kinds of value. In other words, we tend to see morality as having overriding force. Moreover, failing to act on one's moral reasons justifies the reactive attitude of guilt, which people usually prefer to avoid. Finally, the reasons must be reasons to be trustworthy, and not reasons to trust, because the only sustainable moral reason to trust is that one believes that others are trustworthy.

A critic might respond that, while trust is a response to perceived trustworthiness, our perceptions of trustworthiness can be colored by inappropriate factors. We are, after all, more inclined to regard the behavior of in-group members as trustworthy merely because the person is a member of the in-group. Social trust is mildly positively correlated with high societal ethnic homogeneity; people are more likely to trust those who look and speak like them.[61] The worry is that establishing that we have an impartial moral motive may not be sufficient to generate trust if in-group bias is significant, since in-group bias may generate a contradictory motive to not trust members of the out-group.

I acknowledge that in-group bias poses a difficult problem for maintaining social trust. And yet we frequently overcome it, especially in developed countries over the last several generations. My suggestion is that we have done so in part by establishing other bases for trustworthy

---

[60] I regard "therapeutic" trust, where we decide to trust others because we think it will incentivize them to act better, as deciding to act *as though* we trust others. Real trust is a response to perceived trustworthiness. See Keren 2014, p. 2597.

[61] Kahneman 2011. For a recent survey article finding either no or a small negative effect of ethnic heterogeneity on social trust, see Dinesen and Sønderskov 2017.

behavior besides in-group membership. Social institutions like liberal rights, democratic government, and open markets all help to sustain trust between diverse persons. So my task is to show how this can occur and how liberal institutions can help to strengthen social trust across difference.

A related concern is that social trust will be *sustained* on largely nonrational grounds, such that *justified* social trust is not a significant contributor to a social order's social trust. In that case, we can still argue that, while real-world social trust is not sustained by rational factors, it *would* be sustained by rational factors; that is, the rational basis of social trust would be sufficient to sustain social trust. So long as social trust can be sustained by rational factors, then we can say that politics in such an order is not war because rational reflection is enough to sustain social trust. Further, rational factors will not undermine social trust and moral peace, since each person will see the social trust in her order as justifiable for each person according to their own moral reasons. When people interrogate or scrutinize their and others' reasons to trust and be trustworthy, they will find adequate rationales for trust and trustworthiness. In brief, *reflection stops defection*. And so, in general, we will have no reason to abandon social trust and return to a "relentlessly self-interested world."[62] Showing that we have no such reason would be a considerable philosophical accomplishment.

A third related concern is that the empirical literature only shows that social trust has teleological value, not that *justified* social trust does. But a system of justified social trust has greater social and relational value than a system of unjustified social trust because social trust is more easily sustained, and its benefits more readily enjoyed, if it is based on the perception of trustworthiness. Further, "mere" social trust may coincide with justified social trust if mere social trust *could* be justified by perceived trustworthiness even if it is motivated by other factors. Finally, even if nonrational factors motivate most real social trust, then insofar as real social trust drives trustworthy behavior, then to that extent mere social trust justifies social trust indirectly; mere social trust motivates trustworthiness, and trustworthiness justifies social trust. In sum, then, social trust has enormous value, and a system of justified social trust will capture further value still.[63]

---

[62] Gaus 2018, p. 8.
[63] Though as we shall see repeatedly, public reason is not intended to maximize social trust; instead, we want free institutions to promote social trust only in ways that respect persons.

We must now locate motivating moral reasons that incentivize trust-worthy behavior and show how public justification might figure into duties generated by these moral reasons. Toward this end, I will argue that, within a system of social trust, respect for persons requires two forms of behavior: *being trustworthy* and *treating others as trustworthy.*

My argument is *not* that respect requires that we trust others. We do not have a duty to trust others, just to be trustworthy and treat others as trust-worthy under certain conditions. I reject a duty to trust for two reasons. First, trust is a belief, not an action like being trustworthy and treating others as trustworthy, and it is hard to make sense of the idea that we are obligated to others to believe *anything* that we do not already believe, given that beliefs are often not under our conscious control. Second, it seems wrong to say that a distrustful person violates her moral duties to others *simply* by being distrustful. She is blameworthy if she fails to be trustworthy or treats others wrongly, but a simple failure to have trusting beliefs is not a failure to do one's duty. A refusal to trust may indicate a character flaw, however, and certainly has great costs, since those who refuse to trust others cannot enjoy rich, stable relations of love and friend-ship with others.

Yet while respect for others does not require that we trust others, respect does require that we be *trustworthy.*[64] Respect requires that we supply others with trustworthy behavior; if we respect those who trust us, we will generally act according to their empirical and normative expectations.[65] Respect also requires that we hold those we trust *accountable* only when we perceive that they have violated shared moral rules. We confine our practice of holding others responsible or accountable to cases where others have failed to be trustworthy. Thus, respect can be connected to trustwor-thiness in two ways, yielding two arguments from respect.

The two arguments from respect will perform a normative double-duty. They will first identify reasons of respect to act in ways that sustain a system of trust, and so help explain what it means to sustain social trust in the right way. They will also show that persons *in a system of trust* can typically access and be motivated by the identified deontic reasons. Duties to be trustworthy and duties to only hold others accountable for

---

[64] My account of duties of trustworthiness and my rejection of a duty to trust thus fits Bicchieri, Xiao, and Muldoon 2011, who argue that trustworthiness is seen as a social norm, but trusting is not. People do not behave as though trust is a norm, but they think most will punish those who fail to be trustworthy.

[65] Though we are not required to be trustworthy in interactions with generally untrustworthy persons when being trustworthy makes us vulnerable to the untrustworthiness of those persons.

their culpable moral mistakes yield fairly obvious deontic reasons that motivate trustworthy behavior within a system of trust.

4. Trust, Punishment, and Accountability

Before developing these arguments, however, we must first understand how a system of trust is ordinarily maintained once we acknowledge reason to participate in such a system.[66] The most obvious way in which humans maintain social trust is by complying with the moral rules that are the object of trust; that is, by being trustworthy with respect to those rules. People then trust because it is a natural cognitive response to perceived trustworthiness. When we see people obeying costly or at least mildly burdensome social norms, like waiting their turn in line, holding the door for someone else, allowing another driver to merge into traffic, throwing away trash in a public park, and the like, we typically form the judgment that others can be trusted to do what is morally required of them because they seem trustworthy to us.

We have reason to be trustworthy not merely because we sometimes have independent moral reason to comply with a moral rule, but because we fear being punished for violations. To understand how punishment works within a system of trust, we must first understand the role of the reactive attitudes in that system. Remember that moral rules are social norms: we not only expect others to comply with moral rules, but think *others* think we all should follow the rules; and in the case of a moral rule, we think others think we all should follow the rules on pain of acting immorally. These normative expectations typically engender emotional reactions to violations of moral rules other than mere frustration or disappointment. We have reactive attitudes toward such persons—we are indignant with them when we observe a violation, and we resent them when the violation hurts us in some way. If someone skips in line, lets the door close in our face, refuses to allow us to merge into traffic, or litters in a public park, we experience resentment and indignation. As Gaus notes,

> we experience resentment because those who fail to meet our demands manifest an ill will toward us; we are indignant when, as a third party, we

---

[66] Typically a system of social trust is already in place, so the central problem is to determine how to maintain and strengthen such a system. I am skeptical that practical reason alone can give us sufficient reason to establish trust where there is none; we have to stumble into a system of trust, but practical reason can require us to maintain it.

do not really have the option of deciding whether or not we care about the attitudes of others toward us in these practices: we cannot help but react to the ill will of those with whom we interact.[67]

And in many cases, we feel guilt when *we* violate the relevant moral rule, since we regard ourselves as under the authority of the rule as well. We feel at least a twinge of culpability when we skip in line, fail to hold a door for someone, cut someone off in traffic, or litter in a public park.

Our reactive attitudes motivate punishment through blame and ostracism. Usually, when people observe violations of social norms, they react with blame and even physical attacks.[68] We'll condemn someone who cuts in line, honk at someone who won't let us merge into traffic, and scold a litterer, or at least scowl at her. We might even imprison someone for a serious crime.

Punishment is critical for maintaining a public moral framework like a system of trust. As Gaus further notes,

> maintaining a public moral framework requires maintaining shared expectations—rebuking people who do not act on the shared rules (their actions undermine empirical expectations) and those who make mistakes about what the rules require (and so undermine shared normative expectations).[69]

Punishment places costs on persons who violate moral rules beyond the costs of frustrating or disappointing others, given that being punished is a cost and often produces public shaming, which we typically prefer to avoid. Punishment is essential for incentivizing people to comply with moral rules because it imposes costs on violators. To maintain a system of trust, we *should* scold a litterer, or at least scowl at them.

A system of social trust, therefore, is a system of *accountability*.[70] In a system of social trust, we jointly trust one another to follow the moral rules of our community, and we hold others responsible or accountable for violating the moral rules that are the object of our trust. We do this because trust involves reliance on others, and a failure to comply with the rules suggests that others bear us ill will or perhaps want to benefit at our

---

[67] Gaus 2016, p. 181.
[68] Ibid, pp. 180–198, 212–218.
[69] Gaus 2016, p. 180.
[70] Brennan et al. 2016, p. 37 argue that norms form a system of accountability; I extend their insight by arguing that a system of accountability can sustain social trust.

expense. This generates the reactive attitudes, and motivates punishment as a response. And sanctioning behavior helps to keep moral rules in force, and so to maintain moral rules as social norms.

More strongly, a system of trust *necessitates* the presence of the reactive attitudes and a practice of accountability. Recall Strawson's distinction between the observer and participant attitudes about other persons.[71] When we have the observer attitude, we see other persons strategically—as obstacles or tools for our ends. The participant attitude recognizes others as moral agents and leads us to see ourselves as on a par with them, that is, as a moral agent as well.[72] From the participant perspective, we see ourselves as somehow in moral relations with those persons.

When we respond to our personal reasons to enter into an ongoing system of social trust and commit ourselves to maintaining and strengthening it, we must take the participant attitude toward others. Recall that in chapter 1, I argued that trust should be defined in terms of reliance on others from the participant perspective in order to distinguish trust from mere reliance. In this way, we see those we trust as moral agents who are accountable for their actions. So a decision to enter into a system of trust invariably involves taking up and honoring a practice of moral accountability. If we want social trust, we must bring the Strawsonian reactive attitudes, blame, and punishment along for the ride.

Punishment keeps moral rules in force by generating two kinds of fear of reprisal: fear of sanction *as such* and fear of *legitimate* sanction. We are driven by a desire to avoid the generic costs of the sanction of the community, which include factors like losing opportunities for personal gain. But fear of legitimate sanction will generate guilt in us and so appeal to our moral motivations. Often these fears coincide: we avoid littering both because we don't want others to disapprove of us and because we don't want to feel bad about ourselves.

The moral motivations generated by legitimate sanction are surprisingly important, and often matter much more than the pragmatic motives to avoid simple sanction. Persons punished for violating the normative expectations set by social norms will modify their behavior if they believe the punishment is legitimate. Bicchieri, Eugen Dimant, and Erte Xiao have found that punishment in line with normative expectations leads to major behavioral modification, but without this basis, punishment often fails.[73] Their finding

---

[71] Strawson 1974, p. 10.
[72] This notion of moral personality is central in Benn 1988, pp. 90–96.
[73] Bicchieri et al. 2018.

fits with a large amount of evidence accumulated over the past twenty years that "strongly indicates that when punishment fails to correspond to what people believe are legitimate normative expectations, punishment is either ineffective, or generates 'anti-social' counter-punishment."[74]

Now that we understand the connection between trust, punishment, and accountability, we can start to identify our moral, motivating reasons to be trustworthy. Once I introduce the respect-based arguments in the next two sections, we will see that a system of trust is maintained by four incentives. First, we often have a private desire to engage in moral behavior that motivates rule compliance on its own. Second, we are morally motivated to be trustworthy out of respect for those who trust us. Third, respect will also morally motivate us to give persons the benefit of the doubt if they appear trustworthy; we will treat them as trustworthy until they violate a moral rule in a way that suggests they are not trustworthy. When others fail to be trustworthy, we will only then hold them accountable, often through blame and punishment. Blame and punishment will motivate trustworthy behavior both out of fear of legitimate sanction and the costs of being sanctioned as such. The desires to avoid both forms of punishment provide the third and fourth incentives to be trustworthy. I now turn to the respect-based arguments.[75]

5. The Argument from Trustworthiness

We can connect respect to public justification by means of two arguments from reciprocal social trustworthiness. First, respect for those who trust us requires that we supply them with trustworthy behavior.[76] We will not ordinarily disappoint the normative expectations of others by engaging in untrustworthy behavior. Morality may permit deception or manipulation of others if we perceive that others are untrustworthy on some issue that puts us at risk of harm. But within a system of trust, respect for others requires that we be trustworthy to live up to the trust that others

---

[74] Barrett and Gaus 2018. Also see Bowles and Gintis 2011, p. 26.

[75] My arguments are meant to demonstrate that we *in fact* have duties of respect to others based on shared relations of trust and accountability. But in terms of providing incentives, people need only be motivated by their *belief* that they have these duties even if they lack those duties. My view is that our belief that we have these duties can be justified by showing that we in fact have those duties based on fairly ordinary and comprehensible moral considerations.

[76] Even, I think, if others trust us irrationally.

have placed in us.[77] Others rely upon us to comply with shared moral rules to achieve their ends. Thus, when we disappoint their expectations and violate what they take to be generally applicable moral requirements, in an important way, we subvert or undermine their rational agency and often deceive, mislead, or wrong them. Moreover, in many cases we should be grateful for the trust others place in us, and this can give us further reason to be trustworthy.[78] So, in relationships of trust and trust-worthiness, the "fact of trust on the part of one party is a reason for the other party to be trustworthy."[79]

However, respect for others does not require that we be trustworthy no matter what, even within a system of trust. We might have personal values or moral ideals that mandate our compliance regardless of our society's social norms. Sometimes respect for others prohibits us from doing what they think is morally required in favor of doing what *we* think is morally required, even if others disagree.[80] If a moral rule conflicts with a person's sincere religious faith, she will often feel as though she *must* disobey it. So when we perceive the violation of a norm *and* the violation is rooted in someone's conscience, typically our perception of trustworthiness is not entirely destroyed, or even lessened. We see that others are acting according to their moral ideal, so we think they are in general decent people who bear us no ill will and who can still be trusted to follow an array of other moral rules. Respect does not prescribe trustworthy behavior when trustworthy behavior would necessitate violating one's conscience or deep moral commitments.

To put things a bit more carefully, we can say that we are not required to be trustworthy with respect to our community's moral rule when our personal ideals and values provide a justification for ignoring the rule.[81] Respect does not require compliance when we have sufficient moral reason of our own to reject the rule in question. This suggests a connection

---

[77] Katherine Sweet worries that respect only requires that we (i) be trustworthy or (ii) announce that we are not trustworthy. But we often have independent moral reason to follow the norm, and we are seldom in a position where such announcement would be effective.

[78] O'Neil 2012, p. 303.

[79] Harding 2011, p. 84.

[80] For instance, as Mullin 2005, p. 322 notes, it will often "be right to betray trust, and the person trusted may be offended to be trusted in this way."

[81] It is, of course, true that if disobeying one norm were taken as evidence that a person would exercise her private judgment all the time, and her private judgment was expected to be at variance with many social norms, then we would be inclined to regard the person as untrustworthy. However, the person who constantly exercises her private judgment, I think, can be held responsible for failing to recognize that we at least sometimes have moral reason to defer to public judgment about what is morally required of us.

between respect and the idea of public justification, for public justification specifies the conditions under which trustworthy behavior is *compatible* with our personal ideals. Respect requires trustworthy behavior regarding shared moral rules so long as the rules are publicly justified for us.[82] Of course, completing the connection requires specifying an account of public justification, but I turn to that task in chapter 3.

We now have a preliminary case for the premises in one of our two arguments from respect. Call this the *argument from trustworthiness*:

1. Within a system of social trust, if A respects other members of the system of trust, then A will be trustworthy by complying with moral rules that are compatible with A's deep commitments and values.
2. A's compliance with moral rules is compatible with A's deep commitments and values if and only if the rules are publicly justified for A.
3. Within a system of social trust, if A respects other members of the system of trust, then A will be trustworthy by complying with moral rules that are publicly justified for A. (1, 2)

We have already seen the case for premise 1. Respect requires trustworthy behavior, but only when the moral rules that we trust one another to follow are compatible with the personal ideals of the agent in question. But there are limits on the deep commitments and values that we think are worthy of respect; a minimal conception of reasonableness, developed in chapter 3, helps draw a boundary between respect-worthy commitments and values and commitments and values that are beyond the pale.

It may appear that premise 1 prevents respect from requiring us to allow our personal ideals to be overridden by the value of a moral rule, as well as ruling out cases where everyone else's compliance with the rule generates reasons for compliance that outweigh objections derived from our deep commitments and values. However, these overriding conditions are addressed in premise 2; respect will require overriding our personal ideals and values when the balance of intelligible reasons favors compliance with moral rules instead of acting on our ideal.[83]

---

[82] Rather, so long as the rules are ones *we think* are publicly justified for others, since we will expect rules that are not justified for others to engender noncompliance, and so to undermine the behavior required to maintain the moral rule as a social norm.
[83] I thank Paul Billingham for raising this challenge.

The above explanation of social trust provides the groundwork for defending premise 2. If and *only* if a rule is publicly justified for an agent, does the agent has sufficient moral reason of her own to comply with the rule (and to internalize it as her own). To vindicate premise 2, however, we must carefully articulate a conception of compatibility. At a minimum, complying with a publicly justified rule is compatible with one's deep commitments and values when obeying the rule does not typically prevent one from living in accord with those deep commitments and values. But there is an ambiguity at work here, since the agent may or may not recognize the conflict, or may perceive a conflict when there is none. An account of moderate idealization, developed in chapter 3, will help explain the compatibility of the reasons to comply with the moral rules that are applied to a person and the reasons generated by one's personal commitments and values. Compliance with a moral rule is compatible with one's deep commitments and values just when a moderately idealized version of the agent detects no conflict between the reasons prescribed by moral rules and personal ideals.[84]

6. The Argument from Accountability

Within a system of trust, we will confine our practice of accountability to violations of shared moral rules, and only to moral rules we think are publicly justified.[85] Recall that if we trust others, we rely upon them to comply with shared moral rules, which we jointly understand as specifying what morality requires. We then build our lives around the belief that people will tend to do what morality requires and comply with these moral rules. And if we trust others to comply with moral rules, we will not ordinarily second-guess them unless they have given us reason to do so.[86] We let our guard down with those we trust and give them the benefit of the doubt.

---

[84] Another complication arises if other members of the public do not see public moral rules as compatible with A's deep commitments and values despite A believing they are compatible.

[85] An interesting case arises if A wants to hold B accountable for violating a moral rule R that she believes is publicly justified for B but not anyone else. One could argue that A should not hold B accountable because that may encourage false beliefs about shared normative or empirical expectations in B and other observers. Typically we hold others accountable to rules that we believe are justified at least for the large majority of persons. I can see the case for prohibiting holding B accountable for violating R when A believes R is defeated for most other people. Fortunately, the main line of argument in this book does not depend on whether there is such a prohibition or not.

[86] As Rose 2014, p. 135 argues, a high-trust order is "based on a convention of presumptively extending trust."

This means that our practice of accountability is only "activated" when we observe a failure in others to do what we regard (and understand that others regard) as the right thing to do. Accordingly, our trusting others means that we will *restrict* our practice of accountability to reprimanding persons whom we reasonably believe recognized, or should have recognized, reason to comply with the moral rule they broke.[87] We will hold other drivers accountable for violating traffic norms, but not if we have reason to believe they are in danger, say if they have their hazard lights on.

But as with the argument from trustworthiness, our practice of accountability must accommodate an exculpatory condition. For we cannot appropriately hold others accountable for violating a moral rule if we think that they believe compliance with the rule is incompatible with their personal ideals.[88] In that case, violations are reflective and sincere, and so the person is not truly accountable for a violation driven by the values she holds dear. Thus, we will hold other moral agents accountable for wrongdoing only in cases where they see themselves as having sufficient moral reason of their own to comply with the moral rule they have violated.[89] If we did not think they saw sufficient reason to comply, our practice of accountability would not make sense.[90] As I noted in the introduction, I do not hold the Amish accountable for holding up traffic in the Lancaster area; they pay great social and economic costs for their form of life. I do not think their mode of travel is blameworthy as a result.

In this way, we identify an exculpatory criterion for *moral responsibility*, specifically responsibility as accountability.[91] One way to understand this criterion is that it is based on the *epistemic condition* of moral responsibility.[92] The epistemic condition holds that a person can be responsible for an action only if she *knew better* than to act as she did, or that she *should* have known better than to act as she did.[93] If we cannot

---

[87] Kennedy and Schweitzer 2017 argue that publicly holding others accountable increases third-party trust in the accuser and reduces trust in the accused, so our practice of accountability may increase trust in many ways. Gaus 2018, p. 11 observes that a person who refuses to allow others to hold her legitimately accountable will undermine the trust that others have in her.

[88] Unless, again, these ideals are beyond the moral pale or that the person is culpable for the ideals she holds.

[89] As McLeod 2000, p. 474 argues, if persons "do not do what we trusted them to do through no fault of their own, then we would not say that they have betrayed us."

[90] Gaus 2011, p. 263.

[91] Shoemaker 2015, pp. 87–117. Also see Watson 1996.

[92] I am grateful to Brandon Warmke for encouraging me to explore the epistemic condition literature.

[93] Haji 1998, pp. 140–150 discusses the epistemic condition, as does Sher 2009. Robichaud and Wieland 2017 offer most current discussion of the epistemic condition.

say that someone knew better or that she should have known better than to act as she did, it seems obvious that we cannot appropriately hold her responsible for her actions. The epistemic condition raises a variety of complications that we must avoid here, so I will focus on defending my claim that conscientious, reflective dissent from a moral rule applied to a person by her society can violate the epistemic condition. If, as I argued in chapter 1, there can be reasonable disagreement about what is morally required of us, then a person can be mistaken about what is morally required of her even after deep and sincere consideration. This strongly suggests that the person in question has done her epistemic duty; she has attempted to gather the relevant information and engage in a respectable enough amount of reasoning that she can no longer be held accountable for not knowing that some moral requirement applies to her.[94] In other words, if a moral agent engages in a respectable amount of reasoning, it is no longer the case that she *should have* known better than to act as she did, such that she is thereby excused from violating the relevant moral requirement. Chapter 3 discusses this condition further, but for now we can see that social norms whose validity is reasonably disputed cannot ground our practice of accountability. As we shall see, the only moral rules that can ground our practice of accountability are ones that each person can see herself as having reason to accept.

People who trust one another will only hold one another accountable for violations of shared moral rules, save in cases where trusters recognize that the trustee is not responsible for the violation.[95] And one case in which the trustee is not responsible for violating a moral rule is when she reflectively and conscientiously dissents from the rule. Respect for persons enters the normative story here because in confining our practice of accountability toward those we trust in this way, we express due regard for them.[96]

---

[94] Gaus 2011, pp. 254–258 works out an account of a "respectable amount" of reasoning. A respectable amount of reasoning involves reasoning of adequate quality, where quality can be understood in terms of inferential success. In this way, we can avoid idealizations where persons embrace conspiracy theories after lots of bad reasoning. I thank Ami Palmer and Katherine Sweet for pressing me to consider this point.

[95] In this way, the person fails to be blameworthy. Mason 2015 distinguishes between "ordinary" and "objective" blameworthiness; ordinary blameworthiness occurs under conditions of moral knowledge, whereas objective blameworthiness occurs when an agent violates a moral rule she could not have known about but whose violation may yet indicate bad will. Here I appeal to ordinary blameworthiness.

[96] Holding others accountable for culpable moral mistakes can be disrespectful in a number of ways. It can be disrespectful because one can choose to engage in such an action based on an authoritarian mindset. Or it could be disrespectful for other reasons, such as a desire to deceive, to cause pain and embarrassment, to signal one's moral rectitude to third parties, and so on.

One might object that we do not need the deontic reasons grounded in our practice of accountability in order to sustain a system of social trust in the right way.[97] The argument from trustworthiness is perhaps enough. But the second argument identifies an important deontic reason that discourages holding others accountable when they are not morally culpable for moral rule violations. If members of the public are sensitive to these accountability-based deontic reasons, then they will hesitate to hold others accountable in cases where holding accountable would undermine the system of trust, both when they know that the trustee is not culpable for her moral mistake, and in cases where her culpability is unclear. A critic could reply that this deontic reason will make members of the public too hesitant to punish, as they might miss cases where persons are genuinely culpable. Yet while there is something lost in failures to hold others accountable for their culpable moral mistakes, the costs of mistakenly holding others accountable are considerable. They not only impose disapproval on trustees, they put the truster in danger of countersanctions from the trustees and from third parties. And by acting inappropriately, and bringing countersanctions on themselves, the truster may appear less trustworthy herself. Giving others the benefit of the doubt, therefore, should improve a system of trust's capacity to sustain itself, at least on balance.

We can now construct the second argument connecting respect and public justification, the *argument from accountability:*

4. Within a system of social trust, if A respects another member of the system of trust, B, then A will only hold B accountable to moral rules compliance with which is compatible with B's deep commitments and values.[98]
5. B's compliance with moral rules is compatible with B's deep commitments and values if and only if the rules are publicly justified for B.
6. Within a system of social trust, if A respects B, then A will only hold B accountable to moral rules that are publicly justified for B. (4, 5)

I have outlined the case for premise 4, which is that we only hold those we trust accountable for violating shared moral rules, save in cases where compliance with the rule is incompatible with one's deep commitments

---

[97] I thank Chad Van Schoelandt for raising this concern.
[98] Here we again confront the complication that arises from the case where A is mistaken about what B regards as compatible with B's deep commitments and values.

and values. That is a precondition for engaging in a coherent practice of accountability. And premise 5 is identical to premise 2 and so is grounded in the same arguments that we will examine in chapter 3. The conclusion follows.

7. Conflicting Obligations

We have two respect-based obligations to other members of a system of trust: we are obligated to be trustworthy with respect to publicly justified rules, and to hold others accountable only for violating publicly justified rules. In short, we are obliged to *be trustworthy* and *treat others as trustworthy*. Since trust is rationally justified by the perception of trustworthiness, discharging our obligations sustains a system of trust over time by providing moral motivation for persons to be trustworthy.[99] These two obligations are conditional on a system of trust having great social and relational value, since our observation of the low value of a system of trust will gradually undermine our motivation for complying with a system of trust's constitutive moral rules. But if we recognize the great teleological value of a system of trust, then our reasons of respect can fuel trustworthy behavior.

One powerful challenge to my trust foundation for public justification is that we have competing moral obligations that may override or cancel the respect-based obligations to be trustworthy and treat others as trustworthy.[100] Perhaps we have an obligation to minimize the suffering of others even if doing so requires that we be untrustworthy. I admit that I cannot show that this normative situation is impossible. But I can nonetheless offer four replies.

First, many of the moral obligations that might be thought to compete with those implied by a public justification principle will be recognized as binding by, and so publicly justified for, members of a system of trust. This is because persons are generally able to recognize which obligations apply to them. Thus, if a person has what appears to be an obligation to violate a *putatively* publicly justified moral rule, this suggests that rule is not justified for that person. Accordingly, the obligations generated by the public justification principle should not typically conflict with our other

---

[99] In the absence of strong nonrational countervailing factors that undermine belief in the trustworthiness of others.

[100] Including, perhaps, other moral obligations that derive from respect for others. I thank Eric Mack and Paul Billingham for this point.

moral obligations because our recognition of those duties will provide adequate ground to think that the putative publicly justified obligations are defeated, and so not obligations at all.

Second, even if we have obligations that would not be recognized by suitably idealized persons, such that these obligations will compete with the obligations generated by our respect-based duties in a system of trust, nevertheless, two *conditional* duties exist. We have duties to comply with publicly justified rules and only hold others accountable for violations of public justified rules in the absence of countervailing considerations. It may very well turn out that we seldom face countervailing considerations in our day-to-day lives, in which case we've established generally applicable duties to act that can appeal to public justification.

Third, even when we have *putatively* competing moral obligations that are strong enough to countervail the respect-based duties that I have identified, we should recognize that duties generated by respect for other persons are generally quite weighty and so are not easy to override. Our duty to be trustworthy out of respect for others, for instance, is quite strong for it enables us to maintain valuable moral relations with others.

Finally, we should bear in mind that actions that undermine a system of trust can have considerable costs by reducing the value realized by that system. Sometimes, of course, we can get away with untrustworthy behavior and such behavior may not threaten the system of trust in general. But when we are caught, we face social disapprobation and punishment from our community. And when we are not caught, we may feel guilt.

Fabian Wendt has worried that public reason liberals do not "allow for trade-offs between publicly justifiability and other values, since rights, justice, peace, etc. can sometimes be more important than respect for persons as it is expressed in publicly justifiable laws."[101] Notice that my first, third, and fourth replies effectively answer Wendt's concern. Respect for persons as it is expressed in publicly justifiable moral and legal rules is sensitive to considerations of rights, justice, etc. because those factors figure into determining what is publicly justified. And so many cases of putative conflict dissolve. The trust foundation for public justification also explains the great weight of respect expressed in publicly justifiable laws. Public reason liberals also have no burden of proof in vindicating the great priority they place on public justification because, on

---

[101] Wendt 2018, p. 14.

my trust-based account of public justification, other moral considerations are not disregarded.[102]

Most fundamentally, however, Wendt can be answered with Barrett and Gaus's critical point that the main reason public reason liberals appear to place undue weight on public justification is because public justification appears to prohibit imposing otherwise attractive *laws* on others. But if we adopt a conception of social order that places great importance on the role of social norms, then many unjustified laws will simply be infeasible or largely ignored unless they are publicly justified. Recognizing the limited conditions under which law can be effective lessens the conflict between public justification and imposing attractive laws.[103]

8. The Deontological and Teleological Value of Trust and Peace

We can now briefly summarize the teleological and deontological value of social trust and moral peace and how those values are interrelated.[104] A system of trust has *teleological* value because of the goods it encourages: effective institutional functioning and relations of romantic love and friendship. The system has *deontological* value because it is sustained by means of duties of respect to engage in certain lines of conduct.

The presence of each kind of value is necessary but not sufficient to sustain a system of trust in the right way. If we appeal solely to the teleological value of social trust, then members of the system of trust will have reason to free ride on the teleological value created by others because individual acts of trust and trustworthiness will not significantly contribute to a society's level of social trust. Further, appealing solely to the teleological value of social trust seems to allow us to maximize social trust in any way we can. But this is a mistake; we would not want to establish social trust by brainwashing, for instance.

If we appeal solely to the deontological value of social trust, then two other problems arise. First, it is not plausible that respect requires public justification in a society without social trust because respect does not require being trustworthy or treating others as trustworthy in a society without social trust. Respect does not require trusting and trustworthy behavior unless some degree of social trust already exists. Second, the very

---

[102] Wendt 2018, p. 5.
[103] Barrett and Gaus 2018, p. 2.
[104] I thank Chad Flanders for pressing me to clarify the relationship between the two types of value.

idea of treating persons we trust with respect is not possible unless a certain threshold of social trust has been reached.[105]

The idea of a threshold of social trust raises a challenge because problems arise if we set the threshold too high or too low. If we set the threshold too high, respect seldom requires trusting or trustworthy behavior; and treating others with respect plays a limited role in sustaining and increasing social trust. But if we set the threshold too low, trust may play no explanatory role in determining what respect requires, nor can we expect the duties of respect to generate social trust given how little trust there is in the first place.

Based on my account of the state of war in chapter 1, I argue that respect requires trustworthy behavior and a confined practice of accountability even with a relatively low threshold of social trust. Even if persons exhibit a relatively low level of social trust, trustworthy behavior is still expected and its absence is resented. Low trust societies are not conditions where all recognize that each person is out for herself such that "all is fair in love and war." Instead, persons' expectation of trust suggests that a low-trust society is failing its own standards, and not that such a society has dissolved into violent conflict. The hope, therefore, is that the duties of respect are activated by low levels of social trust and every degree of social trust above that low level, despite the fact that the duties of respect do not apply in the absence of social trust.

There is also a *causal* connection between the teleological and deontological value of social trust. Compliance with the duties of respect should cause social trust levels to rise over time.[106] For compliance with the duties of respect means that people will be trustworthy with respect to moral rules. They will be trustworthy based on four motivating factors. First, respect requires trustworthy behavior. Second, respect requires treating others as trustworthy until shown otherwise. Third and fourth, untrustworthy persons will fear the legitimate sanction of their community for failing to follow the rule, as well as the other social costs of being sanctioned. And social trust is a response to the perception of trustworthiness. This means that social trust will have the opportunity to accumulate. Moral peace, a state of society with a high degree of social trust, is the result.

We can therefore say that the deontological value of social trust *piggybacks* on the teleological value, since a threshold of teleological

---

[105] I thank Colin Manning for helping me to see the importance of the threshold of social trust.
[106] Or, more weakly, compliance with the duties of respect will increase social trust in the absence of strong countervailing forces and counteract factors that otherwise would reduce social trust.

value must be reached in order to realize the deontological value. The deontological value of social trust also *constrains* the teleological value; it prohibits methods of increasing social trust that treat others disrespectfully. And finally, the deontological value of social trust *increases* the teleological value, since the duties of respect generate trustworthy behavior, which generates social trust and, eventually, moral peace between persons.

Many contractarian theories relate teleological and deontological values in this way. For example, Rawls is concerned both with maintaining a system of social cooperation and with treating persons within that system with adequate respect. Rawls's version of public reason liberalism therefore appeals to a teleological value (stable social cooperation) and a deontological value (respect for persons as free and equal within a system of stable social cooperation). The deontological value piggybacks on the teleological value, since respect for persons only requires certain lines of conduct within a cooperative social order. The deontological value constrains the teleological value because social cooperation cannot be promoted by any means that would increase it; and the deontological value increases the teleological value since respectful behavior creates and sustains a stable system of social cooperation over time. So my contract theory is no more evaluatively complex than Rawlsian political liberalism.

Public justification factors into my evaluative categories because only publicly justified moral rules can sustain social trust in the right way. If the arguments from trustworthiness and accountability are successful, then we respect others by complying with publicly justified moral rules and only holding others accountable for violating publicly justified moral rules. So a publicly justified system of moral rules will sustain social trust respectfully.

Public justification therefore realizes teleological and deontological value. A system of publicly justified moral rules sustains social trust (the teleological value) in a respectful manner (the deontological value). The duties prescribed by publicly justified moral rules therefore piggyback on meeting a threshold of social trust because public justification is not required outside of a system of social trust. The duties prescribed by publicly justified moral rules also constrain the promotion of social trust; they prohibit increasing social trust by breaking publicly justified moral rules, they prohibit punishing others for breaking unjustified moral rules, and permit punishing others for breaking publicly justified moral rules. And the duties prescribed by publicly justified moral rules increase the level of social trust and so establish moral peace. Obeying publicly justified moral rules and punishing persons for violating publicly justified moral rules jointly increase trustworthy behavior and so increase the perception of trustworthiness in the population, which in turn increases social trust over time.

As we will see in the next chapter, compliance with moral rules is compatible with an agent's deep commitments and values if and only if the rules are publicly justified for her. This means that the idea of public justification must specify the compatibility relation between the reasons we have to comply with moral rules and the reasons we have to act on our first-personal commitments and values. I hope to show that specifying the compatibility relation involves appealing not merely to public justification, but to a particular interpretation of this contested idea. With a good interpretation in hand, we will have a teleological and deontological foundation for public justification and, eventually, for liberal institutions.

CHAPTER 3 | Public Justification

THIS CHAPTER DEVELOPS AN account of public justification, specifically the public justification of moral rules. I do so in order to explain the compatibility relation at work in the arguments from trustworthiness and accountability. I have to explain when complying with moral rules is compatible with our personal values and commitments. I claim that when a moral rule is publicly justified, complying with it flows from one's personal convictions. And this means that persons see themselves as having reason to be trustworthy by complying with the rule, and that a system of accountability can be applied to them, and others, to motivate obeying the rule. Justified social trust forms through the perception of this properly incentivized trustworthiness, which in turn drives the formation of moral peace between persons.

The compatibility relation specifies the compatibility of our *practical reasons*, our reasons for action. These are reasons of two types: our social reasons to comply with moral rules and our personal reasons to comply with our own values and commitments. Thus, the compatibility relation is understood in terms of a congruence of two types of reasons—*first-personal* reasons to act on our personal norms and values, and *second-personal* reasons to comply with publicly recognized rules.

Both types of reasons must be in some sense psychologically accessible, and morally motivating once accessed. The person who has the reasons must be able to see, on reflection, that the reasons are hers and motivate her to act morally in accord with either her personal moral standard or the public moral standard prevalent in her social order. If she cannot see the reasons as hers according to her moral standards, then her reasons cannot drive socially trustworthy behavior, since trustworthy behavior requires an appreciation of moral reasons. In the same way, her reasons cannot render her the appropriate subject of accountability. We cannot rightly insist that others comply with a moral rule, for instance, based on reasons that they cannot access and that are not moral reasons. Thus, inaccessible, nonmotivating reasons cannot drive trustworthiness, nor can we appropriately hold others accountable for failing to act on such reasons. So our aim is to specify the compatibility of a person's psychologically accessible, morally motivating reasons with her other reasons of that kind.

This chapter divides into four parts. First, I must address what is to be publicly justified, which I have thus far understood as a moral rule. I claim that the unit of public justification is an authoritative, public moral rule binding among free and equal moral persons. I do this in sections 1–4. Second, I must explain what sorts of reasons complete a public justification. I develop an account of sufficient *intelligible* reasons determined by the reasons grasped by *moderately* idealized agents. I must also address how to understand the idea of eligible and defeated moral rules that result from the account of justificatory reasons I advance. I do this in sections 5–11. Section 12 explains how public justification specifies the compatibility relation, which vindicates the arguments from trustworthiness and accountability. In section 13, I address concerns about how we can determine what is publicly justified. I then argue, in section 14, that my approach to public justification can withstand some common criticisms of public reason views, especially the claim that public justification requirements are self-defeating. Section 15 concludes.

Before I begin, note that my account of moral order supposes a deeply social account of the human person, one whose nature involves the disposition to comply with certain kinds of rules, the vast majority of which are not consented to in the way that traditional social contract theorists understand consent. In fact, even the institutions that confer psychological identity on persons are comprised of unchosen social rules, such as rules governing the family. Social rules are prior to individualist identity.

I also do not offer a metaphysic of human nature, and my project does not require that I offer a full philosophical anthropology. Instead, I merely assume that people are morally emotional rule-followers, and as such can jointly form a system of trust. I thereby make some verifiable claims about our moral psychology, and so about human nature, but I do not go beyond these claims. Consequently, my defense of liberalism should in no way depend upon the much-maligned "atomistic" individualism.

I also think that we have moral duties other than those derived from publicly justified moral rules. My aim in this work is to analyze a subset of the normative order, namely binding public moral rules that we hold others (and ourselves) to on pain of the reactive attitudes, blame, and punishment.

My defense of liberalism does offer a theory of the bases of obligations between equal persons, but I do not rule out the possibility of obligations to animals or to God. In this way, I again avoid objectionably individualist assumptions.

1. The Object of Public Justification: Moral Rules Revisited

As we saw in chapter 1, moral peace between persons obtains when significant justified social trust prevails among them, and social trust is justified when community members recognize that they have sufficient moral motivation to comply with moral rules. Moral rules are understood as social norms, practices publicly believed to be in effect and publicly recognized as grounding empirical and normative expectations. This means that moral rules must meet a publicity condition, where persons recognize that each person sees herself and others as having reason to comply with the norm.[1]

The public reason literature focuses largely on justifying broad moral principles rather than mid-level moral rules that specify particular classes of behavior. This raises the question of *individuation*, of how to specify the rule or principle that is the object of public justification. The public reason literature also usually focuses on the public justification of *legal* rules rather than moral rules.[2] And many of the arguments for individuating the object of public justification to fine-grained units like legal rules rather than coarse-grained units like principles of justice apply only to the law, and not to moral rules. This means we need new arguments for why moral rules are the prime object of public justification, which will involve explaining why we should justify moral rules rather than legal rules alone. We have already seen why moral rules are at the heart of public justification—because they are the central unit in sustaining and justifying social trust. So this leaves us to offer further arguments that we should justify moral rules rather than broader moral practices or principles.

Our cognitive limitations provide the simplest reason for fine-grained individuation at the level of moral rules. People are built to evaluate rules with quick applications of implicit cognitive judgments and emotional reactions. We are better at evaluating rules than lofty political principles, and our judgments about acts are governed by rule-based cognition,

---

[1] Though unlike Rawlsian accounts, they need not see themselves as having the same or similar reasons for endorsing the relevant norms. Rawls 2005, pp. 66–72.

[2] Ibid., p. 140. For a discussion of this controversy, see Quong 2011, pp. 273–287.

where rules classify all kinds of percepts and evaluations and dictate many of our actions.[3] It is harder to evaluate principles given all the factors that go into justifying one, rather than evaluating a local social regularity like a social norm. In the same vein, it is much more difficult to detect and punish *violations* of principles and constitutions than it is to detect and punish violators of rules. Principles and constitutions are extremely general; determining violations often requires a theorist or a judge. But nearly everyone can determine, and frequently does determine, whether someone has violated a moral rule. Instead, we need units of justification "that are sufficiently fine-grained to serve as the basis of our actual social life."[4]

Similarly, it is much easier to assess the *effects* of a single moral or legal rule than, say, the effects of constitutions and conceptions of justice, for we can develop relatively simple models of the effects of a law or moral practice. Obviously such judgments are fraught with difficulty, but evaluating rules against a backdrop of other rules is still easier than evaluating principles and constitutions.

A second reason to justify rules is that any more general level of individuation will require assuming or imposing some sort of harmonization upon its constituent rules that may not exist; this means that justification at the level of principles could foreclose paths to moral peace between persons. Moral peace might be reached through a patchwork of distinct and often unrelated rules, and not just through a unified system of rules that can be described by generic principles.

Some will object that rule-following is irrational when it sets back one's interests. I do not have the space to develop an account of the rationality of rule-following here.[5] Instead, I simply assume that such an account can be given such that our best account of practical rationality permits complying with rules simply because compliance with the rule is morally required. I make this assumption to develop a coherent account of the foundations of moral and political authority in terms of moral peace between persons, not to provide a full theory of practical reason.

Note here that I have not provided a criterion for individuating moral rules beyond the conditions for moral rules as social norms that I developed in chapter 1. A reader familiar with the public reason literature might wonder whether I need to explain how to individuate moral rules. We do not need such an account here because we have a clear enough

---

[3] Gaus 2011, pp. 101–122 reviews arguments to this effect.
[4] Ibid., p. 42.
[5] But see ibid., pp. 131–163.

idea of the level at which social norms operate to proceed with my argument. However, I will need to be more specific when individuating *laws* since laws often have a range of parts that do not always congeal into specific norms or even into coherent wholes of norms. Chapters 4 and 6 revisit this issue.[6]

2. The Authority of Moral Rules

A critical part of creating, maintaining, and reforming a system of social trust is the practice of issuing *moral demands* or demands that persons comply with the moral rules of their society.[7] Moral demands sustain moral rules because they help to sustain the empirical and normative expectations of compliance by clarifying in a public way what expectations are in place.

One form of moral demand plays a special and central role in sustaining a system of trust. We can identify it by looking at other kinds of moral demand. Consider John's simple *command* that Reba eat meat at his dinner party;[8] perhaps he thinks that Reba, his vegan guest, is being disrespectful by refusing to eat the meal he prepared. So John commands Reba to eat meat when he insists that Reba comply *regardless* of her attitude about eating meat. That the rule frustrates Reba's deep commitments and values matters little to John. He merely wishes to alter her behavior whether or not the demand has any rational uptake for her. John does not care whether Reba is actually culpable for her veganism, and so whether she sees herself as having reason to comply with a rule requiring that one eat a host's meal at a dinner party. John's command thereby undermines the system of trust since he insists that Reba violate her own code. Moreover, the action is disrespectful, since respect requires that we confine our actions in accord with our practice of accountability.

What if John were to issue meat-eating orders while *fully* realizing that the order is incompatible with Reba's deep commitments and values—in this case, her veganism? This would be even more problematic, since in this case, John flagrantly disregards Reba's perspective. Perhaps John is trying to prod or tempt Reba into violating her conscientious convictions. This is an active refusal to take Reba to be a source of reasons.

---

[6] And in much more detail in the next book.

[7] Adams 2018, pp. 8, 17 claims the authority of a commander is grounded in the judgment of the commanded that the commander is trustworthy.

[8] Maybe the demand is issued subtly by means of an offended look.

John may act in yet another way by issuing a moral demand *with regard* to Reba's perspective. In such a case, John issues a moral demand sincerely believing that the demand is rooted in a rule that Reba accepts, or should accept given *her*, not necessarily John's, commitments. Only this third sort of demand is capable of sustaining a system of trust. And so only this sort of moral demand can be part of a social system that establishes moral peace between persons. If John issues the command without having any way to know that Reba is a vegan, then his demand misfires, but it is not trust-undermining since he will cease his social pressuring when he grasps Reba's deep commitments. And were Reba not a vegan, then if there is a moral rule requiring that guests eat the meal that a host has prepared, John's demand would be appropriate.

If Reba were not a vegan, then John may have issued an *authoritative* moral demand. A moral demand has authority for Reba when her values and principles commit her to compliance. A moral demand derived from a rule has authority over Reba when she is committed to the rule. Thus, others are permitted to demand that Reba comply with the rule in question because their demands are simply demands to comply with Reba's own standards.[9] Consequently, authoritative moral demands will not typically lead Reba to experience the demand as alien or authoritarian. Instead, these demands will likely drive feelings of guilt and, accordingly, evoke motivation to behave differently or to defend one's actions as justified. If Reba is not a vegan, then she may feel guilt for refusing to eat John's meal; so she may eat the meal anyway, despite thinking the food tastes bad.

To be more precise, moral authority is a claim-right that the demander has for the demandee to comply with the demand.[10] If John makes an authoritative moral demand of Reba, then Reba owes it *to John* (and others) to comply with the demand. That is just part of what it means for a person to have authority over another—that the person *under* authority owes compliance to the person *in* authority. That said, in a system of moral rules, authority does not run in one direction, from authorities to subordinates. Instead, moral authority is equal and reciprocal: we may all insist that others comply with our social order's moral rules.

Authoritative moral demands issue from *obligations*, distinguished from mere duties. Duties are moral requirements, but they are not

---

[9] There will be cases where John is not permitted to demand that Reba live up to her own standards when there is a justified right of personal discretion to follow one's personal norms or when there are publicly justified standing rules, rules that govern who can hold others accountable. I discuss standing rules in the next book.

[10] Vallier 2014, pp. 25–26.

necessarily requirements that others are permitted to enforce through criticism, ostracism, or punishment; nor is a duty necessarily the appropriate subject of the reactive attitudes when violated. John may have a duty to worship God, but his failure to comply with the duty does not license the reactive attitudes in others. On my view, obligations are a type of duty with an inherently social component. Obligations are duties *to others* that others may hold us to; obligations thereby generate the rational reactive attitudes when violated.

Most public reason liberals understand public justification as vindicating the state's *liberty-right to coerce*, though not already each person's *claim-right to make moral demands*.[11] My approach to public justification differs from the mainstream because the master values are the value of a system of social trust, what respect requires of persons who trust one another, and the resulting state of moral peace. If our aim is to use public justification to establish justified social trust and moral peace, then our conception of public justification must reach beyond the law to all moral rules.

3. The Presumption in Favor of Moral Liberty

Liberals of many stripes endorse a presumption in favor of liberty with respect to *political coercion*. Without a good justification, political coercion should be regarded as unjustified. I contend, following Stanley Benn and Gaus, that social morality contains a parallel presumption in favor of *moral* liberty.[12] If we wish to ostracize others and order them around, our actions are only appropriate if others have some sufficient reason to endorse the rule upon which the ostracism is based. Without sufficient reason, persons are at moral liberty to act as they see fit.

To be more specific, persons are at moral liberty vis-à-vis *one another* to act as they see fit, since genuine moral requirements may apply to them even in conditions of moral liberty. John might have a duty to act in some fashion while no one has the permission to demand that he does so. So "moral liberty" occurs when someone is free from the legitimate interference of others. Consequently, a state of moral liberty is *not* a morality free zone,[13] but a *social* morality free zone. This distinction matters. If the presumption in favor of moral liberty applies to moral requirements *as such*, it

---

[11] For example, Rawls 2005, p. xliv adduces a liberal principle of legitimacy that specifies when the state has permission to coerce but not when a citizen is obligated to comply. Ibid., p. xliv.

[12] Benn 1988, p. 112; Gaus 2011, pp. 341–346.

[13] Gauthier 1986, pp. 83–112.

would be extremely implausible. The presumption in favor of moral liberty only applies to what others may demand of us.

Gaus characterizes the presumption in favor of liberty as follows:

> (1) agents are under no standing moral obligation (in social morality) to justify their choices to others; (2) it is wrong to exercise one's liberty so as to interfere with, block, or thwart the agency of another without justification.[14]

The presumption assumes that there is no moral obligation to justify all of one's actions to others, just actions that involve interfering with the agency of another, either through coercion or other forms of social control, like ostracism.

Why think that the public evaluation of moral rules contains this asymmetry between the justification of action and the justification of interference with action? One argument, first explored by Stanley Benn, asks us to imagine situations where one agent interferes with another and then to locate where *appropriate resentment* lies. Appealing to our shared understanding of the appropriateness of resentment is supposed to be evidence that some agent or another has committed a moral violation. Benn's case involves Alan splitting pebbles while Betty casually observes him; Betty then demands that Alan justify his behavior to Betty. Yet it seems clear that Betty is the one who owes Alan a justification because she is interfering with Alan's agency when Alan is not bothering her or anyone else. Consequently, the "burden of justification falls on the interferer, not on the person interfered with. So while Alan might properly resent Betty's interference, Betty has no ground for complaint against Alan."[15]

Benn's case illustrates that it would be inappropriate for Betty to resent Alan for failing to justify his pebble-splitting activities, but that it would be appropriate for Alan to resent Betty for interfering with his pebble-splitting. If you reject a presumption in favor of moral liberty, then you should also reject the idea that Alan's resentment of Betty is appropriate, since he is under a standing moral obligation to justify his actions to Betty and, by supposition, he has not done so. But it seems rather plain that he is not under such an obligation.

Another argument for the presumption against interference and in favor of moral liberty is that conforming our behavior to a presumption in favor of moral liberty helps to sustain a system of trust, and so create the

---

[14] Gaus 2011, p. 341. Also see Benn 1988, pp. 87–90.
[15] Benn 1988, pp. 344–345.

conditions for moral peace. Abiding by a presumption against interference means that we recognize that we need a reason to interfere with others; and we will generally take ourselves to have such a reason when other persons violate the moral rules of our community. Waiting for a good reason to interfere is a way to treat others as trustworthy and to allow others to respond to their reasons to act as we trust them to act.

The presumption in favor of moral liberty does not imply that moral rules must all be explicitly justified to those subject to them. Requiring express justification of all moral rules would be far too demanding. Instead, the presumption is met when a moral rule that legitimizes interference is *justified for* the person subject to the rule. Given the great benefits of moral rules, many of them meet the presumption rather easily. This explains why the presumption in favor of moral liberty can be hard to see, since it is frequently and easily met in most cases.[16]

The presumption becomes visible when members of a society reasonably disagree about what morality requires. For instance, when a restrictive norm begins to break down through challenge, such as social prohibitions on sex between two men, it is clear that if we are to *properly* hold men accountable for having sex with each other, men engaged in these acts must see themselves as having sufficient reason to refrain from those sex acts. Otherwise, we must regard them as confused or excused.

There are objections to the idea of a moral presumption in favor of liberty that I cannot review here.[17] My aim in this section has rather been to motivate the idea of a presumption based on both their familiar grounds and the value of social trust and moral peace.

4. Liberty and Equality

Liberty and equality are an integral part of a properly constructed order of moral rules. One way in which the value of liberty is recognized is by endorsing a presumption in favor of moral liberty, an unrebutted permission to act on our own judgment. Liberty has value because an abrogation of liberty must be justified. This is a form of negative liberty.[18] As we will see, some reasons can justify interference, and when others insist or force

---

[16] For a criticism of the presumption in favor of liberty, see Lister 2010, pp. 163–170.

[17] Paul Billingham suggests that one may not need to publicly justify interference that attempts to *resist unjustified* interference on the part of others. My account allows that such defensive interference need not be publicly justified.

[18] Vallier 2014, pp. 30–31 explores a related presumption against coercion.

us to comply with those justificatory reasons, we remain free. This is positive liberty—liberty with respect to practical rationality. On a classical positive liberty view, a person is free when she can act on her best reasons, when she can do what it is rational for her to do.[19] Public justification, therefore, employs two conceptions of liberty: a negative presumption in favor of liberty that can be overcome via the establishment of rules that enable our positive liberty. In this way, I contend that one's total liberty is preserved by a publicly justified moral order; what we have lost in negative liberty, we gain in positive liberty. This, I think, is what Jean-Jacques Rousseau was after: a way to preserve something like the liberty of the state of nature in civil legal society despite the fact that the latter requires restricting the liberty of persons.[20] Rousseau revives the idea of positive liberty from the ancients in order to pull off this trick.

We can also see a thin idea of equality at work. Following many others, I contend that moral authority is essentially reciprocal, and that moral rules are essentially reversible. As such, they do not refer to particular persons, and so will have authority only if they have authority for all members of the relevant moral community.[21] Moral rules should also ground relations of mutual accountability, where each person may make publicly justified demands of others. So no person has more justificatory power than anyone else. At this stage in my argument, the notion of equality is compatible with strong forms of social hierarchy, so long as the moral rules that exist in that order are rationally validated from multiple points of view.[22] Liberal theory requires thicker, more substantive egalitarian commitments, such as the possession of equal rights, a position I defend in chapters 5 and 7.

5. Intelligibility and Convergence

We have established that moral demands, and the interference associated with them, must have moral authority if they are to sustain a system of trust by incentivizing trustworthiness and accountability. We must now identify

---

[19] Plato thought a person's freedom is diminished when, for instance, he "enslaves the best part of himself to the most vicious" See Cooper 1997, p. 1197 (589e).

[20] Rousseau argues that once we establish the social contract and government, persons trade their "unlimited right to everything that tempts him and he can reach; what he gains is civil freedom and property in everything he possesses." See Rousseau 1997, pp. 9, 54.

[21] Darwall 2006, p. 21. Following Darwall, though with some revisions, Gaus 2011, pp. 22–23 argues that public justification solves the puzzles of moral authority and mutual, equal authority.

[22] Subordinates are unlikely to see hierarchy-preserving rules as justified for them, and so prevent these rules from being publicly justified. I discuss hierarchy and public justification in more detail in my discussion of associations in the sequel to this book.

the kind of reasons that determine when a moral demand is authoritative by meeting the presumption in favor of moral liberty. Toward this end, we must determine which reasons specify the compatibility relation. By specifying the contours of this set of *justificatory* reasons, we take a major step toward establishing a conception of justification that explains when moral rules are an appropriate basis for trustworthiness and accountability.

Recall that the set of justificatory reasons can only contain reasons that are psychologically accessible and morally motivating on reflection. Otherwise, we do not have an adequate account of the compatibility between following moral rules and our personal norms and values at the same time. Consequently, we will lack a philosophically attractive story about when we have reason to abide by (and, we shall see, to internalize) a moral rule.

In fact, my account of the set of justificatory reasons will specify both the justificatory reasons of particular persons and the justificatory reasons for members of the public as a whole. That is, we will have an account of when each person has sufficient reason of her *own* to comply with a moral rule, which can in turn be used to explain when the public has sufficient reason to comply with the rule. Thus, the set of justificatory reasons will determine when a moral rule is justified for each person, and so for every person subject to the moral rule. Social trust based on justificatory reasons will accordingly be based on the fact that all persons generally have sufficient moral reason that they can see to comply with the moral rules applied to them.

The set of justificatory reasons is broad because it is determined in part by recognizing the fact of evaluative pluralism, such that persons will have deeply divergent projects, plans, and principles, which will generate diverse and incompatible reasons for action. Thus, we cannot restrict the set of justificatory reasons too much and then only allow these privileged reasons to figure into public justifications for moral rules or as reasons to object to moral rules. If we wish to establish justified social trust among diverse persons, we must establish a scheme of moral rules that take each person's full deliberative perspective into account. This does not mean that we must take another person's reasons and values as serious options for us; we need only take her reasons and values to give *her* morally motivating and psychologically accessible reason to act.

Many public reason liberals insist that justificatory reasons be shared, shareable, or accessible.[23] In contrast, I defend a convergence conception

---

[23] For my critique shared and accessible reasons requirements, see Vallier 2014, pp. 104–111, and for criticisms, see pp. 121–123. Convergence approaches bypass many of the concerns raised in

of reasons that allows inaccessible and unshared reasons into public justification.[24] In this book, my defense of convergence is based on an account of trustworthiness and accountability. First, justified social trust must be driven by the reasons that each person sees as morally motivating for her. This means that she must be able to appeal to her full panoply of moral reasons. Were we to appeal merely to the reasons other agents share with us, we could show neither that they have reason to be trustworthy with respect to a moral rule nor that we can appropriately hold them accountable for violating the rule.

Second, if we restrain the reasons people may appeal to in order to justify endorsing moral rules, restraint will prove incredibly burdensome. Restraint would bar persons from using their diverse reasons to shape their shared moral order, in discourse and in action, inside and outside the traditional strictures of the public square. Most worrisomely, persons would be prevented from building their lives around diverse values that other persons have no shared reason to accept because they could not legitimately demand that their fundamental rights be protected on the basis of their deep values and commitments.[25]

We can also answer a new complaint about convergence views advanced by Watson and Hartley, who claim that convergence public justifications are versions of a "mutual advantage" view where agreements are not based on a shared, collective will.[26] A convergent public justification is moral since it appeals to the moral reasons of persons. Thus, convergent justifications form more than arrangements of mere mutual advantage. Further, a convergent justification is a way of forming a collective will on how to live together; it just offers a different interpretation of the idea of a collective will since it describes a collective agreement on moral and legal rules, even if people converge on them for different moral reasons.

6. The Intelligibility Requirement

I turn now to a positive account of the scope of the set of reasons that can figure into a public justification. The set must be restricted to recognizably

---

Enoch 2017, pp. 147, 160, since the epistemology of public reason doesn't have to ground what Enoch calls an accessibility requirement.

[24] Vallier 2014, pp. 124–130.

[25] One could reject restraint with respect to the reasons that justify moral rules but accept shared reasons requirements on public discourse about political decisions.

[26] Watson and Hartley 2018.

moral reasons, or at least reasons that the person in question can see as moral rather than as immoral. Call this the *moral criterion* on justificatory reasons. The set must not exclude the deep, personal reasons of citizens, either. To explain when diverse persons have sufficient reason to endorse a moral rule, we must allow persons to appeal to a wide range of personal practical reasons. Call this the *diversity criterion* on justificatory reasons.

My account of the set of justificatory reasons can be understood as an *intelligible reasons requirement*. The intelligible reasons requirement expands the set of justificatory reasons to its outer limit. In other words, it counts as justificatory any reason that can be recognized as such by members of the public. If R_A can be seen as a reason for agent A to act, then it can play a justificatory role, so long as R_A is relevant and not overridden or undercut by another justificatory reason. To put it another way, R_A can figure into a public justification if it is relevant and sufficient.

I take a reason R_A to be relevant just in case it counts in favor or against some proposed moral rule that members of the public are presently evaluating. For example, John's reason to refine his ability to pitch a fastball does not speak to whether his country should enforce the moral obligation to vaccinate children. Similarly, Sarah's reason to go on a bike ride neither supports nor undermines the case for a rule concerning morally offensive clothing. Further, reasons must be sufficient in the sense that they are not rebutted or undercut by other reasons. They must be sufficient reasons to justify action and belief. Sufficient reasons are those that remain undefeated, in that they are neither rebutted nor undercut.

Qualifications made, we can now define the intelligible reasons requirement. I define the requirement in terms of the property of intelligibility:

Intelligibility: A's reason R_A is intelligible for member of the public P if and only if P regards A as entitled to affirm R_A according to A's evaluative standards.[27]

The *Intelligible Reasons Requirement* (IRR) counts all and only intelligible reasons as justificatory.

IRR: A's reason R_A can figure in a justification for (or rejection of) a moral rule M only if it is intelligible to all members of the public.

---

[27] I here modify the definition of intelligibility found in Vallier 2014, pp. 104–108 and Vallier 2016a.

Intelligibility has four elements that require explication: (i) the idea of members of the public, (ii) the idea of regarding an individual as entitled to affirm a reason, (iii) the idea of an individual's evaluative standards, and finally (iv) the moral restrictions on what counts as a justificatory reason.[28]

Regarding (i), members of the public are rational representations of those persons on whom moral rules are imposed and the reasons moral persons affirm. Thus, John is represented among members of the public as an idealized version of himself, one that only affirms reasons based on adequate information and valid inference. John is said to have a reason, on this view, if he would affirm it in light of adequate information and reasoning. In this way, John is characterized as a reason-possessor at the appropriate level of idealization. As a group, then, members of the public denote the set of all reason possessors on whom moral rules are imposed, and so whose endorsements bear on the justification of a moral rule.[29]

The IRR requires unanimity because if members of the public cannot see the reason as intelligible, it is hard to understand how they can see it as a reason at all. If members of the public cannot even regard the reason as having epistemic credibility based on the evaluative standards of the person who offers it, then they cannot regard it as even minimally epistemically credible, and so cannot ascribe it normative force.[30] Further, without epistemic credentials, it is hard to determine whether the reason is held sincerely or, perhaps, even genuinely affirmed at all. A final consideration is that if we were to weaken the IRR to allow, say, a majority to regard the reasons as justified, then reasons can enter into public justification even if some members of the public cannot ascribe them epistemic credibility. This implies that members of the public would allow the moral order to be shaped by considerations that they cannot regard as normatively binding. Such an allowance does not comport with a commitment to respect the diverse perspectives of members of the public rather than their utterances or nonrational sentiments.

Regarding element (ii), we must explain what it means for a member of the public P to regard an agent A as entitled to affirm the reason based

---

[28] I have expanded on these conditions in Vallier 2016a.
[29] Gaus 2011, pp. 232–258 explains what it means for a member of the public to "have" a reason.
[30] Here I allow members of the public to ascribe epistemic credentials to a member's proffered reason based on that member's testimony, insofar as they recognize the member as a reliable testifier about the epistemic credibility of her own reasons.

on A's evaluative standards. Remember first that P is idealized in accord with a here-unspecified notion of idealization, so the notion of regard is epistemic, not factual. P regards A as entitled to affirm a reason by judging that a suitably rational and informed A is permitted to affirm the reason based on A's evidence. Idealization occurs twice: P is idealized such that she can construct a plausible model of the reasons A is entitled to affirm based on what A could rationally choose to affirm were A suitably idealized.

Epistemic entitlement refers to one having a right or permission to believe a claim versus having a duty to believe a claim.[31] Many entitlement theorists also hold that one can have an epistemic right to believe something for which one has no articulable or recognizable evidence.[32] Infants are presumably epistemically entitled to trust their perceptions, even if they are not cognitively sophisticated enough to make themselves aware of any evidence for their views. Epistemic entitlement does not require that, in being entitled to hold a belief, one be able to engage in "some sophisticated mental exercise."[33]

On to (iii): an evaluative standard is a set of prescriptive and descriptive norms a member of the public takes to justify her reason affirmations by providing standards that enable her to generate and order her moral and political proposals. Consider Roman Catholicism as providing a set of evaluative standards. Roman Catholic social thought is rooted in complex notions of natural law and the common good, which has led to a variety of social and political positions, many of which are hard to classify along traditional left-right spectra. Pope Francis has argued against abortion and in favor of restrictions on carbon emissions based on doctrines that he believes lie at the core of the Catholic social thought.[34] He sees no tension between the two views but rather a substantial unity. Catholic evaluative standards, then, are partly modes of prescription—moral and political considerations that lead Catholics to make certain proposals and reject others.

But notice that Catholic doctrine also has a descriptive component. Catholics believe that God imbues fetuses with souls at conception, or more accurately, that in the act of the creation of a human person, God creates a being with both substantial form (the soul) and matter. Catholics,

---

[31] I use the terms "entitlement" and "epistemic entitlement" and their respective grammatical variations interchangeably.
[32] Wolterstorff 2010, pp. 86–117 provides an overview of epistemic entitlement.
[33] For a general overview, see Altschul 2014.
[34] Francis 2015.

thus, rely heavily both on theism and Aristotelian metaphysics, most often in the combination developed by Thomas Aquinas. So Catholics develop and order their moral and political proposals not merely in accord with their values but by their beliefs about the nature of the social world, which for Catholics includes God and the unborn. In fact, arguably much of Catholic opposition to abortion is not based on unique moral evaluative standards, but rather descriptive ones. It is because human fetuses are persons that it is wrong to kill them. Everyone agrees that innocent persons should not be killed without a good reason, but in the Catholic social world, fetuses are persons, hence the moral and legal prohibition on abortion.

Finally, consider (iv), the intuitive moral limits on what reasons count as relevant to some justificatory question. Gaus puts the moral limits condition thus: "Certainly we must exclude . . . evaluative standards that disvalue the very idea of morality, value immoral acts qua immoral acts, disvalue conformity to justified moral rules, or value forcing people to conform to unjustified moral rules."[35] But on what basis may we do so and still establish justified social trust between members of the public? The traditional answer appeals to "reasonableness," where parties are interested in the moral enterprise of building a cooperative order with others who have a functioning sense of justice, who affirm the value of reciprocity, and who recognize the depth of pluralism.[36]

But appeals to reasonableness run afoul of a dilemma. The only way that reasonableness can give us a basis for excluding some evaluative standards from public justification is if it has some intuitive content, such that it is more than a mere term of art. Otherwise "reasonableness" only has normative force by stipulation. But public reason liberals build a great deal of content into the idea of the reasonable, which potentially renders it a normatively inert term of art. Accordingly, uses of reasonableness are torn between the intuitive notion, which lacks specific and substantive content, and the technical notion, which leaves reasonableness's normative force unexplained. Rawlsians maintain both that the idea of the reasonable is intuitive and can be fleshed out in specific ways. But I submit that this is a challenge that has yet to be met.

The best alternative, in my opinion, is to work with a more deflationary or thin moral notion that, while less able to rule out certain evaluative standards as immoral, will in combination with other features of a theory of public justification justify the negative reactive attitudes, blame, and

---

[35] Gaus 2011, p. 282.
[36] Rawls 2005, pp. 54–66 outlines the dominant account of reasonableness.

appropriate punishment. One key feature of reasonableness is that reasonable agents are normally prepared to be reciprocal cooperators.[37] An agent will cooperate when she believes others are prepared to do likewise even if she could do better by defecting. In Rawlsian terms, contractors are prepared to go beyond appealing to their threat advantage—the minimal share required to make cooperation in their instrumental interest.[38] Rawlsian contractors are reasonable in a second sense as well, for they must recognize the burdens of judgment.[39] My theory, however, does not require that contractors recognize the burdens of judgment for themselves.

My deflationary notion of reasonableness is capacious. To illustrate, consider the ethical egoism advanced by followers of Ayn Rand's Objectivism. Rawlsians could maintain that Objectivism is not a genuinely moral view, as it purportedly has no built-in notion of other-concern. But the Objectivist position resembles familiar forms of eudemonism; it is distinct in emphasizing that one can flourish in commercial activity and that the expression of ingenuity in the form of profit-seeking is a great life good.[40] Rawlsians may worry that Objectivists are not interested in developing a common, cooperative, public framework for social life. But Objectivists champion the voluntary formation of complex social orders based on positive-sum games and innovation. They are reciprocal cooperators. Objectivists just have a different conception (even if false and ultimately unjustified) of what it means to form a cooperative order, rather than no conception. I think it is rather difficult, then, to show that Objectivists are unreasonable in any but the technical sense, which, again, doesn't get us very far.

A deeper Rawlsian concern might be that allowing Objectivist reasons into public justification would generate injustice or justify illegitimate social and political arrangements. But remember that permitting reasons into public justification does not imply or even render probable that members of the public will be resented, blamed, punished, or coerced solely on the basis of those reasons. If Objectivists insist on implementing strong rights of private property, then whatever their reasons, Rawlsians will have their own reasons to object, in which case the Objectivist proposal is defeated. As a result, even if we allow Objectivist evaluative standards to count as reasonable, we are a far cry from being stuck with a publicly justified

---

[37] Gaus 2008b provides a useful formulation of reasonableness as a willingness to play assurance games rather than prisoner's dilemmas.
[38] Rawls 2002, p. 15.
[39] Rawls 2005, pp. 54–58.
[40] For a review of Rand's position, see Badhwar and Long 2014.

Objectivist legal order. However, if Objectivism is a reasonable comprehensive doctrine, then Objectivists can reasonably reject the large states Rawlsians typically endorse.[41]

While a deflationary notion of reasonableness rules out few evaluative standards, our intuitive notion of reasonableness prevents obviously defective evaluative standards from generating justificatory reasons. As we have seen, being reasonable requires being prepared to propose reciprocal terms of cooperation. If you insist on getting your own way and are unwilling to compromise in the formation of moral institutions, then it is natural to say that demands made in accord with those terms are morally inappropriate. As a result, evaluative standards that directly imply the permissibility of such demands can be ruled out of bounds as sources of justificatory reasons.

Similarly, and more generally, normal moral persons are interested in sustaining social trust with others, and within a system of trust they see others as ends and not as mere means. So, reasonable evaluative standards recognize that people are interested in moral relationships with one another. In this way, we can rule out deeply egoistic evaluative standards as unable to generate justificatory reasons. We can rule out sadistic and masochistic evaluative standards on the same basis because both kinds of standards endorse destroying goods for their own sake, either goods for others or for one's self.

Beyond this we cannot say much. But I do not think this is problematic, as there are many ways to block moral authority and moral demands other than condemning a host of evaluative standards as unreasonable. Given that the standard for allowing reasons into the justificatory process is not the only factor determining when rules and laws are justified, intelligibility theorists are not committed to regarding immoral or wicked proposals as just, legitimate, or authoritative.[42]

A perhaps stronger objection is that people with immoral evaluative standards will *veto* what we would normally regard as morally essential proposals, which is akin to Quong's worry that convergence views may not guarantee sufficiently liberal outcomes.[43] However, we are able to rule out some evaluative standards as unreasonable, and the rest of the book argues that liberal institutions are in fact publicly justified to persons with diverse evaluative standards. My approach does not conceptually

---

[41] I address which economic structures can survive this contest in the next book.

[42] I have more to say about reasonableness in Vallier 2014, pp. 146–151.

[43] Quong 2012, pp. 55–58.

guarantee that liberal institutions are justified, however, but I think this is a cost worth paying vis-à-vis using the idea of the reasonable to guarantee liberal outcomes directly.[44]

Now that we have specified the intelligibility requirement, we can see why it plays a central role in specifying the compatibility relation between a person's reasons to comply with a moral rule and her reasons to act on her deep commitments and values.

The intelligibility requirement excludes a range of reasons that run counter to moral behavior and that cannot be ratified by reasonable evaluative standards. So intelligible reasons will be recognizably moral reasons, or at least recognized as moral by the person who has the reasons. The intelligibility requirement therefore satisfies the moral criterion.

The intelligibility requirement also places few restrictions on the set of justificatory reasons, allowing a wide range of diverse reasons to figure into public justifications for moral rules. Thus, the intelligibility requirement, unlike more restrictive requirements, allows persons to appeal to their private reasons derived from their personal commitments and values in determining which moral rules apply to them. The diversity criterion is thereby satisfied.

In this way, our reasons to follow moral rules and our personal reasons are both typically intelligible, and so a person's intelligible reasons must be compatible with one another—congruent—for a moral rule to be publicly justified. When a moral rule is so justified, then complying with the rule is compatible with our personal reasons, and so establishes the basis of trustworthy behavior and our practice of accountability.

We must now show that intelligible reasons are adequately psychologically accessible and motivational. This can only be accomplished by appealing to a conception of idealization.

7. Idealization

To achieve adequate psychological accessibility and motivation, justificatory reasons must be all and only those reasons that a person can reach by a sound inferential route that is not beyond her ordinary cognitive capacities.[45] Thus, intelligible reasons should not be whatever reasons we presently accept, but ones that survive some degree of rational scrutiny.

---

[44] Muldoon and Vallier 2019 explain the costs and benefits of different approaches to public reason with regard to guaranteeing liberal outcomes.

[45] To simplify the argument, I here assume persons have roughly equal cognitive capacities.

At the same time, they should be reasons that ordinary persons can reach through reflection, and not reasons that would only be endorsed after a great amount of cognitive exertion. Call this the *cognition criterion*. The cognition criterion is critical if we are to identify reasons that are adequately motivating for normally functioning members of the public. If we require too little cognition to justify endorsing moral rules, it is hard to see how we have identified bona fide reasons for action, rather than mere present acceptances that may be based on no reasoning at all. But if we require too much cognition, then people will have to exert inordinate effort to arrive at an affirmation of these reasons. Consequently, it is hard to see how these hard-to-access reasons can explain the compatibility of our reasons to follow moral rules and our personal reasons in a way that explains when persons should be trustworthy. We can only expect persons to be trustworthy with respect to rules that they can ordinarily see a point in following.

Further, the cognition criterion also explains which reasons can ground our practice of accountability. We can only hold persons accountable for failing to respond to reasons that they can reasonably be expected to *know about*, or that we reasonably think they *should* have recognized as relevant and applying to them. Again, as noted in chapter 2, idealization must specify a kind of epistemic condition on moral responsibility-as-accountability; the reasons identified by idealization must be all and only those that a person can be held responsible for failing to act on or failing to recognize.

Idealization is used to characterize the relevant justificatory public and the idea of a sufficient reason to endorse or reject a moral rule.[46] Idealization is not meant to provide an account of all our normative reasons, or even all reasons relevant to justice and right action. Instead, idealization focuses entirely on identifying the reasons that can justify public moral and political authority, and their associated forms of ostracism, coercion, and punishment. Further, it is critical to recognize that idealization is not an attempt to defend a hypothetical consent theory. Instead, hypothetical models in public reason, going back to Rawls, are *heuristics* for determining the reasons real persons—"you and me"—possess.[47] So idealization works as follows: a justificatory reason is one that an individual would endorse if she were suitably idealized, perhaps as fully rational,

---

[46] In Vallier 2014, chapter 5, I developed a detailed conception of moderate idealization Here I expand that account to the public justification of moral rules.

[47] Rawls 2005, p. 28. I return to this point in my discussion of veils of ignorance in chapter 5.

informed, and reasonable in the Rawlsian sense, or perhaps as moderately rational, adequately informed, and minimally reasonable. Either way, the endorsements of the idealized person are *models* that output the reasons that apply to us in justifying moral and legal rules.

Public reason liberals idealize to avoid attributing reasons to persons based merely on what real-world persons presently endorse.[48] We should not tie the justification of moral rules to these nonrational factors, not only because we would end up with worse moral orders, but also because it is hard to see how such reasons could form a bona fide justification for ostracism or punishment in the first place. So the pressure to idealize is the pressure not to base a moral order on ignorance and irrationality.

Standard conceptions of idealization contain two epistemic dimensions, a rationality dimension and an information dimension.[49] These dimensions regulate what citizens believe about what they have reason to do. The rationality dimension regulates how citizens reason with respect to their beliefs, i.e., how they draw inferences from more fundamental beliefs to more complex beliefs and how they revise their beliefs in response to new data. The information dimension determines the nonnormative facts that persons can access—facts about the world and their present circumstances. The radical approach to idealization pushes both dimensions to their limit, assuming the public's reasons are modeled by what their perfectly rational and informed representatives would affirm.[50] The reasons identified by this process should comprise the most coherent and plausible harmonization of real-world persons' considered judgments. For example, Rawls's idealization, the original position, ascribes reasons to real persons, in particular reasons to comply with the two principles of justice, based on the reasoning of fully rational parties with a great deal of information, even behind the veil of ignorance.

But there are moderate conceptions of idealization that rely on more modest notions of rationality and information, such as the rationality and information necessary for real moral agents to navigate their social world given normal environmental constraints.[51] Individuals are boundedly rational and informed. I cannot here review all the reasons that one might

---

[48] Or, at least, the reasons real-world persons *claim* they endorse, since what current individuals *claim* to endorse is separated from what they *in fact* endorse by inferential errors and ignorance.
[49] Rawls 1999a, pp. 16–17, pp. 102–105 and Gauthier 1986, pp. 233–258 provide two influential models of idealization.
[50] Rawls 1999a, pp. 118–123.
[51] Gaus 2011, pp. 244–258. Also see Vallier 2014, chapter 5. Rosati 1995 advances an account of moderate idealization for subjectivism about the good.

radically or moderately idealize along both epistemic dimensions. But the trade-offs are relatively simple to state. If we radically idealize, public justification will not be subject to any irrationalities or ignorance, but the model of idealization will generate reason-ascriptions that are too far removed from ordinary agents' concerns. If we moderately idealize, we allow reason-ascriptions to be based on some nontrivial amount of irrationality and ignorance, but the reasons we ascribe to agents are connected to their real concerns.

The case for idealization in justifying moral rules is that idealization is required to satisfy the cognition criterion. The relevant cognition means that an agent can begin with her own evaluative commitments and trace an inferential path toward endorsing (or at least not rejecting) a moral rule her society applies to her. Radical idealization cannot satisfy the cognition criterion because it involves changing far more beliefs than is plausible for specifying when persons can see themselves as having reason to comply with a moral rule. We need a conception of idealization that shows that persons, *as they are*, can assess moral rules from their own perspectives. Radical idealization permits dramatic revisions to our beliefs and values. A radically idealized individual may lack the core commitments of her real-world counterpart, such that the reasons ascribed to her are not a plausible specification of the compatibility relation.

In the same way, we must idealize some if we are to establish that persons have reasons to act at all. Persons can only be said to have good reason to comply with a moral rule if their putative reasons have at least some epistemic virtue or merit. Present acceptances frequently lack any epistemic virtue or merit because they are based in bad inference or in culpable failures to gather relevant information. So if we are to insist on the rational endorsement of moral reasons, we must insist on using idealized accounts of the reasons we have.

Further, and critically for the argument from accountability, only moderate idealization can plausibly specify the epistemic condition on moral responsibility-as-accountability.[52] First, and most obviously, we

---

[52] Anthony Taylor has recently argued that the normative presuppositions of our practice of accountability and the associated reactive attitudes need not appeal to reasons that a person can necessarily come to grasp or appreciate through reflection and inference. Our practice is instead neutral between appealing to psychologically accessible reasons on the one hand and a person's capacity to be sensitive to her external reasons on the other. Taylor then argues that his "susceptibility to reasons" alternative is best. For Taylor's view, see Taylor 2018, pp. 107–110. Taylor's position is a nonstarter for my trust foundation for public justification, as reasons to trust must be internally accessible; they must be reasons we can psychologically access.

can appropriately hold persons accountable for acting on their present acceptances if their acceptances lead them to violate moral rules when the wrongdoer could have recognized reasons to abide by moral rules given some reasonable amount of reflection. If a person violates a moral rule by acting only on the reasons she can immediately see, she will often be insensitive to moral considerations that she plainly *should* have been sensitive to in deciding how to act. So that means we must idealize some in order to identify the moral reasons that a person can be held accountable for failing to act upon.

Critically, however, we must not hold Reba accountable for failing to act on moral reasons that she can only see if she were radically idealized. We cannot plausibly say that Reba *should have known* about reasons that she could only see if she were perfectly informed and fully rational because we cannot hold *anyone* responsible for not being perfectly informed or fully rational. In this way, I side with those who hold that some kinds of *moral ignorance*—a failure to recognize the true moral reasons that apply to a person—excuse.[53]

Moral ignorance excuses because our practice of accountability is only appropriate if Reba can recognize the moral reasons that apply to her after following plausible *duties of inquiry* rather than duties of belief.[54] That is, the responsible agent doesn't necessarily have a duty to believe in the moral reasons that apply to her, but rather a duty to inquire into the evidence that would lead her to form the belief that some moral reason applies to her; so we are not violating doxastic voluntarism in excusing some kinds of moral ignorance.[55] Moral ignorance only excuses if a person is not blameworthy for her ignorance; however, she may have engaged in what some in the literature call a "benighting" act where she willfully ignores evidence or fails to look for it.[56] So that means moral ignorance is blameworthy only if a person's ignorance is due to a benighting act at some point in her past, such that her ignorance can be *traced* to that act.[57]

Given the fact of evaluative pluralism, a person's failure to identify her *true* moral reasons is often morally excused. The Rawlsian and Hayekian

<hr />

[53] For recent discussion of whether moral ignorance excuses, see Wieland 2017. Also see Haji 1998, p. 173 and Zimmerman 1988, pp. 75–83.
[54] Tyndal 2016.
[55] Wieland 2017, pp. 6–9.
[56] Ibid., p. 12.
[57] For a recent critique of some tracing accounts, see Rudy-Hiller 2017, though Rudy-Hiller agrees with tracing accounts which allow that one can be responsible for one's ignorance in certain cases.

burdens of judgment plague our ability to identify these reasons. Even exemplary moral reasoning by real-world persons will sometimes lead to false moral beliefs; false moral beliefs, therefore, cannot always, or even usually, be traced to a benighting act.

Moderate idealization plausibly specifies what it means to take another to be a source of reasons and so to treat her with respect by treating her *perspective* with respect. A person's perspective is not merely her present set of acceptances, but rather consists in the reasons a person has given her core values and commitments. If we do not idealize, then the justificatory reasons we ascribe to persons may bear no necessary inferential connection to that person's core values and beliefs. By responding to those reasons, we would therefore not take her perspective into account, just her present acceptances, however biased or irrational. Similarly, we cannot appeal to radical idealization because radical idealization threatens to erase a person's values and commitments. Consequently, by responding to the radically idealized reasons of persons we would not be responding to *them* at all.[58] Similarly, if trusting others is a way of taking their perspectives into account, then if we appeal to radical idealization, we will not trust the person in question, but a rationally exemplary phantom.

Given the importance of properly incentivizing trustworthiness, and so providing the foundation for justified social trust, I do not think we need to worry that the moral reasons involved lack the best epistemic credentials. If our aim is to establish justified social trust among diverse persons by motivating trustworthiness, then moderately idealized reasons seem a better source of motivation than rationally exemplary reasons. For exemplary reasons cannot be plausibly ascribed to the real persons with whom we have established relations of trust.

Before turning to address a common concern about idealization in public reason, I want to stress the connection between idealized reasons and real-world trust because it may appear as though an account of idealized reasons will only drive *idealized* trust and trustworthiness, not *actual* trust and trustworthiness. Remember from chapter 2 that one goal of the trust model is to show that the social trust that we have, or that we could have with adequately liberal institutions, is compatible with the reason of all. People will have plenty of nonrational motives to be mistrustful and untrustworthy, as well as nonrational motives to be trusting and trustworthy. But rational reflection on their trust and trustworthiness

---

[58] Dorsey 2017 makes a similar point about how subjectivists about the good should limit idealization.

will not yield any good reason to be mistrustful or untrustworthy. This means that a morally peaceful polity is based on the reason of the public because members of the public see no reason to reduce or end their trusting and trustworthy behavior. These reasons can sustain social trust in the absence of countervailing factors.

On this view, then, moderate idealization establishes the conditions under which trust and trustworthiness are rationally justified. The fact that a moderately idealized agent has sufficient intelligible reason to accept and internalize a rule means that an agent who has internalized a rule will have no reason to reject it. It also implies that a reflective person will see that she has reason to internalize a rule that she has yet to internalize. Moderate idealization does not guarantee that some real person will accept or internalize the rule, only that a real person will, on reflection, find no reason to reject the moral rules on which social trust and trustworthiness are based.

Real persons are therefore addressed in two ways. They find no reason to be *less trustworthy* by defecting from a rule they have sufficient reason to accept. And they find no reason to be *less trusting* based on their assessment of whether others will defect from a rule they have sufficient reason to accept. Again, *reflection stops defection*.[59]

8. Wolterstorff and Enoch contra Idealization

Christopher Eberle, Enoch, and Nicholas Wolterstorff have all complained that idealization risks authoritarianism and paternalism by forcing people to comply with laws or moral rules that they would accept if properly idealized despite the fact that they in fact reject them.[60] I have elsewhere offered a generic reply to these criticisms, but here I want to defend my account of idealization against them.[61]

---

[59] Though, importantly, not *all* reflection stops defection, since cognitively demanding forms of reflection go beyond what moderately idealized agents will see, and so may yield complex and abstract reasons to defect from a system of trust. But given that moderately idealized agents are better proxies for our best reasoning than radically idealized agents, *most* reflection will stop defection. I cannot rule out the possibility that some intensely reflective people will find reason to defect from a system of trust, if for no other reason than that it is hard to know what intensely reflective people will tend to believe. The most intensely reflective people in human history tend to believe rather strange things, so they should probably not set our standard for reflection.

[60] Eberle 2002, pp. 209–233; Wolterstorff 2012, pp. 31–35, 68–75, 83–85, 103–110; Enoch 2013, pp. 159–160.

[61] Vallier 2019b.

Wolterstorff has worried that idealization severs the connection between respecting persons' rational autonomy and taking the concerns of their idealized counterpart into account. Wolterstorff writes:

> Why does respect for a person's rational autonomy, thus understood, justify us in ignoring his views, if he in fact disagrees with the legislation, and in coercing him? For that is what the proposal amounts to: ignoring the actual views of all those who are not fully rational. Why do only the rational people, along with everybody's fictional rational counterpart, count in the political calculus? Do we not deserve respect in our actuality as persons with political beliefs?[62]

For Wolterstorff, there is no clear argumentative connection between respecting persons and basing law on reasons those persons would affirm if idealized. In fact, there is serious risk of disrespect.

Similarly, Enoch complains that moderate (Gausian) idealization permits us to treat persons in a condescending fashion. If we treat people in accord with what their idealized counterparts would endorse, rather than what they actually endorse, we are patronizing. By treating people in accord with moderate idealization, we do something morally worse than treating them in accord with a mind-independent, transcendentally true moral principle. For the treatment literally "adds insult to injury." Gaus is both "willing to coerce his interlocutor based on a rule she doesn't endorse" and tells her "she misunderstands her own deep normative commitments." We certainly do not treat her as free and equal by acting in this way. As a result, Enoch claims, "the thought that by offering such a response [as Gaus's] any progress at all has been achieved in dealing with authoritarianism sounds ridiculous."[63]

What unites Enoch's and Wolterstorff's criticisms is the idea that the grounding value of public reason (be it respect or antiauthoritarianism) prohibits treating people according to what their idealized counterparts endorse. Wolterstorff cannot see how the value of autonomy permits us to disregard what persons actually, freely claim to endorse, whereas Enoch cannot see how the value of avoiding authoritarianism permits us to disregard what real persons freely claim to endorse. If we want to respect autonomy and prevent authoritarianism, appealing to idealization *frustrates* those aims.

---

[62] Wolterstorff 2012, p. 33.
[63] Enoch 2013, p. 166.

But the form of idealization I favor is meant to identify *reasons that properly incentivize trustworthiness*. Trustworthiness that flows from these reasons will justify social trust, which in turn gives rise to moral peace between persons. To establish moral peace, diverse persons must rationally endorse their social order's moral rules, or be disposed to endorse them when the basis for their trust is challenged, such that the rules survive the criticism of each person's moral point of view. Idealization tells us which reasons help the rules survive those criticisms. Thus, idealization is not a proxy for consent or autonomy, nor does it seek to avoid authoritarianism. In sustaining a system of trust, we should care about what others say they endorse, if for no other reason than that what others say they endorse may be our best indicator of what reasons they have. If we're going to idealize, we should do so humbly by appealing to others for information about their reasons. But the right account of the reasons that incentivize trustworthiness is not settled by what others presently endorse, but rather what they would endorse when moderately idealized. Because trust and trustworthiness explain the normativity of public justification on my view, rather than consent, autonomy, or nonauthoritarianism, we have good reason to idealize members of the public.

Consider again the Amish example. Suppose that Reba is frustrated that John, her neighbor, drives a horse and buggy instead of a car. She is frequently stuck behind him while driving, and John has made her late several times. Now suppose that John is Amish, that Reba knows this, but that John is still figuring out what being Amish requires. Imagine that Reba proposes that John drive a car instead of a horse and buggy to be kind to other drivers, and that trust is able to form around such a norm. The problem is that the terms of social trust will be dishonest or insincere. This is because John's compliance is not based on his psychologically accessible moral reasons given that his religion forbids driving electrical vehicles. Reba secures John's agreement on a moral rule while simultaneously believing that her best model of his reasons would lead him to reject the terms, since she knows about his Amish faith. Reba knows that John agrees to comply with the moral rule of driving cars on the road only because he has not thought things through, perhaps because he is new to the Amish community and does not recognize that driving cars is forbidden. Like a disreputable car salesman, she must close the deal before John thinks too much about the requirements of his faith. In an important sense, then, Reba pulls the wool over John's eyes and the eyes of all other people who cannot interrogate, or have not rationally interrogated, their moral rules. In this way, basing moral rules on what we presently claim to accept cannot establish long-term and stable trustworthiness, since even modest reflection will lead John to reject the moral rule that he would otherwise think he should follow. He need merely speak with his bishop to see his reasons to change his behavior.

In contrast, when Reba insists that John comply with moral rules that Reba believes could survive John's rational evaluation, such as requiring that he at least display reflector lights and turn signals on his buggy, she can validly hold him accountable for failure to comply with those moral rules. For he will be culpable for his failure to comply with the relevant moral rule because he has failed to be trustworthy. John recognizes the need to display reflector lights, and his bishop even requires that he do so out of love for his neighbor. This rule is one that John can accept and internalize and that will survive his own rational scrutiny. And we could know that this rule would fit John's commitments because we can develop an idealized model of John's reasons based on our understanding of his faith. Even if he initially misunderstood his commitments and agreed to drive a car, we could know, through idealization, that this was not a stable basis for mutual trust and trustworthiness. To identify the terms of a sustainable trust, then, we must idealize. Failing to idealize would lead us to base social trust on rules that cannot survive rational evaluation.

Part of the force of Wolterstorff's and Enoch's critique arises from imagining Reba browbeating John based on what the Reba believes John has most reason to do, even when John is telling Reba otherwise. But this is not an objection to idealization; instead, it is a complaint that Reba has misunderstood John's reasons. That is why it is vital to listen to real people. Reba is surely prone to error regarding John's evaluative standards; she may not know he is Amish or know what being Amish requires. Wolterstorff and Enoch worry that Reba discounts the complaints of real-world John when she appeals to idealization to discount John's real-world objections to her demands, or at least that public reason *permits* Reba to discount John's objections. But Reba only discounts John if she makes moral demands of him despite realizing that he lacks sufficient reason to endorse the moral rule that Reba demands John follow, as he arguably does in the case of driving a car. If Reba sincerely and carefully considers his objection to her demands, and her best model of his commitments indicates that John is mistaken about what he should value, then she can make a demand of him anyway. This is because her actions are shaped by her decision to take John to be a source of reasons, even if he explicitly disagrees with her demand.

To buttress the point, consider any case where we make moral demands of persons that they *know* better than to ignore. We think they're making excuses and trying to justify themselves based on bad reasons. A common example would be an addict who refuses to check into a rehabilitation facility so that she won't lose her children to child services. If Reba demands that John go to rehab, and John refuses, she may nonetheless demand that he go anyway, since she knows that he does not *really* want to keep hurting his children because of his addiction. Chapter 4 argues that in some cases, we may coerce persons to comply with laws on similar grounds.

9. Internalization and *Modus Vivendi* Moral Orders

When moral rules have authority based on the intelligible reasons of moderately idealized members of the public, they morally incentivize trustworthiness, justifying social trust and building moral peace. With this understanding, we can explain what endorsement involves: publicly justified moral rules should be *candidates for internalization*, rules that people accept as their own and hold themselves to given their own moral emotions. The idea of internalization is critical for distinguishing a morally peaceful society from one whose stability and persistence is based on mere power relations. In the latter *modus vivendi* society, people have *some* reason to comply with the rules to which they are subject, but these are not reasons to internalize those rules. Accordingly, any peace imposed is not *moral* because it is based merely on coercion, fear, and intimidation. The idea of internalization should help us distinguish between a polity based on a moral peace treaty from a *modus vivendi* truce that arrives when one group surrenders to another or a cease fire is established.

Sometimes *modus vivendi* regimes are understood as those whose stability is based primarily on a contingent balance of power rather than the fact that people can see themselves as its authors.[64] This is why *modus vivendi* regimes are said to rest on mere force rather than reason. In contrast, a publicly justified moral order should be stable based on the *moral* reasons of persons.

David McCabe, who defends a version of *modus vivendi* liberalism, argues that public reason liberals draw too hard-and-fast a distinction between our pragmatic reasons to follow laws under a *modus vivendi* regime and our principled reasons to follow laws in a publicly justified polity. The only way to defend such a distinction is to accept the

---

[64] Rawls 2005, p. 147.

"power-independence" assumption, which holds that "one's endorsement of some policy or principle is morally grounded only if one would not support a different policy or principle under a different balance of power."[65] On the power-independence assumption, a regime can only be publicly justified if citizens would support their favored laws if power relations differed. McCabe rightly points out, however, that every regime's stability depends on a balance of power because our moral judgments are often contingent on arrangements of power, and that it is hard to imagine laws that are *not* contingent in this way. For instance, we might support a law based on the fact that our favored party is out of power, but my reasons for such support are surely consonant with living in a publicly justified polity.

I agree with McCabe that it is hard to distinguish our pragmatic reasons for supporting laws under a *modus vivendi* regime from our principled moral reasons for supporting laws in a publicly justified polity. A *modus vivendi* regime provides us with powerful reasons to comply with its laws. Similarly, a *modus vivendi* moral order—one whose moral rules are stabilized by nonmoral factors—also gives us powerful reasons to act. We act to avoid ostracism and resentment, but not because we think the moral rule at issue is authoritative for us. Thus, if we are to characterize a morally peaceful society correctly, we must distinguish between the reasons that stabilize moral rules in publicly justified moral orders and the reasons that stabilize moral rules in *modus vivendi* regimes.

Fortunately, an answer is at hand. A morally peaceful society is one with a high degree of justified social trust, and trust necessarily involves the truster's belief that the trustee has moral reasons that are alone strong enough to motivate compliance with moral rules. This means that a *modus vivendi* order cannot stably establish trust because it is grounded in nonmoral reasons to act. While we can form reliable expectations about how others will act in a *modus vivendi* order, and so establish a measure of social stability, social trust will be low, which will give rise to considerable opportunism, that is, private defection.

In this way, the moral reasons that constitute relations of trust are not merely reasons to comply with moral rules. They are moral reasons to adopt the relevant moral rule as one's own. In fact, these are reasons to internalize the rule.[66] An agent internalizes the rule when she takes it to be personally binding, which will often generate guilt and other moral emotions when she fails to meet the requirement, "even if by doing so she

<hr />

[65] McCabe 2010, p. 126.
[66] Gaus 2011, pp. 202–204.

gets what she wants."[67] The person who complies with the rule based on a simple balance of reasons may well refuse to accord the rule authority over her. Again, a person can have a balance of reasons to comply with moral rules in a *modus vivendi* regime: she sees herself as having good reason to avoid legal and social penalties. But social trust requires that people endorse the rules that apply to them as their own.

I follow a number of theorists in understanding internalization as involving the reactive attitudes and responsibility claims.[68] A failure to comply with an internalized moral rule licenses others to resent John and hold him responsible for violating the rule. If John has internalized the rule, say a new rule to hold the door for both women and men and not just women, then, in an important sense, he *knows better* than to violate it by helping no one or helping women alone. He accepts the rule as morally binding on his actions, not merely as posing an external threat if he fails to comply. If we justify a rule based solely on reasons to comply and do not appeal to reasons to internalize the rule, then we may as well count reasons to fear reprisal as justificatory. So if John holds the door for men only because he doesn't want someone to be angry with him, we count his fear-based reasons as justificatory. By appealing to internalization via the reactive attitudes and our practices of trusting and holding responsible, we can distinguish reasons based on a *modus vivendi* from reasons that comprise a publicly justified polity.

Here, then, is how I understand the connection between trust, idealization, and internalization. Real trust can be sustained when people internalize moral rules and act on them for moral reasons (or at least they have sufficient moral reasons to motivate them to be trustworthy). Idealization therefore tells us when trust can survive rational scrutiny, such that no truster can see a reason to reduce her trust in others or to be untrustworthy with respect to internalized moral rules.

We now have a normative basis for distinguishing between *modus vivendi* regimes and publicly justified polities, between societies at *moral peace* and societies *at war*. We can say that a moral rule is publicly justified for John when John has sufficient, intelligible reasons to comply with and internalize the rule. Let us, therefore, understand publicly justified moral rules as the building blocks of a morally peaceful society. A *modus vivendi* regime can be defined as one where some sizeable portion of moral

---

[67] Ibid., p. 203. See Nunner-Winkler and Sodian 1988.
[68] Such as Taylor 1985, p. 85.

and legal rules fail to be publicly justified, but whose institutions are none-theless stable and effective.[69]

10. Eligible Sets and Social Choice

Evaluative pluralism implies that intelligible reasons can vary dramatically between persons. In a homogenous society, where people have the same religion, philosophy, geography, education level, family structure, race, and sexual orientation, we *might* be entitled to assume that people have more or less similar intelligible reasons. But in any large-scale social order, intelligible reasons are bound to differ greatly. Let us then further specify the fact of evaluative pluralism as a fact that persons' intelligible reasons will differ dramatically in a free, mass moral order.

The fact of evaluative pluralism implies that persons will disagree about which proposals are best. For this reason, my conception of public justification will take the diverse reasons of persons as inputs and generate an *eligible set of proposals* as its output. An eligible set of proposals is a set of moral rules that no suitably idealized member of the public has sufficient intelligible reason to reject. No member of the eligible set is defeated; all members of the public regard the proposals in the eligible set as superior to no proposal at all. This specifies a justificatory baseline of no rule, which I address in more detail in the next section.

An eligible set can be narrowed with a Pareto criterion, which holds that if each member of the public believes that a is superior to b, then the eligible set ranks a over b. If a proposal is Pareto superior to another, then the latter proposal is *dominated* and, by dominance reasoning, we can remove the dominated option from the eligible set of proposals in order to generate an *optimal* eligible set.[70] Dominated proposals are still *socially* eligible in the sense that members of the public regard the rule as better than nothing. But they can nonetheless be excluded from the optimal set.

Now, given evaluative pluralism, how many elements should we expect the optimal eligible set to contain: zero, one, or more than one? An optimal eligible set cannot be empty if the socially eligible set has at least one member, since the optimal eligible set is formed by all proposals superior to otherwise socially eligible proposals. Thus, when the optimal eligible

---

[69] I have characterized an ideal public justification as a *congruent* justification, one that realizes the ideal of congruence found in Rawls and other public reason liberals in Vallier 2015. For Rawls's analysis of congruence see Rawls 1999a, pp. 434–441.
[70] Gaus 2011, p. 323.

set is empty, we can infer that all moral rules are defeated, such that no moral rules have authority, and so cannot be the object of justified social trust. Given enough diversity, null sets abound.

Some optimal eligible sets will contain one and only one member, but this state of affairs should prove exceptional. Diverse intelligible reasons will arguably place more than one eligible proposal in many optimal eligible sets. Evaluative pluralism will also ensure that members of the public rank members of the optimal eligible set differently (if they ranked them identically, Pareto shrinks the set). Consequently, we can expect more than one eligible moral rule for regulating harmful, noncooperative behavior in many cases.

Optimal eligible sets with more than one member raise the question of how we are to select a proposal from the set, given that members of the public will want to institutionalize at least one member of the set as a real-world rule. Given the diverse reasoning of members of the public, further reasoning is unlikely to generate consensus. This means that we need some publicly justified *decision procedure* for social choice.

Loren Lomasky addresses the possibility of an optimal eligible set of proposals with more than one member.[71] On Lomasky's view, there are many combinations of rights that adequately split the difference between our desire to protect our holdings and to aggress against the holdings of others. A social contract cannot tell us which option is best, so we must appeal to social evolution to converge on a scheme of basic rights. Gaus develops a similar insight and applies it to public reason liberalism. And Rawls would eventually admit that multiple conceptions of justice are eligible and that reasonable persons will rank them differently, so he too can be understood as advancing an optimal eligible set with more than one member.[72]

In *Justificatory Liberalism*, Gaus argues that we should use publicly justified decision procedures to select a proposal from the optimal eligible set, which he understood as a set of "inconclusively justified" proposals.[73] So long as we can publicly justify a decision procedure, appealing to that procedure to select a member of the optimal eligible set is permitted and can lead to the conclusive justification of at least one proposal because the proposal is both undefeated and is selected by a publicly justified decision procedure.

---

[71] Lomasky 1987, p. 79.
[72] See the introduction to the paperback edition in Rawls 2005, pp. xxix–xxxvi.
[73] Gaus 1996, pp. 223–226.

In *The Order of Public Reason*, Gaus identifies a problem with using decision procedures in this way: if one procedure is publicly justified, others might be as well.[74] This raises the question of how members of the public are to choose decision procedures.[75] We might attempt to solve this problem by employing a *second-order* decision procedure to select a first-order decision procedure from an optimal eligible set of procedures. But this will generate a regress by requiring a third-order decision procedure to resolve dissensus about second-order decisions procedures, a fourth-order decision procedure for third-order dissensus, and so on. Gaus attempts to avoid the regress by denying that we must publicly justify the processes by which we settle on a moral rule and that we can converge on inconclusively justified moral rules via cultural evolution.[76] So Gaus now denies that we must conclusively justify decision procedures. I will follow him in this.[77]

11. Veto Power and the Justificatory Baseline

We can now see that evaluative pluralism means that different people have different intelligible reasons and that, as a result, many proposals may be optimally eligible even if members of the public rank them differently. But intelligible reasons also *defeat* many proposed moral rules. Defeat can be understood as *veto power*.

When a person has sufficient intelligible reason to reject a proposed moral rule, then the rule has no authority over her and, as a result, holding her to the rule violates our practice of accountability. That is all the presence of a member of the public's defeater reasons implies. This raises the distinct question of what we must do to repair our practice, which in turn should give us a sense for what should happen to a defeated moral rule. The most obvious thing to do is to stop demanding that the person with defeater reasons comply with the moral rule and to stop interfering with her to ensure that she complies.

In so doing, however, the moral rule may remain a social norm if people continue to affirm that all persons are normatively expected to comply

---

[74] Gaus 2011, pp. 391–393, 407 discusses related concerns.

[75] Since it is also possible that the eligible set of decision procedures is empty.

[76] Gaus 2011, pp. 389–409.

[77] I do not deny that some methods of settling on a member of the optimal eligible set might be unacceptable, but I am not aware of such a method. D'Agostino 2013 discusses the possibility of morally questionable methods of settling on a member of the optimal eligible set.

with the norm. Thus, the normative expectations might persist despite a failure of external sanctions. Giving up on external sanction, however, will probably tend to undermine normative expectations, since those tempted to defect will be able to defect without negative consequences. And, eventually, defection will weaken the belief in the prevalence of normative expectations. That said, Bicchieri allows that social norms might not be enforced by external sanctions, but perhaps motivated by other factors, such as a belief in the prudence of following the norm.

So the bare minimum behavioral requirement in response to the perceived defeat or veto of a social norm is to cease sanctioning norm violators. This might undermine the social norm, or it might not. Beyond this, however, members of the public might take three further courses of action. (a) They could selectively apply the rule only to persons who lack defeater reasons. (b) They can downgrade the social norm to a descriptive norm by rejecting normative expectations altogether. (c) Or they can seek to deprive the social norm of its empirical and normative expectations, destroying the norm.

My sense is that members of the public will assume that if the moral rule lacks authority for one individual, it probably lacks authority for many others who are not disobeying the rule. Moreover, tracking and distinguishing between people who have reason to go along with the norm and those who do not is quite cognitively demanding.[78] So for the most part, option (a) is off the table. Option (b) will be hard to maintain if the costs of following the norm are especially high, since people will not think that one another should follow the norm, just that they will. As a result, option (b) is most likely in cases where the costs of following the social norm are low relative to the benefits. This means that option (c) is most likely in cases where the costs of following the social norm are high relative to the benefits. Therefore, in cases where a moral rule is defeated, it may remain a social norm for some, become a descriptive norm for all, or cease to exist. The future of the norm depends on the persistence of normative and empirical expectations in the absence of external sanction.

So we can understand the defeat of a moral rule as implying that external sanctions on rule violators should not be applied because the moral rule cannot appropriately structure our practice of accountability. The violator cannot see, after a respectable amount of reasoning, that she has

---

[78] Though see the idea of standing rules in the next book.

sufficient intelligible reason to comply with the rule. The consequences of removing external sanctions for the social norm will vary.

In this way, when a moral rule is defeated, the presumption in favor of moral liberty is not met. And a defeated moral rule should not be backed by external sanction out of respect for the violator, since by supposition she lacks reason to be trustworthy with respect to the rule. Persons with defeater reasons for the relevant moral rule should be at moral liberty with respect to other members of the moral order to violate the norm without external sanction, blame, or punishment. Thus, the justificatory baseline is a state of moral liberty, and the presumption in favor of liberty is overcome only when a moral rule is publicly justified.

One might object that this justificatory baseline is too easily met. Some members of the public might regard a moral rule as barely superior to no rule but still deeply objectionable. Unless the other members of the public agree, and so all jointly prefer an alternative rule, the concerned members will be stuck with an unattractive rule. But we should question this objection. Recall from chapter 1 that all moral rules, by definition, must be seen as both reciprocal and promoting mutual benefit. It is not clear why moral rules meeting these conditions will be so deeply objectionable that adhering to a no-rule baseline will stick these members with a rule they despise. And if we raise the justificatory baseline, we will deny moral authority to many rules that can form the basis of social trust between persons because we will hold that such persons have adequate moral reason to disobey the rule even if they expressly regard the rule as superior to no rule. With a more demanding model of public justification, therefore, we may miss opportunities for identifying when social trust can be rationally sustained.

More common, however, is the converse concern, what we might call the *anarchy objection*.[79] The anarchy objection maintains that achieving public justification among diverse persons is exceedingly difficult, so much so that we can expect far more empty sets of proposals than we can tolerate. This is because an absence of eligible rules will prevent a society from performing its most basic functions, or at least prevent a society from *permissibly* performing its most basic functions. As Enoch puts it, *"everything*

---

[79] I have addressed this as an "empty set" objection in Vallier 2014, pp. 132–134. I thank Will Lugar for pushing me to mention this objection here, and Marcus Schultz-Bergin for helping me to understand the form of the objection.

is controversial" and so under any plausible idealization, "*nothing* is justifiable to all the reasonable." Given the plurality of diverse reasons in a diverse public, how could Enoch be wrong?[80] My first reply is that the conditions for eligibility are rather low, as noted earlier in this section; they're so low, in fact, that one may reasonably worry whether my account of public justification will ascribe authority to *too many* rules. This is because many *purported* cases of defeat are just cases where a member of the public regards a moral rule as highly suboptimal based on her own evaluative standards. The member of the public will object to both defeated and highly suboptimal rules, and theorists may fail to distinguish between those two types of objection.

That said, I concede that if we determine the eligible set of proposals solely by attending to reasons derived from each person's ideals and comprehensive doctrines, the anarchy objection may remain a serious threat. But members of the public are not concerned with living according to their evaluative standards alone, since they also value cooperating with others. And members of the public may also include among their evaluative standards the need to get along and even be reconciled to others. This means that many members of the public will acknowledge a trade-off between institutionalizing their values in the moral, legal, and political orders and being able to cooperate with diverse persons that do not share their values. One attractive feature of the trust foundation for public justification is that we have a rough idea of what the costs to cooperation will be—the lost opportunity for forming relations of social trust with others. In this way, a desire to live in a high-trust order can make more proposals eligible than otherwise.

Finally, the fact that some have defeaters for a moral rule does not imply that we must get rid of the rule if we can *exempt* the person with defeater reasons from being subject to the moral rule. One important role of freedom of association is to create a social context where persons are free to live under distinct and complex moral rules that do not apply to members of the public as a whole. So we can address some cases of defeat by allowing groups with defeaters to form their own subcommunities and live in accord with different sets of rules.[81]

---

[80] Enoch 2015, p. 122. For Enoch's full treatment of the anarchy objection, see pp. 118–130.
[81] I explore the conditions under which defeater reasons require exemptions or the repeal of *laws* in Vallier 2016b.

12. Public Justification and the Compatibility Relation

So far I have outlined the object of public justification (authoritative, internalized moral rules), the currency of public justification (a positive balance of intelligible reasons to comply with and internalize moral rules as authoritative), and the subject of public justification (moderately idealized members of the public with the commitments of real persons). It is now possible to define when a moral rule is publicly justified. To do so, consider the idea of a public justification for a single agent, which we can understand as *personal* justification:

> *Personal Justification*: a moral rule is personally justified for a member of the public only if the member has sufficient intelligible reason to comply with and internalize the rule.

To ensure that the reader connects my convergence and moderate idealization conception of public justification to the justification of each individual person, I have decided to use the somewhat less than ideal language of a moral rule being "publicly justified for an agent," despite the fact that many in the public reason literature restrict the meaning of "publicly" to refer to the public as a whole.

When a moral rule is publicly justified for each member of the public, we can say that the rule is publicly justified *full stop*:

> *Public Justification*: a moral rule is publicly justified only if each member of the public has sufficient intelligible reason to comply with and internalize the rule.

Public justification matters because it specifies the compatibility of the reasons one has to comply with a moral rule and the reasons one has to pursue one's personal commitments and values. If a moral rule is publicly justified for John, then it is practically rational for him to internalize and comply with the rule, so long as others do likewise (given that the rule is a social norm based on conditional preferences that others comply), even when compliance comes at some cost to him. This is because the set of intelligible reasons identified by moderate idealization are appropriately *moral, diverse, and cognitively accessible*. Reasons to comply with moral rules and the reasons to comply with one's personal commitments and values are thereby rendered consistent by establishing that the balance of reasons favors going along with the rule, and so that the reasons generated by one's personal commitments and values do not override the rule. We have established, therefore, that public justification is a *sufficient* condition for the compatibility of one's reasons to follow moral rules and the reasons derived from one's personal commitments and values.

Public justification is also a necessary condition for compatibility. To see this, note that the categories of public justification and defeat exhaust the justificatory valences of a moral rule. An extant moral rule must count either as defeated or as a member of the eligible set of proposals. If the rule is a member of an eligible set, then it will be publicly justified when it is in effect.[82] There is no middle ground because we never encounter a moral rule that we have no reason to obey or disobey. Following a rule often restricts our choices and licenses interference from others when we disobey the rule, so there is usually at least some reason to want to dissolve a moral rule in favor of a blameless liberty to act. It is equally rare, if not impossible, that the balance of our reasons to follow a rule and our reasons to reject the rule perfectly neutralize each other given all the ways in which diverse reasons can be weighed vis-à-vis one another. Thus, again, an extant moral rule must be either publicly justified or defeated. And one is free to disobey a defeated rule and refuse to internalize it, so a defeated moral rule is a poor basis for social trust and trustworthiness.

We can now formulate an argument that public justification is necessary for establishing the compatibility relation.

1. An [extant] moral rule is either publicly justified or defeated.
2. A's compliance with a publicly justified moral rule is compatible with A's deep commitments and values.
3. A's compliance with a defeated moral rule is not compatible with A's deep commitments and values.
4. Therefore, A's compliance with a moral rule is compatible with A's deep commitments and values only if the moral rule is publicly justified.

I have just argued for premise 1, and premises 2 and 3 are defended throughout the chapter. Since the conclusion follows and is the necessary condition of the second premise of the arguments from trustworthiness and accountability, we have established that public justification is necessary

---

[82] This is to assume that, because moral rules are in effect by definition, then if a moral rule exists and is a member of an eligible set of proposals, no two of which can be in effect simultaneously, then that moral rule will count as publicly justified since none of the others are in effect.

for establishing the compatibility relation. Thus, my conception of public justification vindicates premise 2 in the argument from trustworthiness and the identical premise 5 in the argument from accountability.

What this means is that moderately idealized intelligible reasons appropriately morally incentivize trustworthiness and are the only reasons that do so. Intelligible reasons explain both when a person has sufficient reason to be trustworthy by complying with a moral rule and when it is appropriate to hold another person accountable for violating a moral rule. In this way, publicly justified moral rules have the *unique power to sustain a system of trust* and establish relations of respect between persons in such a system. Because such reasons incentivize trustworthiness, and justified social trust is a rational and natural response to perceived trustworthiness, only publicly justified moral rules are a suitable basis for trustworthiness and the trust that follows. Since justified social trust generates moral peace, only publicly justified moral rules are capable of creating and sustaining moral peace between diverse persons. And because the rules are publicly justified, treating persons in accord with them is compatible with and even required by respect for persons within that system.

To illustrate, if John believes that a moral rule limiting driving speed (say not to exceed the legal limit by seven miles an hour or more) is publicly justified for other people on the road, then he believes that persons see themselves as having sufficient reason to comply with the rule. That means that they will be disposed to comply with the rule, and so be trustworthy with respect to it. Consequently, John can justifiably trust that persons will comply with the rule; so when he observes compliance, his resulting trust is strengthened or at least not diminished. Further, if John observes excessive speeding, he will regard others as culpable for violating the rule, and so as violating the public trust. John's extension of a presumption of trustworthiness to the speeding driver is undermined, and holding the speeding driver accountable becomes an appropriate response to the violation.

The main argument of this chapter can be summarized as an attempt to establish the following claim:

A's compliance with a moral rule is compatible with A's deep commitments and values if and only if the rule is publicly justified for A.

Again, this is the key second premise in both the argument from trustworthiness and the argument from accountability. The reason that the premise is true is that the moderate idealization / intelligible reasons approach to public justification offers an attractive specification of the compatibility relation because the approach satisfies the moral, diversity, and cognition criteria. The reasons are moral because they are recognized as such by a range of reasonable evaluative standards. The reasons are diverse because intelligible reasons are remarkably varied reasons. And the reasons are cognitively accessible because they are arrived at by moderate rather than radical idealization. Defeated rules, in contrast, do not render compliance compatible with a person's deep commitments and values because the rule is not endorsed by diverse, cognitively accessible moral reasons.

13. Knowing What Is Publicly Justified

In chapter 1, I argued that the Rawlsian and Hayekian burdens of judgment make it hard for us to know what others believe themselves to have reason to do. Further, I have claimed that public justification can proceed only in terms of intelligible reasons, many of which will not be shared. Accordingly, the reader is bound to wonder whether we can ever know what is publicly justified for members of the public given how hard it is to know their reasons.[83] And if we can't know when a moral or legal rule is publicly justified, then that is a problem for my view.

In response, I interpret the point of public justification somewhat narrowly in the following sense. Public justification is not meant to construct a full, complete account of which moral and legal rules are justified for particular members of the public. It is, rather, a standard for addressing social conflicts as they arise. Once someone complains about being subject to a rule, we can use a public justification principle to determine whether her objection is legitimate and what sort of social reform must be pursued to address that objection. We can call this approach a "testing conception" of public justification because it involves testing rules in light of objections to see if the rules meet the standard of public justification.[84] I adopt a testing conception because, on my view, when complaints about rules arise, public justification helps to determine whether those controversial rules undermine relations of trust and whether reforming the rule, or dissolving it, improves our social order's capacity to sustain a high level of social trust in the right way.

If we adopt a testing conception, how might we determine what is publicly justified in the real world? There are several methods. First, we

---

[83] I have addressed this concern in my previous book, but it is worth renewing what I said there given the importance of this objection. See Vallier 2014, pp. 172–177.
[84] Gaus 2011, pp. 424–427.

can consult the deliberation between members of the public to see which arguments and reasons they offer for their positions. Second, we can study rule compliance to determine whether people in practice take themselves to have reason to comply with a moral or legal rule. Third, we can examine specialized forms of media, as movies, television shows, and novels can often track important social conflicts and can represent the arguments for how those social conflicts might be resolved.

Finally, we can use political philosophical models to determine whether certain central rights can serve as normative guidelines for objecting to particular rules. In particular, we can model a choice situation that identifies rights that members of a system of trust should recognize and institutionalize. In chapters 5 and 7, I will use develop such a choice situation to argue that some kinds of rights, what I call *primary rights*, are so essential for life in modern, free social order that they are likely to be publicly justified for a wide range of perspectives. If so, primary rights can serve members of the public in evaluating particular moral and legal rules because members can ask whether a social rule violates a primary right. If they determine that the rule violates the right, then the rule should probably be rejected or modified. So while primary rights are too vague and general to allow theorists to determine in the abstract whether certain social rules are publicly justified, they provide a rational basis for members of the public to determine which rules to keep, which to modify, and which to dissolve. In making those determinations and reforms, people will sustain social trust in the right way, and so create moral peace between persons.

Some readers will remain skeptical, but we will pursue this fourth method in future chapters, so there will at least be further argument.

14. The Self-Defeat Objection

I have already implicitly answered a large range of other objections because they were never aimed at my account of public justification. These objections include the incompleteness, indeterminacy, antidemocratic, integrity, unreasonableness, asymmetry, insincerity, theoretical indeterminacy, and arbitrary idealization objections.[85] I have already addressed the anarchy objection, which holds that my view permits too many defeater

---

[85] For a review of the objections and citations to those who advance them, see sections 5.1–5.6, 5.10–5.12 in Vallier 2018b.

reasons for proposed laws.[86] My view at least partly resists the allure of political perfectionism.[87] The forms of coercion and social control perfectionists typically support will frustrate a system of trust and undermine the relations of respect that persons have within such a system.

I would like to end the chapter by addressing a common concern about public reason liberalism that has attracted recent attention—the self-defeat objection.[88] The self-defeat objection holds that public justification requirements are somehow self-defeating.[89] Steven Wall claims, for instance, that the rationale for public justification requirements entails that the requirements themselves must be publicly justified.[90] But given that many, if not most, reasonable people reject public justification requirements, due to evaluative pluralism, such requirements cannot be publicly justified. Define public reason's *reflexivity requirement* as the view that public justification requirements must be publicly justified if they are to determine which laws (or, in our case, moral rules) are publicly justified. The self-defeat objection combines the reflexivity condition with the plausible claim that many reasonable people do or would reject public justification requirements.

To run a successful self-defeat objection against my trust foundation for public reason, we need an argument that establishing trust and trustworthiness between persons requires the public justification of my public justification requirement. Wall's arguments can be retrofitted for this purpose. He argues that we must endorse the reflexivity condition because public reason liberals implicitly use public justification requirements to justify moral rules and coercive laws.[91] We are not entitled to assume "that people can be given a reasonably acceptable justification for coercive political authority, independently of whether they have been given a reasonably acceptable justification for the condition that legitimates it."[92] Public justification requirements, for Wall, are components of the justification of much moral and political authority for public reason liberals. In short, the justification for a moral rule and the justification for its justificatory test cannot be separated.

---

[86] I have addressed this objection with respect to expressly political public reason in Vallier 2014, pp. 130–134. Also see Rawls 2002, pp. 124–128; Gaus 2011, pp. 303–333, 389–408, 424–447.
[87] Wall 1998, pp. 29–43.
[88] This argument has also been addressed in Billingham 2017 and Bajaj forthcoming.
[89] I have addressed the self-defeat objection in more detail in Vallier 2016c.
[90] See Wall 2002, Wall 2013 and Enoch 2013, pp. 170–173.
[91] Wall 2013, p. 388.
[92] Ibid., pp. 388–389.

To answer Wall, we can weaken the reflexivity condition to the point where the self-defeat objection no longer succeeds. The reflexivity condition says that a given public justification requirement is a genuine moral requirement only if it is publicly justified. But Wall demonstrates only the weaker claim that a public justification requirement cannot be a genuine moral requirement only if it is used *as a reason* to impose publicly *unjustified* demands, punishment, or coercion on others. Further, the self-defeat objection succeeds only if we propose to control or coerce others based on a principle they reject and that they have no *other* sufficient reason to accept. John and Reba will not be at moral peace with one another if John forces Reba to comply with laws that *only* a public justification requirement can ground if she has sufficient reason to reject the public justification requirement, but that is an unusual circumstance. If John sticks to coercing or controlling Reba based on her sufficient reasons other than those directly provided by a public justification requirement she endorses, then social trust is preserved because the motives for trustworthiness are preserved, since Reba has sufficient reasons to comply with the rule.[93]

The self-defeat objector must also show that the defeat of a public justification requirement in particular cases will undermine the justification of critically important moral and legal rules. If public justification requirements cannot justify relatively minor laws and norms, then we do better to simply reject those laws and norms than to give up on public reason.

Extrapolating from these arguments, I contend that, on my account of public reason, self-defeat is a problem only if five conditions hold. Members of the public must have views at the right level of idealization about public justification requirements in the relevant cases. Members of the public must have sufficient reason to reject the relevant public justification requirement at the right level of idealization. The moral or legal rule proposed must not be able to be publicly justified on any *other* basis than those that include the endorsement of the relevant public justification requirements. The moral or legal rule must be sufficiently necessary for

---

[93] I acknowledge that Reba's sufficient reasons may be affected by her model of her own reasons; sometimes our understanding of what we have reason to do is inaccurate, and in some of *those* cases our inaccurate understanding may determine that we have new reasons and motives. In that case, Reba's model of her own commitments may affect her actual commitments, and so may appear to reintroduce a reflexivity requirement by causally or inferentially tying her first-order commitments with her commitment to a public justification requirement. John's model can incorporate this metasource of reason formation, though, so he can avoid coercing her in that case of intermingling reasons.

the moral, legal, or political order to function. And the group of members of the public in question cannot be trivially small. These conditions will almost never be satisfied given the noetic structure of most members of the public.

15. On to Legal Systems

How does this account of public justification apply to coercive law? As we will see, an order of moral rules that forgoes the public use of coercion will suffer from a number of critical defects. Legal rules can help to remedy those defects. A society at moral peace, then, must have publicly justified legal institutions.

PART II | A Liberal Constitutional Order

CHAPTER 4 | Legal Systems

RESPECTFULLY MAINTAINING A SYSTEM of trust requires that our moral rules be publicly justified. Coercive laws are required in order to strengthen a system of social trust by incentivizing trustworthy behavior in cases where a system of moral rules alone cannot provide strong enough reason to be trustworthy. Most moral rules are not backed by publicly authorized coercion, but the use of such coercion can help to stabilize moral rules that might otherwise collapse or create new moral rules that otherwise might not have existed. The law can be an efficient means of maintaining a system of trust by providing persons with additional incentive to engage in trustworthy behavior, as well as by codifying and stabilizing what a moral rule requires in particular circumstances, and form the obligations prescribed by informal moral rules.

The argument of the last three chapters implies that we should generally insist that coercive laws be publicly justified. After all, legal rules, like moral rules, constitute a kind of interference with the moral liberty of persons, such that there is a presumption against such interference that must be met with a public justification. So if legal rules are to give persons moral reasons to comply with them, they too must be publicly justified. Unjustified legal rules cannot establish social trust, therefore, since those who must comply with the law cannot on reflection uncover motivationally sufficient moral reason to comply with them.

In this way, the case for publicly justifying the law proceeds in two steps. Step one is to establish that a system of coercive law is necessary for having an adequately effective order of moral rules, and so to maintain a system of trust. Step two involves establishing both why laws *must be* publicly justified and *how* law can be publicly justified. Before

I can take either step, however, I must explain how I understand laws and legal systems.

1. Law and Legal Systems

I understand a law or *legal rule*[1] as a social rule generally regarded as supremely authoritative and that is typically enforced through official coercive sanction by publicly recognized norm-interpreting institutions like courts. Laws are social norms in much the same way that moral rules are social norms.[2] Legal rules come with empirical and normative expectations; we ordinarily expect others to comply with the law and we think they ought to do so. Raz remarks that "all agree that a legal system is not the law in force in a certain community unless it is generally adhered to and is accepted or internalized by at least certain sections of the population."[3] Raz's recognition dimension implies empirical expectations, whereas his internalization dimension implies normative expectations.

Law is authoritative in that it "does not request: it commands."[4] Like moral rules, legal rules are also de facto regarded as obligatory; those who violate them are usually thought guilty. So most laws are not mere advice or counsel, or good rules of thumb. They purport to have de facto authority over those to whom they apply. But legal rules go beyond moral rules because legal rules are often regarded as the "supreme authority within a certain society."[5] This means they have authority over the obligating power of competitor rules.[6] This supreme authority implies that, if laws are efficacious, those who apply and enforce the law will typically have the de facto power to impose the law in opposition to any challenge. In virtue of having supreme authority, laws attempt to provide decisive practical reasons to comply with them.

We can further specify the authority of law by observing that the law provides the "machinery for the authoritative settlement of disputes" that cannot be effectively resolved by other rules or practices.[7] Law necessarily implies the existence of "adjudicative institutions charged with regulating disputes arising out of the application of the norms of the system."[8] We

---

[1] I will use the terms "law" and "legal rule" interchangeably.
[2] Murphy 2006, p. 4.
[3] Raz 2009, p. 43.
[4] Murphy 2006, p. 9.
[5] Raz 2009, p. 43. I expand Raz's scope restriction to most community members.
[6] Laws can only sometimes legitimately limit moral rules.
[7] Ibid., p. 110.
[8] Ibid.

distinguish law from custom because law is formalized by an adjudicative system. Laws require courts, or what Raz calls "primary law-applying organ[s]" which are "authorized to decide whether the use of force in certain circumstances is forbidden or permitted by law."[9] This determination includes the capacity to determine what the law is by settling interpretative questions, and to determine whether a law has been violated. Primary organs include all norm-interpreting institutions, like the court system, and norm-enforcing institutions, such as the police.

According to Brennan et al., the difference between legal and moral rules runs parallel with the difference between formal and informal norms. Persons subject to informal norms jointly enforce them. "[N]o agent in particular who is duly authorized to 'issue' the orders, or interpret them, or apply them" can bring moral rules into existence.[10] Laws are formal rules, where there are secondary rules that "create a structure of formal mechanisms for the creation, modification, application, and interpretation of the norms that belong to the relevant network."[11] Legal rules therefore create "mediated accountability" where some third party is charged with holding violators accountable, whereas moral rules are governed by nonmediated accountability.[12]

Legal officials usually enforce the law through coercion and coercive threats. In some cases, laws do not claim coercive authority, such as laws passed by legislators to celebrate a national holiday or mint coins in a certain way. But the vast majority of laws with which we are concerned are authoritative social rules backed by the threat of violence from enforcement units that follow the dictates of the official adjudicator.

I do not adopt a specific conception of legal coercion. I understand legal coercion as an attempt to use force or violence to get persons to follow the law in question through a method of coercion specified as appropriate by another legal rule. However, I prefer an account of legal coercion similar to Robert Nozick's account of coercion *simpliciter*, which I modify as follows. P uses legal coercion against Q if and only if

1. P aims to keep Q from choosing to perform legally prohibited action A;
2. P communicates a claim to Q;

---

[9] Raz 1970, p. 192.
[10] Brennan et al. 2016, p. 43.
[11] Ibid., p. 42.
[12] Ibid., p. 41. For a further discussion of differences, see p. 51.

3. P's claim indicates that if Q performs A, then P will bring about some consequence that would make Q's A-ing less desirable to Q than Q's not A-ing, specifically the standard forms of legal sanction, like deprivation of life, liberty, or possessions, through punishment provided by a duly authorized legal official;
4. P's claim is credible to Q;
5. Q does not do A;
6. Part of Q's reason for not doing A is to lessen the likelihood that P will bring about the consequence announced in (3).[13]

My revision of Nozick's account raises a variety of complex questions that I cannot address here, such as whether coercion requires actually discouraging Q from doing A, or just making it less likely, and whether the baseline of noncoercion is understood in terms of what Nozick called the "normal or natural or expected course of events" which can be interpreted in both moralized and nonmoralized ways.[14] For our purposes, then, we can leave these debates open until it becomes clear that this definition of legal coercion affects the plausibility of my main lines of argument in this book.

Coercive legal sanctions, in contrast to informal social sanctions, must be serious, such that they should lead to deprivation of life, liberty, or possessions. And the imposition of the sanctions should be "guaranteed by the use of force to prevent possible obstructions" in contrast to moral rules, where ostracism is often nonviolent. Further, the sanction is "determined with relative precision in the law, and only a small and predetermined number of sanctions are applied for each violation" of the duty associated with the law.[15] Ostracism in response to the violation of moral rules is less limited and formalized. Finally, only certain persons, expressly determined by the law, may apply legal sanctions. Ostracism in response to the violation of moral rules is more open-ended; violations are in some sense everyone's business.[16]

Legal systems combine laws with adjudicative institutions. Adjudicative institutions regulate "disputes arising out of the application of the norms of the system."[17] Adjudicative systems must claim supreme authority over other institutions to interpret and apply the law, and when they are

---

[13] Nozick 1969, pp. 441–445.
[14] Ibid., p. 447.
[15] Ibid., p. 151.
[16] Gaus 2011, pp. 188–192.
[17] Raz 2009, p. 43.

efficacious, they have the recognized authority and power to impose and enforce laws. A legal system therefore "mark[s] the point at which a private view of members of the society . . . ceases to be their private view and becomes (i.e. lays a claim to be) a view binding on all members notwithstanding their disagreement with it."[18]

Property disputes are illustrative, as a legitimate judge can, through a ruling, make one party's belief that she did not damage her neighbor's property authoritative for both parties to the dispute. The legal system's public character provides "publicly ascertainable ways of guiding behavior and regulating aspects of social law" such that "law is a public measure by which one can measure one's own as well as other people's behavior." Legal systems should also be understood as consisting of laws "which the courts are bound to apply and are not at liberty to disregard whenever they find their application undesirable, all things considered."[19] As such, legal systems have the de facto power to make "binding applicative determinations."[20]

While we should adopt some features of Raz's understanding of law and legal systems, we can develop an original, trust-based account of the functions of the law.[21] Since, on my view, the legal order is a supplement to the moral order, the function of the law is to aid and structure that order. Therefore, the central function of the law and legal systems is to *incentivize trustworthy behavior by controlling moral rules* through processes that maintain, revise, suppress, or create legal rules.

One of my aims is to provide an account of legal obligation to vindicate a strong form of legal legitimacy where legal systems are not only morally permitted to enforce law, but citizens are obliged to follow them.[22] I will not provide an account of the justification or obligatory force of *legislation*, however. This is because, as John Hasnas notes, "the duty to obey the law is not the same thing as political obligation," since legal systems can and do exist "that are not associated with any particular government or centralized political structure."[23] As Hayek famously stressed, law and legislation are not the same thing.[24] Law can exist without legislative bodies.[25]

---

[18] Ibid., p. 51. Though, in contrast to Raz, I also think that moral rules perform a similar demarcation function.

[19] Ibid., p. 113.

[20] Ibid., p. 110.

[21] Ibid., pp. 167–168.

[22] In this way, legitimacy is grounded in public justification, so public reason liberalism ties legitimacy and justification close together. For the classic analysis of justification and legitimacy, see Simmons 1999.

[23] Hasnas 2013, p. 451. I will defend legislative legitimacy in the next book.

[24] Hayek 1973.

[25] Raz 1970, p. 191. Also see Hasnas 2013, p. 450.

My theory of legal obligation builds legal obligation out of our obligations to follow moral rules and the need for legal rules. Like moral rules, legal rules are justified in terms of intelligible reasons. Sections 2 and 3 develop these points. But legal obligations can only be generated by publicly justified legal rules, and legal rules can only be publicly justified when moral rules cannot themselves perform the functions members of the public want them to perform, as argued in section 4. So, in section 5, we will find that laws and law-applying bodies have authority if they *efficiently* enable persons to fulfill their publicly justified moral obligations. Law and legal systems must improve upon our capacity to satisfy our moral obligations on balance; the moral benefits of the law must outweigh the moral costs. As a result, section 6 develops revised arguments from trustworthiness and accountability to include legal and not just moral rules. In this way, I offer an "obligation-in, obligation-out" approach to legal obligation because legal obligations must be justified in terms of moral obligations. Section 7 explains how legal obligation mediates moral and political obligation. And section 8 derives legal obligations from moral obligations. Section 9 contrasts my approach to legal obligation with Raz's familiar approach.

2. The Legal State of Nature

Imagine that an advanced alien species descends upon the earth and abolishes all legal systems. All courts are destroyed, as are all legislative bodies and executive offices. No coercive laws may be authoritatively imposed on anyone by anyone. The aliens leave humanity with the capacity to create, alter, remove, enforce, or resist moral rules, but not by means of law as I have defined it. So the aliens permit moral orders to continue, such that systems of moral rules can generate some social order via ostracism, shunning, and blame. Assume, as is likely, that many of these moral rules are publicly justified; they are genuinely morally authoritative.

Private parties may use coercion, but only as a liberty-right, a moral permission, not as a claim-right, where others have a moral duty to allow a person to permissibly use coercion. Private parties may use coercion to defend themselves or others from attack or to punish transgressors, and aggressors are permitted to use coercion to prevent counterattacks. Each person has a liberty-right to coerce in many cases, but no one has public authorization to engage in either action via a recognized system of moral rules.[26]

Call this social order a *legal state of nature*. In Lockean terms, we have created a social contract that creates *society* by establishing a justified set of moral rules.[27] But there is no social contract between society and public agents with the authoritative power to coerce. There is no system of public judgment that can back society's decrees with publicly authorized legal force. Thus, a legal state of nature exists when we have an order with authoritative moral rules but no such legal rules.

We should now envision how such a social order will function. Some may contend, as Hobbes did, that the moral order must collapse unless backed by a publicly recognized unitary state. Others may have more Lockean intuitions, where the legal state of nature has a high degree of social order but still fails to produce critical social goods. I imagine a moral order more in line with Locke than Hobbes, though I think it is hard to determine who is correct given that context will heavily influence the behavior of the resulting order. But we can agree that such a social order will face huge social costs, especially in supporting large-scale institutions that local moral rules cannot sustain. Moral rules will be able to sustain local orders only where ostracism and blame are successful modes of social control since interactions with total strangers are sharply limited, leaving people to interactions with their families, churches, civil associations, and small commercial institutions.

The work of a variety of social scientific researchers can substantiate these claims, such as anthropological studies of social cooperation in societies without states, as well as work on the formation of legal rules in the absence of state power.[28] Economic approaches to private law drive similar conclusions.[29] There is also important evidence, much of it new, that moral rules play the most important role in promoting social cooperation, given the limitations of political coercion.[30]

---

[26] The ground of these liberty-rights is that there are not justified claim-rights that morally prohibit persons from exercising their liberty; in that sense, at least, this state of nature is Hobbesian in that there are at least no legal norms that are publicly recognized as mutually binding.

[27] Locke [1690] 1988, p. 324.

[28] Scott 1999, 2009.

[29] Benson 2011; Leeson 2014; Stringham 2015.

[30] See Ostrom 1990, North 1990, pp. 125–129, and especially Bicchieri's discussion of the limitations of the law in structuring social norms. Bicchieri 2017, p. 144.

3. The Advantages and Shape of Legal Systems

With that said, the legal state of nature has three general problems: the order of moral rules will probably be *uncertain, static*, and *ineffective*.[31]

A merely moral order leaves its members in crippling uncertainty. If people disagree about what moral rules require in certain cases, there are no formal, decisive means for resolving the disagreement. In a legal order, institutions and officials are expressly devoted to formalizing and harmonizing legal rules and generating authoritative, final judgments. These institutions can act relatively rationally and quickly. Further, the punishments imposed in the legal state of nature are haphazard and potentially numerous. Courts can impose regular punishments in an ascertainable fashion through a limited group responsible for imposing one or a few legal sanctions. As Brennan et al. put it, there are sometimes "epistemic reasons to want mediated accountability" given that courts can solve various unclarities about the content of the law and how it should be enforced.[32]

A legal state of nature is also exceedingly *static* in that bad moral rules can be hard to change. As Mark Murphy notes, social rules "possess tremendous inertia."[33] In many cases, oppressive moral rules can last for centuries, such as rules that permit slavery and serfdom.[34] It is true that influential social groups, large or small, can change moral rules. But the changes imposed are unreliable, since these groups can lose public favor in a variety of ways that courts ordinarily do not. The rules suppressed by the popular group can return when the group loses public favor.

Stasis is explained by the fact that moral rules are social norms. If a bad or unjustified rule is in equilibrium, then it will resist change because few have an incentive to unilaterally deviate from it. And so, it may be the case that "only the political order is apt to be an adequate engine of moral reform as it can move us to a new equilibrium much more quickly than informal social processes."[35] Coercion can stabilize norms that our

---

[31] Murphy 2006, p. 29. For a classic discussion, see Hart 1961, chapter 4. I use the term "ineffective," whereas Murphy uses the term "inefficient," because I want to reserve the term "efficiency" to denote when the balance of moral reasons favors complying with a law, and "inefficiency" to denote the denial of efficiency.

[32] Brennan et al. 2016, p. 52.

[33] Murphy 2006, p. 28.

[34] Though in actual practice, such rules are typically strengthened by legal enforcement.

[35] Gaus 2011, p. 437. Here I mean to focus on the legal order, whereas Gaus does not sharply distinguish between the legal and political orders.

noncoercive moral practices cannot, so a legal system should have the special power to create new legal rules and enforce them with coercion.

Finally, a legal state of nature can be *ineffective* because its mode of enforcement, the court of public opinion, is unreliable, clunky, and unclear. A legal system can respond faster and with greater accuracy to violations of moral rules than the moral order can. When violations are detected, institutions are in place to quickly identify and enforce the law with expressly formalized legal sanctions. Legal institutions can therefore stabilize empirical expectations about which rules apply to them quickly and effectively. Another attraction of legal rules is that people can form short-term and long-term plans to pursue their diverse ends because they can make reliable predictions about how social life will proceed in the future. Consequently, uniform public legal systems can generate substantial social and economic benefits by propagating laws and enforcing them uniformly.

Having a legal system is especially important when it comes to the recognition, codification, and enforcement of rights claims. We need a legal system to protect rights because rights claims are especially strong moral demands that can lead to severe social conflict if they go unrecognized. Since moral rules by themselves can be vague and ineffective, a legal system can help assess rights claims through the relatively quick and effective application or extension of law to render a decisive decision. Practically every society that recognizes rights has a legal system to protect them, even if the protection is not enumerated in a constitution or written statutes, so this point is widely understood.

We can see then that a legal state of nature composed solely of rules unsupported by a legal order will exhibit undesirable degrees of uncertainty, stasis, and inefficacy. A legal system can remedy these defects. Only a legal system can properly control and modify the moral order because legal systems possess greater certainty, adaptability, and efficacy than social institutions in the legal state of nature. A legal system can substantially improve a society's ability to provide certain, adaptive, and effective tools for discouraging the violation of moral rules. We can therefore say that a moral order has three *central functions*—to be adequately certain, dynamic, and effective, especially when it comes to recognizing, codifying, and enforcing rights claims. A legal system can substantially improve a moral order's capacity to execute these central functions. This means that a social order with a legal system will better promote social (and legal) trust than a mere moral order.

All of these problems arise even if everyone in the legal state of nature complies with publicly justified moral rules. But in the real world many people will disobey justified moral rules, and this will be its own source of social problems. Part of the justification of legal order is, thus, to force people to comply with justified rules. Since this is obvious enough, I set the problem of forcing persons to comply with justified moral rules aside, though I will address noncompliance in a constitutional order at some length in chapter 6.

We must not be too quick to assume that law can improve or alter social norms. Citizens will often break laws when there are real risks of punishment. Tom Tyler argues that "fear of punishment, social norms, and moral convictions all explain some variance in legal compliance, with moral convictions best explaining such variance, peer disapproval (or social norms) coming second, and fear of punishment last."[36] People usually obey the law because they think doing so is the right thing to do, or that they think others think they should do so.[37] So law is often insufficient to motivate compliance. People will sometimes ignore laws, even those backed by punishment, if laws violate entrenched social norms.

Legal systems *significantly* improve a moral order's capacity to execute its central functions. By "significance" I mean that the improvement must meet a threshold that makes the improvement *detectable* to all moderately idealized agents and that the improvement is seen as nontrivial. Thus, significance is understood as a function of the evaluation of members of the public.

We can now establish the importance of the *rule of law*. On my view, and following Lon Fuller, legal rules that comprise the rule of law have a range of defining characteristics, such as generality, publicity, exclusion of retroactive legislation, clarity, stability, exclusion of legislation requiring the impossible, and the congruence of official action and declared rule.[38] Legal rules must apply to the public generally. They must be publicly accessible; members of the public should be able to determine what the law is through ordinary legal inquiry, such as speaking with a lawyer or judge, examining case law, etc. Consequently, ex post facto laws cannot contribute to the rule of law. Laws must also be clearly worded and stable, enduring over time. They cannot demand the impossible and should be understood as applying to both citizens and government officials.

Laws of this sort can stabilize public expectations in a way that will help ensure that they can be publicly justified, and laws that violate these

---

[36] Barrett and Gaus 2018, p. 10. See Tyler 2006, p. 45.

[37] See Kronenburg et al. 2010 and Robinson 2000.

[38] Fuller 1969, chapter 2. Also see Rawls 1999a, pp. 206–214 and Gaus 1996, pp. 195–214.

conditions are likely to be defeated. We can also see that the legal state of nature lacks key mechanisms for generating the rule of law, given that it cannot generate a uniform public, and publicly justified, legal system.[39] So a publicly justified legal system should embody the rule of law if it is to improve upon the legal state of nature in the right way.

Second, while the legal system will recognize many rights claims, it will not recognize them all. Evaluative pluralism leads sincere, informed people of goodwill to disagree about what rights we have and the extent to which these rights should have public status. Publicly justified legal systems will only raise rights to public status if all have sufficient reason to endorse those rights. An example is a right against harm, which I discuss in chapter 7. Though societies understand harm differently, they agree on some core cases. A right not to have one's hand amputated by one's neighbors is almost always the subject of public recognition and should receive rational validation by all moderately idealized members of the public.[40] No one wants to be vulnerable to losing her hand for no reason. Protecting a right to not have one's hand amputated thereby establishes moral peace between persons. A moral order is limited in its ability to recognize and codify these rights, however, so another reason that a moral order needs a legal system is to determine, with some efficiency, clarity, and short-term finality, which rights are to be recognized. Codifying rights claims in public statements and defending them with violent, yet authoritative, means can stabilize the protection of rights and so answer those claims.

An example of a rights claim that a publicly justified legal system will not recognize is the claim of many socialist parties that workers have a right to own and operate capital. This claim never achieved public recognition in a liberal democratic order because socialists were unable to convince enough people that the right is justified for the public. This does not mean that moral reality contains no such right; the true moral theory may contain the right of workers to own the capital they use. Nonetheless, sectarian rights claims are not part of a publicly justified legal system.

---

[39] To give equal weight to the badness of a publicly authorized system of law, we must remember that a publicly justified legal system also rules out certain *governmental* actions that undermine it. So once the rule of law is established, we will have moral *and* legal rules to prevent the government from violating the rule of law and disrupting public expectations. I return to legal limits on government power in chapter 6.

[40] We find strong defenses of bodily integrity rights in Rawls 1999a, p. 53 and Gaus 2011, pp. 357–358.

Moreover, unjustified rights claims may *undermine* the moral order when people begin to ostracize and interfere with others who have sufficient reason to reject the rights claim in question. Consider a small band of Marxists who ostracize local business owners for not handing their capital over to their employees. The Marxists might be correct that there *exists* an objective right for workers to own and operate capital, but their proposed right has no public status. As T. H. Green noted, such claims are equivalent to invoking the "name of a fallen dynasty exercising no control over men in their dealings with one another."[41] If I tell most American business owners to fork over their capital based on my Marxist reasoning, my position is normatively identical to insisting that American business owners fork over their capital because the Soviet Union has passed a law requiring capital redistribution. The rights claim has no rational uptake; the demands misfire. Since sectarian rights claims are not rationally validated, they will therefore tend to undermine, rather than support, moral peace.

Public legal systems are subject to error. They frequently fail to extend publicly justified rights to those entitled to them and in still more cases violate recognized rights. So while we need a public legal system to protect, recognize, and institutionalize rights, the legal system must be limited to stop the recognition or enforcement of defeated claims. I will address these limits further in chapters 5–7.

4. Why Publicly Justify Legal Coercion?

Legal rules must be publicly justified because we want them to be part of the basis for genuinely trustworthy behavior. To see this, first recall that a legal system must be authoritative. Its practices and the laws it enforces and interprets impose de facto claim-rights on persons to comply with these laws. However, unless those de facto claim-rights are publicly justified, forcing persons to comply with the law is morally equivalent to private coercion or coercive threats. The enforcement of a law that lacks justified authority, therefore, does not give persons intelligible moral reasons for action, and so cannot be an ongoing basis for trustworthy behavior or justified social trust. It is true that law can give persons self-interested reasons to comply with various moral and legal rules. But since unjustified laws do not generate moral reasons, they not only cannot drive genuine trustworthiness, they face a number of other problems. First, even normally

---

[41] Green 1895, p. 105.

moral and compliant persons will tend to defect from such a law when they believe that they can get away with it, creating an incentive for opportunistic free-riding that can undermine social trust. This also means that they will not be as trustworthy with respect to the law as they would if they recognized sufficient moral reasons to comply with the law, since they will obey the law only when they recognize a nontrivial risk of being caught. In general, then, the law may not only be less effective than we might want, it may not be generally observed at all. As we have seen, laws will often be ineffective when they conflict with social norms. In contrast, publicly justified laws are ones that each person sees herself as having sufficient moral reason to comply with, such that publicly justified laws help morally incentivize trustworthiness. This, in turn, engenders justified social trust and the moral peace that arises from it.

Second, we must publicly justify laws because they are generally supposed to obligate, and so the presumption in favor of moral liberty will apply to laws too. We can only establish moral obligations by overcoming the presumption in favor of moral liberty, and so if we have moral obligations to follow legal rules, then legal rules must be publicly justified. Moreover, legal rules, like moral rules, interfere with the behavior of others, and interference with others must be publicly justified to overcome the presumption. In this way, I adopt not only a presumption in favor of moral liberty, but a presumption in favor of *legal liberty* as well. The *presumption against legal coercion* is an extension of the presumption in favor of moral liberty.

Lastly, the law must be publicly justified because there may be a publicly justified *moral right* against legal coercion, such that there is an authoritative moral rule which specifies that coercive actions taken by members of a system of trust must be publicly justified.[42] We thereby provide another moral justification for a presumption against legal coercion. I will explore this line of argument further in chapter 7.

A critic could argue that some laws are sufficiently necessary that they should be imposed even without a public justification.[43] Sometimes too much is at stake to hold legal coercion hostage to public justification and the desirability of maintaining a system of trust. Perhaps some group of persons promotes a sufficiently dangerous cause that we cannot afford to

---

[42] Gaus 2011, pp. 479–489. In this way, I agree that a public justification principle governing the use of coercion is a principle "within a moral order." See Gaus 2018, p. 21.

[43] Wendt 2018 can be understood along these lines.

allow them to engage in actions that public justification may permit. I acknowledge the point: yes, in some cases, deferring legal action due to a failure of public justification may be a moral mistake. But the only reason deferring legal action would be a mistake is because the need for the law is taken to outweigh the value of a system of social trust and what respect requires of persons who trust one another. Normally, however, the joint teleological and deontological value of a system of social trust is hard to override.

Some opponents of public reason argue that respect does not require the public justification of coercion because psychopaths and the mentally impaired can be stopped from using coercion even if they cannot understand the moral reasons not to use it.[44] But since relations of trust are a necessary condition for the requirement of public justification, if someone is not trustworthy and has no interest in being trustworthy, as many psychopaths might not be, then the fact that they do not recognize the moral value of a system of trust sets them apart from those to whom a public justification is owed. By rejecting membership in a system of trust, such persons have, as Locke thought, declared themselves the equivalent of wild beasts in virtue of their behavior; they are no longer recognized as acting from the participant stance.[45] This means we are not prohibited from coercing them to protect ourselves, though our coercion lacks moral authority. In this way, we do not have to publicly justify using coercion to protect ourselves from coercion that cannot be publicly justified.

5. How to Publicly Justify Legal Coercion

We cannot vindicate the authority of legal systems merely by establishing that the moral order *needs* a legal system. Instead, we must explain how the need for a legal system helps publicly justify legal rules. In my view, moderately idealized members of the public will recognize the need for a legal system, as they can see both the defects in the legal state of nature and how a legal system can remedy those defects. The public justification for the law, then, *is the fact* that the law is seen as necessary to solve the problems faced in the legal state of nature. This implies that if moral rules

---

[44] For a discussion of the moral psychology of psychopaths and its relation to understanding moral rules, see Shoemaker 2011. For a reply to this kind of objection, see Gaus 2014.

[45] As Locke wrote, such persons refuse "to recognize that reason is the rule between men, and that man becomes liable to be destroyed by the injured person and the rest of mankind, as any other wild beast or noxious brute that is destructive to their being." Locke [1690] 1988, p. 96.

alone can sustain our system of trust, the law cannot be publicly justified, since it is unnecessary for the sort of social life that members of the public want to share with one another.

If this seems like too high a bar for the justification of law, remember that the evaluation of whether a law supplements the moral order is made by moderately idealized members of the public who have access to social scientific information. In the case of empirical evaluations of this type, we can expect some convergence on social scientific judgments about whether law can supplement the moral order. That is, evaluative pluralism should not lead to unmanageable disagreement over the effects of a law on a social norm like a moral rule given that this is an empirical fact subject to scientific verification that is not typically beyond present social science.

We can now see a critical difference between how we justify moral rules and how we justify law. If members of the public decide that a moral rule is superior to all alternatives and to no rule, then it is publicly justified. However, to have no law on some issue is not to say that there will be no *moral rule* governing the issue. To have no law regulating an issue is to leave the matter to social morality. So, in many cases, whether a law is publicly justified depends on whether members of the public think it better to use law rather than moral rules alone. If a law is publicly justified, then, members of the public must justifiably regard the law as an *improvement on the legal state of nature*, and not on a state of nature with no moral rules at all (a truly fantastic scenario). And more strongly, the law must be justifiably regarded as an *efficient* improvement. An efficient improvement is one where the net benefits of the law, which includes all of its moral benefits and costs, is greatest. To put it another way, an efficient improvement is one that has the greatest balance of moral reasons in its favor in comparison with alternatives.

In many cases, moral rules alone determine ownership claims since property norms sometimes form without the law, such as the details of property lines. But property disputes are bound to be unstable and ineffective in a legal state of nature because enforcement and resolution of disputes is difficult, as is enforcement and resolution of changing norms. Members of the public should be able to apply a legal system to their property disputes to improve upon the legal state of nature. If they then comply with the rulings of the legal system, they will have efficiently improved on their circumstances in the legal state of nature.

The prelegal moral order, then, has a kind of *priority* over the law. If the moral order is effective enough, then no law is needed, and so no law is justified, given the presumption against coercion in social morality.[46] If we do not need legal coercion to supplement or alter the moral order, then the presumption against coercion is not met.[47] What can be done well in the legal state of nature should not be done by the legal order. The priority of the moral order is not absolute, however, since sometimes the order of moral rules cannot perform the functions described above. Instead, law can be justified when members of the public reasonably believe that the moral order falls below a threshold of efficient functioning.

6. Trustworthiness and Accountability Extended

We have arrived at a critical junction in the book, for I have largely completed my argument that coercion requires public justification. This means that we can extend the two main arguments from chapter 2 to cover the justification of legal rules as well as moral rules. Let us modify these two arguments by introducing the idea of legal rules and a system of *legal trust*. A system of legal trust, like a system of social trust, is trust that persons will comply with the social rules of their society, but in this case the social rules include legal rules as well as moral rules.

> *Legal Trust:* a public exhibits legal trust to the extent that its participant members generally believe that other participants are necessary or helpful for achieving one another's goals and that (most or all) members are generally willing and able to do their part to achieve those goals, knowingly or unknowingly, by following legal rules where moral reasons are sufficient to motivate compliance.

While my definition of legal trust resembles my definition of social trust, legal trust involves trust in legal officials and not just trust in other citizens. Trust in other citizens to follow moral and legal rules can therefore be distinguished from trust in legal officials. It is possible to trust your fellow citizens to abide by moral and even legal rules while thinking that the judicial system and the police are corrupt and unjust. The empirical literature on trust, however, suggests a strong tie between trust in legal institutions and social trust.[48] To see this, we have to once again distinguish trust in

---

[46] See chapter 2, section 3 for a defense of the presumption in favor of moral liberty, and see Gaus 2011, pp. 456–460 for his version of the priority of social morality.

[47] This does not mean that no private party can use coercion to defend herself, just that we cannot justify the imposition of coercive *law* without a public justification.

[48] Bradford et al. 2017.

government and political officials from trust in the legal system.[49] When legal systems are believed to have erred, especially when they treat persons unequally, social trust often falls; Rothstein and Stolle claim to find "a rather strong relationship between aggregate levels of confidence in [legal] institutions and generalized trust."[50] And generalized trust "is destroyed by widespread corruption, inefficient institutions, unreliable policy, and arbitrariness and bias of courts."[51] Bicchieri also finds that abandoning harmful practices in the general public is strongly correlated with "trust in formal institutions."[52] So while trust in *elected* officials may come apart from social trust, trust in the legal system seems tightly empirically tied to social trust.

Legal trust, like social trust, has great social and relational value. Since legal systems are required to help the moral order efficiently perform necessary and valuable social functions, the social and relational value of a system of moral *and legal* trust is greater than the value of a system of mere social trust. That means our reasons to maintain a system of moral and legal trust are stronger than our reasons to maintain a system of mere social trust.

Further, respect for persons appears to play the same role within a system of legal trust that it plays in a system of social trust alone. Consider a revised argument from trustworthiness:

1. Within a system of legal trust, if A respects other members of the system of trust, then A will be trustworthy by complying with legal rules that are compatible with A's deep commitments and values.
2. A's compliance with legal rules is compatible with A's deep commitments and values if and only if the rules are publicly justified for A.
3. Within a system of legal trust, if A respects other members of the system of trust, then A will be trustworthy by complying with legal rules that are publicly justified for A. (1, 2)

Regarding premise 1, we have good reason to be trustworthy with respect to legal rules for much the same reason we have to be trustworthy with respect to moral rules. Compliance with either kind of rule is generally

[49] Rothstein and Stolle 2008, p. 445.
[50] Ibid., p. 450.
[51] Ibid., p. 451.
[52] Bicchieri 2017, p. 145.

required by respect for persons who trust us to comply with the rule. We also only have reason to be trustworthy with respect to publicly justified legal rules because we have sufficient moral reason of our own to comply with the legal rule, and otherwise not.

A revised argument from accountability is a bit more complicated, since a system of legal accountability differs in important respects from a system of moral accountability. A system of moral accountability consists in our social practice of expecting others to comply with moral rules and subjecting persons to informal moral sanctions and punishment when we observe violations of these rules. But a system of legal accountability invokes the idea of a legal system, which includes courts and formalized enforcement mechanisms, like a police force. Even so, the required modifications of my main argument are relatively modest:

4. Within a system of legal trust, if A respects another member of the system of trust, B, then A will only insist that B be held legally accountable to legal rules compliance with which is compatible with B's deep commitments and values.
5. B's compliance with legal rules is compatible with B's deep commitments and values if and only if the rules are publicly justified for B.
6. Within a system of legal trust, if A respects B, then A will only insist that B be held legally accountable to legal rules that are publicly justified for B. (4, 5)

Notice first that I appeal to the new ideas of legal rules and a system of legal accountability. Most significantly, this means that A does not *directly* hold B legally accountable by physically forcing B to follow the law. Instead, she must *call upon* the legal system to hold B accountable. We generally want to prevent unauthorized persons from engaging in legal punishment since legal punishment presents far greater danger than the forms of moral ostracism that we use when we observe violations of mere moral rules. Moderately idealized members of the public will easily see the wisdom in this arrangement.

Premise 4 holds for *members of the system of trust*, and not necessarily all persons who live within a particular society. If someone has set herself outside of the system of trust, then we may be permitted to use the law to control her behavior even if the law and the associated legal system are not publicly justified for that person. But it might nonetheless appear that we have good consequence-based reasons to impose a law on everyone in a system of trust so long as the law is publicly justified for the large majority of people within that system. This is a mistake for two reasons. Respect for others within a system of trust requires public justification to all within that system. And free societies are generally prepared, and often morally required, to issue legal exemptions from laws that are seen as violating the conscience of a minority of citizens. This practice is arguably based on the recognition that the moral reasons a person has to disobey the law are sufficiently strong that imposing the law on her would be wrong.[53]

Since premise 5 is established in the same way as premise 2, by appealing to the kind of public justification that will justify adding a legal rule to the order of moral rules, we can vindicate the conclusion of the new argument from legal accountability.

7. Legal Obligation

We should now explore the implications of my argument for our obligations to obey the law. Since publicly justified moral rules prescribe moral obligations, publicly justified legal rules must prescribe moral obligations as well. But legal obligations derive their validity from publicly justified moral obligations. That is, we have legal obligations because we have more fundamental moral obligations.

I develop the connection by appealing to the idea of a *morally efficient* means of discharging one's obligations. A morally efficient means is one that has the greatest net benefits in terms of the intelligible moral reasons favoring the means and the moral reasons that disfavor the same means. It is the means that a person's balance of moral reasons most favors. We will see below that persons generally have a duty (not necessarily an obligation) to choose what they reasonably regard as the morally efficient means of discharging their moral obligations, which is a crucial step in the argument.

Complying with a law is often the morally efficient means of discharging moral obligations specified by publicly justified moral rules. Accordingly, we have obligations to comply with publicly justified laws because, in complying, members of the public have chosen the morally efficient means for acting morally. In this way, legal obligation piggybacks on moral obligation.

---

[53] For my approach to legal exemptions, see Vallier 2016b.

The duty to obey the law is typically thought to have four features.[54] (1) The duty is pro tanto, implying that the duty holds under normal circumstances, but it can be overridden by serious moral considerations. (2) The duty to obey the law is said to be *comprehensively applicable*, so that those under the law have an obligation to obey all laws; people cannot pick and choose the laws they wish to follow. (3) The duty applies to everyone within the jurisdiction of the law, such that it is *universally borne*. (4) Finally, the duty to obey the law is *content-independent*, which means that the law must be obeyed because it is the law, and not because the relevant laws have a particular content. As William Edmundson notes, "A content-independent duty effectively preempts the subject's individual assessment of the merits of the action required by law and is categorical in the sense that it is not contingent upon any motivating end or goal of the subject."[55] There are many accounts of the duty to obey the law, but none of them seem able to explain all four of these features.[56]

My account of the duty to obey the law is limited; like Raz, I advocate a piecemeal approach. The only laws that obligate are ones compliance with which is a morally efficient means of discharging our moral obligations. So the duty will not be comprehensively applicable in some cases, nor will it always be universally borne; nor will the duty be wholly content-independent. It will not be comprehensively applicable or universally borne because some laws will not be justified to many members of the public. And it will not be wholly content-independent because the public justification of laws will be based at least in part on their content.

I should also stress that my account of the duty to obey the law is not yet an account of whether an entire legal system, understood as including judicial and enforcement institutions, has moral authority. After all, one might have a duty to obey the law but no duty to comply with the legal system that interprets and enforces it. Further, there may be times when a judge's interpretation of a law needs to be authoritative over our own private interpretation of a law, and an account of legal obligation should explain legal obligations to defer to the judgment of legal officials regarding what the law is, the penalties for violating the law, etc. Similarly, my account of a duty to obey the law is distinct from duties to obey political officials and

---

[54] This review is based on Edmundson 2004, pp. 216–217 and Hasnas 2013, p. 451.
[55] Edmundson 2004, p. 216.
[56] Ibid., pp. 230–249 provides an overview of problems with three main types of accounts, natural duty accounts, volitional accounts, and associative accounts. Many of the theories simply haven't successfully answered the classic objections found in Simmons 1981, along with Wolff 1970. Michael Huemer's recent work continues that tradition. See Huemer 2013.

state legislation.[57] All these sources of authority involve further duties and powers that must themselves be publicly justified. I think we can justify these thicker forms of authority, but we can only do so if we first develop an account of legal obligation, and then build further legal obligations, and then political obligations, out of basic legal obligations. The primary way in which legal and political systems gain authority is based on their capacity to protect primary rights, produce justified laws under normal conditions, and exhibit certain kinds of stability.[58]

I have already explained the authority of moral rules. Therefore, if we can explain how the authority of moral rules gives rise to the authority of legal rules, then we should be able to explain the authority of legal rules.

8. The Derivation of Legal Obligation

My account of legal authority begins with the assumption that there are justified moral rules that prescribe moral obligations. In this way, I offer an approach to legal obligation that does not proceed directly from natural duties, the volition of individuals, or shared association.[59] Instead, authority follows from justified moral rules, which members of the public already have an obligation to follow.

The first step toward establishing the existence of legal obligations is to argue that when an agent, John, has an obligation to Φ, he has a subduty to choose necessary means toward discharging the obligation. John's subduty might not be a moral obligation itself, in that a failure to do his duty might not give others standing to criticize him, but it must be a moral duty. This step has the characteristics of a conceptual truth. For Reba's obligation to Φ implies a duty to choose necessary, available means to Φ, since she cannot otherwise discharge her obligation.

In this way, I follow Edmundson's characterization of one kind of argument for a duty to obey the law, which he describes as follows:

(P1) Whatever is typically a necessary means to a morally compelling end is at least a pro tanto duty;

---

[57] For a review of these different notions of authority, see Shapiro 2004.

[58] I explore these conditions in chapter 6.

[59] Though I can appeal to elements of all three considerations insofar as they figure into the justification of moral rules.

(P2) Law-abidingness is typically a necessary means to a morally compelling end; therefore,

(C) Law-abidingness is at least a pro tanto duty.[60]

On my view, the morally compelling end at stake is complying with justified moral rules and so with our moral obligations. Complying with legal rules is typically a necessary means to this morally compelling end due to the defects of the legal state of nature. And since whatever is typically a necessary means to complying with our moral obligations is at least a pro tanto duty, then complying with the relevant legal rules is at least a pro tanto duty.

That said, I would like to expand the conditions of legal obligation to cover cases where compliance with the law is not the only means of discharging one's moral obligation. It may be the case that one can discharge her moral obligations by complying with moral rules alone. However, if the balance of all of one's intelligible moral reasons favors complying with the law over moral rules, perhaps because the agent can see that complying with the law has various benefits that she has reason to care about, then she should comply with the law over the alternative moral rule. And if the balance of her moral reasons favors complying with the law, we can expand Edmundson's argument schema to cover not only necessary means but morally efficient means. Of course, this does not mean that there is no better law *in principle*, just that the moral benefits of the law most exceed the moral costs in comparison with alternative norms.

To illustrate, consider duties to obey laws that resolve disputes and award damages but that private parties might have resolved informally, such as laws requiring arbitration that results from property damages. In many cases, the relevant parties might have chosen an informal dispute resolution mechanism, but they can see that were they to appeal to formal judicial means, they will be much more likely to successfully resolve the dispute. This is so if for no other reason than courts can ensure impartiality and finality, which in turn implies that the parties' balance of moral reasons favors going to court and abiding by the court's decision.

Now consider three qualifications. First, it may be that members of the public can see that more than one law allows a person to efficiently discharge her moral obligations, and yet only one of these laws is in effect.

---

[60] Edmundson 2004, p. 235.

In that case, one is obligated to comply with the law because it is the only game in town, even if it is a member of a set of several rules that are publicly justifiable, where some of these rules might even be more morally efficient means were they in effect. This is because extant rules provide persons with additional reasons for compliance in virtue of the benefits from following a law that is already in effect.

Second, it is important that we not settle for merely *effective* means of improving upon our legal order. We do not want to settle for effectiveness because it makes laws too easy to justify. The moral costs of the law, such as the undesirability of coercion, would have no power to undermine the law if its mere effectiveness could give it authority. Consequently, persons would have obligations to comply with laws that, in their view, are likely defeated. Compliance with the law must be morally efficient; the balance of one's accessible moral reasons must favor compliance.

Third, laws can also be morally efficient by either (a) *transitioning* members of the public from one practice to another or (b) *stabilizing* a practice that would otherwise not be a stable norm. Focusing on (a), a law might significantly improve the moral order by moving members of the public from an unjustified rule to a new and justified moral rule. The unjustified rule may permit persons to enforce a social practice that cannot be publicly justified to those subject to the rule. Thus, by engaging in the practice, we violate our moral obligations to others. By complying with a law that transitions the social group from the unjustified rule to the justified rule, compliant agents better fulfill their moral obligations, since complying with the old rule violates our moral obligations and complying with the new rule, let's suppose, does not.[61] In case (b), we presume that, prior to the ratification and enforcement of the law, a social group wishes to engage in a justified moral practice. But the practice is not, by itself, in equilibrium, perhaps due to a failure of common knowledge. If we wish to maintain the practice, then, we may need a coercion-backed law to keep the moral rule in place, say by ensuring that members of the public recognize that the rule is in effect based on legal punishment of violators.

There is no need for a one-to-one mapping between moral and legal rules such that any authoritative legal rule must have the same content and govern the same behavior as an already existing moral rule. Cases (a) and (b) allow multiple relationships between the moral and legal domains. A

---

[61] Alternatively, as we have seen, a law might transition members of the public from a justified rule to a superior justified rule that is the best rule from the perspective of many members of the public.

law can either reinforce or codify an already existing moral rule with its attendant obligations, transition or stabilize a new moral rule that comes with its own moral obligations, or create a new method of discharging more generic moral obligations.

In light of the foregoing, we can define the conditions for legal obligation:

> A person has a moral obligation to comply with a law iff she is entitled to believe (i) that *general* compliance with the law will significantly improve her moral order's capacity to perform its central functions and (ii) that *her* compliance with the law will allow her to morally efficiently discharge her moral obligation(s) prescribed by justified moral rules.[62]

Some comments are in order. First, recall that Reba is epistemically entitled to believe p when she makes no rational error in believing p, not necessarily when her evidence uniquely favors p. The law has authority when an agent is entitled to believe that the law will have the relevant effect. But this authority can be overridden if the law does not turn out to perform its requisite function and the agent can recognize the relevant failure on reflection.

Notice the key distinction between conditions (i) and (ii). Condition (i) requires that Reba believe that *general* compliance will produce some good, whereas condition (ii) requires that Reba believe that *her* compliance will produce some good *for her*. These conditions flow from the idea of a social norm. If Reba does not believe that the law significantly improves upon her order's ability to perform its central functions, then she is unlikely to believe that the normative expectations that back the law are justified or appropriate, which implies that Reba will not believe that the legal coercion can be publicly justified. And if Reba does not see her compliance with the law as enabling her to do what is morally required of her, or as enabling her to do what she is morally permitted to do, it is hard to see how Reba can think that the relevant normative expectations apply to her.

Condition (ii) is important for a second reason as well, for it shows that legal obligation is grounded in a law being a morally efficient means of discharging moral obligations. If Reba does not believe that her compliance with a law will efficiently enable her to comply with her moral obligations, and that she can efficiently discharge her obligations without

---

[62] Legal obligations also involve the internalization of a law as the agent's own, but I omit discussion of internalization here.

complying with the law, then she has no legal obligation. Unless, of course, her failure to so believe is an epistemic failure where her evidence requires that she believe her compliance will have the relevant enabling effect.

My first-pass definition of a justified legal obligation, however, is not satisfactory. It does not recognize the fact that a person's legal obligations depend upon whether others are complying with the law or not, and hence whether there are empirical expectations. The law must generally be followed, or else it is not a social norm based on intelligible reasons. In the case of widespread disobedience, then, I submit that the legal obligation in question is undermined. A second problem is that Reba cannot be obligated to comply with a law that requires that she violate her other moral obligations, or at least those obligations that have greater or equal weight with respect to the obligations derived from the moral rules that apply to her.

An expanded account of legal obligation:

> A person has a moral obligation to comply with a law if and only if she is epistemically entitled to believe (i) that *general* compliance with the law will significantly improve her moral order's capacity to perform its central functions and (ii) that *her* compliance with the law morally efficiently improves upon her capacity to discharge her moral obligation(s) prescribed by justified moral rules, so long as (iii) she reliably observes that sufficiently many other agents are complying with the law and that (iv) complying with the law does not violate her other moral obligations of equal or greater weight.

If we recognize that generally obeyed laws are legal rules, we can drop reference to general obedience to the law. We can shorten the improvement conditions and contract the entitlement condition to rational belief. I will finally assume that the relevant moral obligations are not overridden, undercut, or otherwise defeated by other obligations to produce a streamlined formulation:

> A person has a moral obligation to obey a law iff she rationally believes that the law significantly improves her moral order and that obeying the law morally efficiently improves upon her capacity to fulfill her moral obligation(s).

The duty to obey the law is *quasi-independent* because it obligates one to comply with a member of a set of legal rules, each of which is publicly justifiable.[63] This set includes options compliance with which Reba might find suboptimal from her own moral point of view, but would be morally efficient means of discharging her moral obligations were they in effect. Thus, if Reba prefers law A, but lacks good objections to laws B and C, then if a publicly justified decision procedure imposes B or C on Reba, she has an obligation to comply with B or C. So legal obligation is content-independent only with respect to the set of potentially justified and morally efficient legal rules.[64]

We can now specify a principle that covers the public justification of law. Recall our definition of public justification for moral rules:

> *Public Justification*: a moral rule is publicly justified only if each member of the public has sufficient intelligible reason to comply with and internalize the rule.

The legal version of public justification is similar:

> *Legal Justification*: a legal rule is publicly justified only if each member of the public has sufficient intelligible reason to internalize the law because each member rationally recognizes that compliance with the law morally efficiently improves upon her capacity to comply with a publicly justified moral rule or rules.

Law is only publicly justified when citizens rationally see it as necessary to improve upon an order of mere moral rules. This does not require, of course, that citizens understand the idea of public justification. Rather, when asked, they express a belief that a given legal rule is necessary to perform an important social function that mere moral rules cannot, and that compliance with the law is the right thing to do. This means that legal rules cannot be publicly justified if they are not seen as required to modify or reinforce a moral rule. *A society's moral constitution has priority; the legal constitution is its handmaiden.*

---

[63] In this way, a legal rule can be different from the prior moral rule but still be authoritative due to being within the eligible set.

[64] This means that a law need not necessarily share the content of the prior moral rule, as the law can change a moral rule in a justified fashion, and gain authority based on its ability to create such a shift.

9. Contrasted with the Service Conception

Raz's service conception of authority is a combination of two theses. The dependence thesis holds that a directive can only have real authority "if it is based upon (or at least reflects) reasons that already apply to the subject of the directive."[65] Practical authority can only arise when obeying the dictates of a legal or political official helps the person better act on reasons that already apply to her. In this way, legal and political officials have authority in virtue of serving ordinary persons by helping them do what they have reason to do. The normal justification thesis holds that a directive typically derives its legitimacy from the fact "that its subjects do better at complying with the correct balance of reasons by obeying the directive than by determining on their own what the balance of reasons requires and acting according to that determination."[66] Any directive that does not serve its subjects by helping them comply with the right balance of reasons lacks authority.

The preemptive thesis follows from the dependence and normal justification theses; it holds that "a subject should treat a legitimately authoritative directive as an action-guiding rule."[67] This involves treating the directive as a "motivating reason for action" and not the considerations that might undermine compliance.[68] Raz's conception of an authoritative reason is also "exclusionary" by being a "second-order reason to exclude reasons one might have not to act in accord with the directive."[69] The reason is a kind of *external reason* in that the reasons need not be "ones that the subject has knowledge of" such that a reason can apply to someone even if she does not realize it.[70] The resulting account of legal authority is piecemeal since directives might be legitimate for some persons rather than others.[71] Legal legitimacy instead requires a kind of respect for the law.[72]

The reader may find it useful to know that I adopt versions of the dependence thesis and the normal justification thesis. Laws have authority only when they enable persons to morally efficiently comply with publicly justified moral rules, either previously existing moral rules or new

---

[65] Ehrenberg 2011, p. 886. See Raz 1986, p. 47.
[66] Also see Raz 1986, p. 53.
[67] Ibid., p. 887. See also, p. 57.
[68] The preemptive thesis also involves setting aside the independent reasons to comply, since the directive rebuts or undercuts one's other reasons to act.
[69] Raz 1986, p. 886; Raz [1975] 1990, p. 39.
[70] Raz 2009, pp. 147–148.
[71] Raz 1986, pp. 74, 80.
[72] Raz 2009, pp. 250–262.

justified rules created by the law. Thus, in complying with a publicly justified law, persons better comply with the balance of reasons that apply to them. I also think that legal authority is piecemeal and limited and that it issues pre-emptive reasons.

However, in contrast to Raz, I insist that justificatory reasons, the reasons that ground legal obligations, must be intelligible reasons. Only intelligible reasons can figure into the justification of moral rules, not unintelligible, yet valid external reasons.[73]

That said, Raz has argued that, because "the point of being under an authority is that it opens a way of improving one's conformity with reason." A person can only achieve this by following the directives of an authority if she has reliable beliefs about whether "the conditions of legitimacy are met" and believes that she "can also have knowledge that they are met."[74] Raz thereby embraces a *knowability* constraint. To have reasons, we must able to know about them.[75] While I require that the reasons must be psychologically accessible rather than knowable, these requirements are similar, and so in the end, our views may not be as far apart as they initially appear.

Justificatory reasons are preemptive in the following sense. We may have external reasons to act, and the balance of *all* our reasons, intelligible reasons and unintelligible external reasons, might speak in favor of some particular action as a result. But on my view, legal authority is only grounded in the balance of intelligible reasons, such that a law has authority when the balance of intelligible reasons favors compliance and internalization. The view allows that the balance of *all* of one's reasons, which could include external reasons, may require one to disobey the law or somehow undermine the preemptive force of intelligible reasons. This means that reasons of legal obligation are not necessarily preemptive *full stop*, though they are *seen as such* by idealized persons.

A third difference between my view and Raz's is that I think legal authority derives from moral authority. So laws only have authority when they help us comply with our moral obligations. Moral authority of this kind is necessary for legal authority.[76]

---

[73] Here I set aside sociopathic persons who often seem to have moral reasons they cannot psychologically access.

[74] See Raz 2006, p. 1025.

[75] Wall has argued this may commit Raz to a conception of reasons closer to public reason liberalism. See Wall, "Razian Authority and Public Reason," unpublished.

[76] I allow for mere personal duties to obey the law to be grounded in other kinds of moral reasons.

Finally, Raz's discussion of legal authority focuses on the authority of the directives issued by legal officials. My theory establishes the authority of moral and legal *rules*, which should enable anyone with the appropriate standing to insist that people comply with the relevant rule. Everyone subject to the rules can demand that everyone follow them even if only some can enforce them. Moreover, the authority persons have to issue directives derives from the authority of the moral rules.

10. On to the Political Order

Chapters 1–3 addressed the constitution of society outside of the state, our moral constitution.[77] Our moral constitution is the complex of publicly justified moral rules that organize social life between persons who prefer to cooperate rather than to conquer. This chapter has shown that without a legal order and enforceable legal obligations, a moral constitution cannot fully promote moral peace and other important social goods. This explains why legal coercion requires public justification, perhaps the main aim of theorizing about public reason.

We must now outline the shape of a political constitution that realizes moral peace between persons. Specifically, we need an account of the highest-order rules of *lawmaking* and how they can be justified.

---

[77] Rawls 1980, p. 539.

CHAPTER 5 | Primary Rights

MY AIM IN THIS book is to show how political institutions can preserve moral peace between persons, and this involves justifying law-altering institutions, bodies that can change the law. This means we need to explain how *constitutional rules* can be publicly justified. Constitutional rules are the highest-order rules of lawmaking and law-alteration. They allow persons to change legal and moral rules. The point of this chapter and the next is to identify a method for publicly justifying constitutional rules as necessary complements to systems of moral and legal rules.

This chapter develops an account of the most fundamental constraints on the optimal eligible set of constitutional rules, which I call *primary rights*.[1] A primary right is a right that anyone with a rational plan of life would want for herself to pursue her conception of the good and justice, and one she is willing to extend to others on reciprocal terms. Primary rights are also moral rights of sufficiently great weight as to merit coercive legal protection; they are rights the legal system should recognize and protect. Moderately idealized members of the public will insist upon rights to pursue their conceptions of the good and justice, and so will have reason to endorse both a scheme of primary rights and constitutional rules that articulate and protect those rights. Publicly justified primary rights thereby remove a vast array of constitutional rules from the optimal eligible set,

---

[1] My decision to begin the political contractarian choice procedure with the selection of rights is common in contemporary contract theory. Rawls, of course, begin his choice process by settling on a list of rights; the same is true for contract theories on the other end of the political spectrum, for libertarian contract theorists like Jan Narveson and Loren Lomasky. See Rawls 2001, p. 42; Lomasky 1987, pp. 56–83; and Narveson 2001, pp. 41–61. David Gauthier, who stands in between egalitarians and libertarians, also begins the bargaining process with setting out a scheme of rights. See Gauthier 1986, pp. 208–222.

since constitutional rules that allow for the systematic violation of primary rights cannot be publicly justified.

My account of rights self-consciously resembles Rawls's account of rights, but it differs in deriving primary rights in light of the fact that moderately idealized persons will endorse different conceptions of justice, and will insist on pursuing their own conception of justice as well as their conception of the good. This means that Rawls's second moral power, the power to develop and exercise one's sense of justice, will lead people in quite different directions, and so will affect the content of the rights they endorse. Evaluative pluralism about justice—justice pluralism—runs sufficiently deep that a society cannot sustain a system of trust by coordinating around one conception of justice, just as a system of trust cannot be sustained by coordinating around one conception of the good.[2] People cannot settle on generic principles of justice to ground social trust, but must instead restrict their focus to determining which particular moral and legal rights can be justified to persons who disagree about justice and the good. Justice pluralism thereby leads to primary rights because only primary rights can form the central basis of social trust among diverse persons.

At the same time, rights are more general than particular laws and policies, which may seem in tension with my commitment to a more fine-grained approach to individuation of moral and legal rules. But in focusing on rights, I am not abandoning my account of individuation. Instead, in showing that rights are publicly justified, we show that members of the public can authoritatively appeal to primary rights to defeat moral, legal, and constitutional rules. For example, suppose we are trying to determine whether a law restricting free speech is publicly justified; if members of the public endorse a right to free speech, then that right serves to generate defeater reasons for the law.

Quong has recently argued that we can treat disagreements about the good and justice *asymmetrically*.[3] His defense is based on two main lines of argument. First, Quong adopts an "internal conception" of political liberalism that expressly restricts the subjects of public justification to a highly idealized constituency of reasonable people who already affirm liberal values.[4] This approach grounds Quong's claim that reasonable disagreements about justice are necessarily based on thick common

---

[2] Rawls 2005, p. xxxvi.
[3] Quong 2011, p. 193.
[4] Ibid., p. 8. See pp. 137–160 for Quong's justification for this restriction by appealing to his "internal conception" of political liberalism.

assumptions about what considerations are relevant to resolving disputes about justice. But, as I have argued elsewhere, the internal conception is in tension with the fundamental aims of public reason liberalism because it limits the number of persons to whom justification is owed to an extremely narrow group of people.[5] This makes Quong's political liberalism objectionably sectarian. Quong also argues that when we impose policies or principles on reasonable persons who reject those policies or principles, we do not violate any plausible principle of legitimacy. So we can publicly justify coercing persons who disagree about justice without wronging them. I have argued that imposing upon persons in this way is, contra Quong, disrespectful and authoritarian.[6] For these reasons, then, I set Quong's alternative approach aside.

In justifying rights, I am not trying to justify a scheme of objective rights that persons have, say, in virtue of their natures. Nor am I denying that such objective rights exist. Instead, I merely claim that those who demand that persons comply with objective rights claims can undermine a system of trust and moral peace between persons if the objective rights are not publicly justified. Thus, my aim is to describe which rights claims should be recognized and protected by a publicly justified legal system.

I leave the derivation of specific classes of primary rights to chapter 7, as well as to the sequel to this book, where I develop a detailed defense of the rights of association, private property, social insurance, and democracy. My aim here is to outline the generic structure of primary rights and the procedure for justifying them in general. I outline the motivation for and definition of primary rights in section 1. I'll connect primary rights to the resources required to exercise these rights in section 2 and then develop a thin veil of ignorance model for identifying publicly justified primary rights in section 3. Section 4 explains how primary rights sustain trust.

1. Primary Rights

The legal state of nature will contain a host of publicly justified moral rules that establish moral rights, both liberty-rights, where agents are morally permitted to act in certain ways, and claim-rights, where agents have permissions to act in certain ways, and can rightly insist that others allow

---

[5] Vallier 2017b.
[6] Vallier 2019a.

them to do so.[7] Some of these liberty-rights and claim-rights will protect interests and choices of great importance to members of the public, and some of those rights will not be adequately protected in the legal state of nature. This subset of our moral rights includes rights that members of the public, at the right level of idealization, will regard as insufficiently recognized and protected in the legal state of nature. They will therefore insist that legal systems protect these rights. In the case of liberty-rights, they will want to upgrade the right to a legal claim-right. In the case of claim-rights, they will simply want to add legal protection to protections provided by moral rules.[8] For this reason, we should expect there to be some permissions and claims in the legal state of nature that will ordinarily merit legal protection *as authoritative claim-rights* due to their importance and centrality for the lives of members of the public.

I call these central rights primary rights.[9] Like Rawls's notion of a primary good, a good anyone would want regardless of her rational plan of life, primary rights are rights that (i) persons will want for themselves to pursue their conception of the good and their conception of justice and (ii) are willing to extend to everyone (and not just the reasonable) on the same terms.[10]

The first condition specifies the potential extent of primary rights as including all rights that persons see as especially necessary or helpful for enabling them to pursue their conceptions of the good by giving them the social space and/or positive aid needed to form life plans and to live out those plans. It also includes the rights necessary or helpful for enabling persons to pursue their conception of justice, so long as that conception

---

[7] I grant that the rules that comprise legal states of nature can vary considerably, but they are overwhelmingly likely to contain some core rights claims that match the scheme of publicly justified primary rights I discuss in chapter 7. Members of the public will want legal protection for their exercise of their agency, taking part in associational life, having jurisdictional protection for private property, as well as access to legal and political procedures for protecting themselves from threats. So legal states of nature will share some central features.

[8] Distinguishing between liberty-rights and claim-rights in the legal state of nature helps us to address a potential objection to my method of justifying rights, namely that some critical objective rights claims in the legal state of nature go unrecognized. But at least some objective rights that morally demand recognition should manifest in the legal state of nature as genuine liberty-rights, where those who have sufficient reason to insist that they have the right will have defeaters for moral rules that require or permit violating the right. They will then sometimes seek legal help in ensuring that the relevant moral rules are reformed or dissolved by legal pressure.

[9] This approach owes much to Lomasky 1987, pp. 56–83.

[10] Rawls adds that primary goods are the goods "persons need in their status as free and equal citizens, and as normal and fully cooperating members of society over a complete life." Rawls 1999a, p. xliii.

of justice, like conceptions of the good, is minimally moral and rational. Given the importance that persons place on pursuing their conceptions of the good and justice, they will want additional legal protection for their ability to pursue those conceptions.

The second condition requires equal primary rights, meaning that all persons have the same rights, enforced in real institutional practice. All primary rights are limited to those that choosers are prepared to extend to others. If, for instance, someone wants to claim a right to free speech for herself, she must be prepared to extend it to others on the same terms. She cannot insist on free speech for herself alone.

The equality constraint does not determine whether the *content* of primary rights privileges some views or values over others, just that everyone will authoritatively hold all chosen rights. The selected primary rights could privilege certain moral norms or values despite being held by all members of the public equally. One could have equal perfectionist rights, for example. This means we will have to derive the claim that primary rights prohibit sectarian or establishmentarian coercion from our thin veil of ignorance device. As we will see, choosers will not risk embracing rights that privilege their own views and values over the views and values of others, lest those with minority or low-status worldviews be oppressed or dominated by those with majority or high-status worldviews. Similarly, the equality constraint does not commit us to distributive egalitarianism, just that, whatever primary rights persons have, they all have them.

Primary rights must therefore be equal because members of the public on the losing end of an unequal scheme of rights will always insist on having as many rights as those held by the most advantaged persons or points of view. They will not choose to coercively protect special rights; in all likelihood, they will either refuse to coercively protect special rights, or insist that such rights be coercively extended to everyone.

The only condition under which members of the public might accept unequal rights is if those with fewer rights benefit more from an unequal scheme of rights than from an equal scheme, following Rawlsian difference principle reasoning. But we have little empirical reason to think that the least advantaged are substantially benefited by an unequal rights scheme, at least in any sense that they could detect when appropriately idealized. For instance, authoritarian regimes, which restrict political participation, do not generally produce better outcomes for their subjects than democratic regimes.

Further, it is not clear how to apply difference principle reasoning to a scheme of rights. How, for instance, could we measure the extent to which different groups benefit from a scheme of rights?[11] We might be able to measure primary rights to resources in this way, but not primary rights generally. It is unclear, for instance, how we can maximize rights to freedom of association or agency rights for the least advantaged by giving more rights to some particular group or sect.

Primary rights must be *authoritative* for moderately idealized persons; they must have practical authority. Accordingly, the paradigmatic legal rights in a morally peaceful regime are claim-rights. So publicly justified rights impose real moral duties on others. This condition is critical because only authoritative rights can preserve a system of trust, just as only authoritative demands and coercion can preserve a system of trust. One implication of authoritative primary rights is to place limits on the rights that can be publicly justified, as people will only endorse rights that they believe justifiably limit their liberty, since protecting rights limits their moral liberty.[12]

Some primary rights go beyond moral and legal claim-rights, however. Many persons, especially those who validly hold a publicly justified legal office, have publicly justified power-rights—rights to create duties and liberties for others. But all powers must be justified as necessary to establish a functional legal system of norm-interpreting and norm-altering institutions. The quick case for publicly justifying power-rights is that a functional legal system requires that officials have the authority to apply and change the law, which in turn can impose new duties and liberties on persons. Chapter 6 provides a case for constitutional authority that includes power-rights.[13]

Primary rights must also be more or less *coherent*, in that there are publicly recognized mechanisms for resolving competing rights claims. This does not mean that all rights are *compossible* in the strong sense that there exist no contradictory, yet valid, rights claims, but rather that the normal operation of a publicly justified legal order harmonizes rights-claims over time.[14] Social change, be it political, technological, cultural, etc., will frequently generate new rights conflicts, so systems of publicly justified rights will probably never reach full compossibility. But a publicly justified legal

---

[11] I thank Adam Gjesdal for this point.

[12] I admit exceptions, such as lifeboat situations where persons are morally permitted to stop each other from pursuing a very scarce resource but neither is obliged to defer to the other.

[13] I further develop a case for publicly justified power rights in the sequel to this book.

[14] Steiner 1977 develops a classic account of the compossibility of rights.

system will gradually render legal rights compossible were other forms of social change to stop. The process is analogous to a market price reaching equilibrium in the absence of constantly changing market conditions. Compossibility draws legal rights into an increasingly coherent whole, even if this current can be thrown off by other factors.

Some primary rights are negative, while others are positive. Negative rights protect liberties and choices from interference or obstacles to action. A negative right to free speech grants one a moral and legal right against anyone interfering with the right-holder's speech.[15] Publicly justified rights are sometimes negative because negative rights are required to protect one's pursuit of the good and justice, and are sufficiently necessary that people will concede rights to others in exchange for securing these rights for themselves. Consequently, at least some negative primary rights should be publicly justifiable to all, and so morally prohibit many proposed forms of interference by government or private parties.

Further, as we saw in chapter 4, legal coercion must meet a presumption against coercion. The presumption against coercion prohibits legal coercion that cannot be publicly justified. Within the domain of moral rules, then a publicly justified rule specifies that coercion needs justification, whereas noncoercion does not. This rule thereby grounds a right against legal coercion.[16]

Primary rights can be positive in one of two senses—the freedom-as-self-rule sense and the welfare-rights sense.[17] The self-rule account construes rights as entitlements to social conditions that protect and promote one's capacity to rule herself, both against external interference *and* against internal blockages to self-rule, such as addiction or poor character. A person is positively free in this sense when her actions are determined by her reason rather than by her own unruly passions. In one way, all publicly justified primary rights enable self-rule, since a right is publicly justified only when rooted in the reasons that persons possess and their prima facie entitlement to act as those reasons direct. But in another way, publicly justified rights are not typically positive in the self-rule sense because persons lack rights to force others to become better self-rulers. People

---

[15] Gaus 2000, p. 82. For the classic formulation of the negative-positive liberty distinction, see "Two Concepts of Liberty" in Berlin 1969.

[16] For discussion and defense of the claim that there is a publicly justified right against legal coercion, see Gaus 2011, pp. 479–487. Notice that this right implies that one can use coercion defensively to stop the initiation of unjustified coercion by another party even if defensive coercion cannot be publicly justified to the initiator.

[17] For a proponent of the freedom-as-self-rule sense, see Green 2011.

can reasonably reject paternalistic interference because antipaternalist members of the public often have sufficient reason of their own to reject paternalistic laws.

The welfare-rights account of a positive right is a right to welfare or some form of means to welfare. In our case, positive welfare-rights are rights to resources, or at least to the conditions under which one can freely acquire certain essential goods and services, such as healthcare, clothing, or shelter. Given the importance of being able to make use of one's negative freedoms, we should be able to publicly justify some rights to resources. But this is not to say that Reba has a right to be provided healthcare by John that allows her to violently force him to help her become healthy. John may have sufficient reason to reject these acts of violence even if he believes he is morally obliged to help Reba because he may not regard himself as having reason to permit the coercive enforcement of that moral obligation. Instead, welfare rights are rights that our fellow citizens act to sustain institutions whose normal operation provide the goods to which persons have a positive right. So if healthcare is best provided to persons through the market, and moderately idealized members of the public can agree upon this fact, then the welfare right to healthcare will likely manifest as the right to participate in a functioning healthcare market.

2. Primary Rights to Resources

Many primary rights simply protect the liberties and choices of rights holders from interference, but, as noted, we should expect members of the public to endorse some welfare rights—rights to resources. This is because, in many cases, being able to make use of one's liberties and to make important choices will require access to certain kinds of goods. However, specifying the kind resources to which persons have a primary right raises some questions that require our attention.

Philosophers have long disagreed about the *distribuendum* of justice— the sort of good distributed by a principle of distributive justice, or in our case, the sort of good to which persons have primary rights. Rawls argued that principles of justice should distribute primary goods, goods that persons will want regardless of their particular rational life plan.[18]

---

[18] Here I speak only to the resources Rawls called "social" primary goods; natural primary goods, such as intelligence and imagination are, as Rawls said, not usually under the control of social institutions. Rawls 1999a, p. 54.

The capabilities approach developed by Martha Nussbaum and Amartya Sen instead proposes to distribute the capability of each person to pursue the life that she has most reason to value.[19] I cannot opt for either approach because members of the public are bound to disagree about which *distribuendum* is appropriate. The best account of the *distribuendum* on my view would be multiperspectival, where different perspectives converge on an eligible scheme of rights despite endorsing different *distribuenda*, but this raises complications that I cannot address here.

Fortunately, distinct accounts of the *distribuendum* endorse many of the same resources that people need to make effective rights-protected choices.[20] These include access to wealth and income, which can be understood as both stocks of money, including cash holdings, and flows of money, including income streams. I would also include access to capital, since capital will include both investments that can grow with time and so provide persons with increasing income and wealth, but also the resources needed to own, operate, or invest in a business. We will see in chapter 7 that some of the rights Rawlsians acknowledge as basic, namely rights to personal property and freedom of occupation, combine to yield a right of self-employment, which in turn will require access to capital goods. So rights to capital are included among the resources to which each person has a primary right.

The goods of income, wealth, and capital should first be secured by negative rights that protect persons from interference in securing income, wealth, and capital for themselves. However, when protection from interference is insufficient to secure an adequate level of these goods, and the moral order fails to solve the shortage, legal intervention can be justified to improve upon the circumstances generated by negative rights alone.

Rawls thought that the most important primary goods include the social bases of self-respect, "those basic institutions normally essential if citizens are to have a lively sense of their worth as persons and to be able to advance their ends with self-confidence."[21] Samuel Freeman further explains that the social bases of self-respect are "features of institutions that are needed to enable people to have the confidence that they and their position in society are respected and that their conception of the good is worth

---

[19] Robeyns 2016 provides a contemporary literature review on the capabilities approach. For early accounts of the capabilities approach, see Sen 1980 and Nussbaum 2001.

[20] Rawls 2001, pp. 58–59.

[21] Rawls 1999a, p. 54.

pursuing and achievable."[22] So we look for institutional rules and goods that give people the ability to secure their self-respect.

Primary rights to resources should supply many of the social bases of self-respect. If people are afraid to appear impoverished in public, they will find at least partial protection in a primary right to the goods required to alleviate poverty. If people feel diminished by their inability to achieve positions with high social status and influence, then procedural rights to certain offices in political and economic organizations can help to avoid such diminishment. Primary rights may undersupply self-respect by failing to reduce public stigma against, say, one's race, gender, or sexual orientation. But my account could include a right to compensation for social or historical disadvantage to rights of agency, if need be. So primary rights can capture many of the social bases of self-respect.

I admit, however, that some bases of self-respect cannot easily be captured by protecting other rights, such as forms of disrespect imposed by unjustified moral rules; the social bases of self-respect might be secured by laws that displace or suppress those moral rules.[23] But since these considerations should not bear greatly on my arguments for primary rights to resources, I will not appeal further to the social bases of self-respect.

3. A Veil with Normative Significance

Legal systems should recognize primary rights that protect and facilitate each person's pursuit of her conception of the good and justice by means of authoritative moral claims on and powers over others. Members of the public will likely endorse both negative rights against interference in pursuing one's conception of the good or justice, as well as positive rights to resources—income, wealth, and capital in particular. But these are rather general constraints on the eligible set of rights. We need a method for determining how to settle on specific primary rights.

The traditional contractarian approach to identifying and justifying rights is to construct a choice situation where idealized agents are denied certain information that would bias the scheme of rights they would choose. The choice situation is structured so as to ensure that the choice is not influenced by factors that are morally irrelevant, like race, gender, or religion. In this way, contractarians often appeal to *veils of ignorance*.

---

[22] Freeman 2014.
[23] I thank my graduate students for this insight.

Contractarian choice models generate simple misunderstandings, so I want to stress that my choice scenario is meant to determine which rights real persons have sufficient intelligible reason to endorse. I moderately idealize contracting parties so that the contractarian choice is based on each citizen's intelligible reasons. In this way, the choice scenario will provide theorists with evidence about what practical reasons real persons have. The choice scenario should therefore pick out the rights that real persons would see themselves as having most reason to respect on reflection.

The veil metaphor in particular invites confusion. It is often said, for instance, that the veil of ignorance argument implies that the rules or principles chosen are morally binding because severely epistemically impoverished persons would accept them. Whether this charge is fair to other contract theorists, it does not apply to the argument of this book. My veil of ignorance is nothing more than a heuristic meant to economize on the search costs of locating a single scheme or small set of publicly justified primary rights. Given the large number of possible rights schemes, we need some way to locate schemes of primary rights that can be publicly justified, and using a veil helps. So let me be clear: *the veil has no normative significance other than as an economizing device.*

By treating a veil of ignorance as a heuristic, I am prepared to acknowledge the existence of other good heuristics, such as veils that deprive contractors of more information than the thin veil introduced below. Since there may be many publicly justified schemes of primary rights, theorists should feel free to use multiple veil heuristics to help each other search the large conceptual space of feasible rights schemes to find the publicly justified ones. This means that the eligible scheme of rights I defend may be *nonunique*. There may be other eligible rights schemes. Some contractarians will frown on allowing multiple bargaining points for contracting parties, but I see little disadvantage in allowing for some indeterminacy, as there will be more trust-justifying ways of organizing society. Fortunately, we should not be left with especially crippling indeterminacy because different heuristics should select at least five classes of rights: agency, association, jurisdiction, procedure, and international rights. There is no space to deploy multiple veil heuristics here, so I develop only one veil heuristic in what follows.

The veil I propose is thin in that parties know almost everything about themselves and their social circumstances. The choosers are moderately idealized members of the public; they know their own conceptions of the good and their conceptions of justice. Feminists may appeal to feminist conceptions of justice, just as Catholics may appeal to Catholic social thought. Persons may offer any of their intelligible reasons to accept or reject proposals in attempting to secure agreement. Instead, below I will only deprive choosers of the knowledge of two sets of facts: (i) facts about the *proportion* of members of society that affirm their conception of the good and justice, or anyone else's, and (ii) facts about the *relative social standing* of any person or anyone's conception of the good or justice; persons do not know whether they *or their worldviews* are high or low status. Parties are therefore asked to choose primary rights without knowing if they are in the majority or a minority, or whether they or their views are socially favored or disfavored.

We need not stipulate that the parties have no knowledge of probabilities of different outcomes, as Rawls does.[24] We must only suppose that the model makes it extremely difficult to single out some person or group for special treatment. Contractors can enter into choice with different levels of risk aversion, but since all will have at least some risk aversion, and cannot be sure of their relative social power, even social and political hegemons will approve of equal schemes of primary rights, since they might not be in power in their society.

The choice situation excludes knowledge of each person's and worldview's relative social and political power to ensure that the rights selected will be reciprocal and equal. If we deprive contractors of their knowledge of their social and political power, they will only insist on schemes of rights that protect the relatively less powerful from the more powerful, primarily by protecting minority or marginal viewpoints from oppression or control by majority or privileged viewpoints.

The choice situation includes basically all other available information to ensure that the selected rights can be justified to each person based on the totality of her intelligible reasons. A thicker veil where persons do not know their conceptions of the good and justice will probably be more prone to select rights schemes that are harder to publicly justify because contracting parties will have access to fewer private, intelligible reasons to ensure that their choice of rights will match what they have sufficient intelligible reason to endorse on full reflection. Some readers will worry that giving parties this much information will allow them to propose biased proposals that benefit a party's particular worldview or social group. However, other groups can veto such proposals, which

---

[24] Rawls 1999a, pp. 132–138, especially p. 134.

should help to ensure that the output of the contractarian procedure remains fair and unbiased.

Our choice model must also include a choice baseline, which is the state of affairs that publicly justified rights schemes must be an improvement upon. For Rawls, the baseline is equality of primary goods, and departures from equality can only be justified if they maximize the position of the least advantaged.[25] For Buchanan, the baseline is the holdings that persons secure following the state of war.[26] I reject both accounts. As noted above, the scheme of primary rights is built from a baseline of the legal state of nature.[27] This is because moderately idealized agents will see the disadvantages of the legal state of nature and will want to use the law to give their liberties and claims additional recognition, specification, and protection.

From the baseline, members of the public will appeal to a Pareto criterion. If all members of the public prefer scheme S_1 to S_2, then the optimal eligible set of rights-schemes contains only S_1. The Pareto criterion has two implications: members of the public will prefer more rights to fewer rights, and they will prefer the scheme of rights that they can agree guarantees the largest feasible bundle of resources, specifically wealth, income, and capital, to each person. Many Pareto-optimal schemes should exist since these schemes will secure different combinations of resources that a society will regard as indifferent to other combinations of resources. These maximal, feasible bundles of resources define the Pareto frontier.

Finally, moderately idealized members of the public choose a scheme of primary rights that not only secures a bundle of resources on the Pareto frontier but also maximizes the growth of the frontier over time. If parties prefer more resources to fewer resources at one time, they should prefer more resources to fewer resources across time. This implies that members of the public can be expected to, but need not always, choose a scheme of primary rights that entitles persons to fewer resources at present in order to secure a larger bundle of resources in the future. We should therefore expect the parties to seek an intertemporal maximization of resource bundles.

Notice that this is not a principle of just "savings," as Rawls described it.[28] Instead, the parties adopt a *principle of sustainable improvements* as an intertemporal Pareto criterion. An authoritative scheme of rights is

---

[25] Ibid., pp. 52–57.
[26] Buchanan 1975, p. 25.
[27] Thus, if someone happens to have more rights than others in a legal state of nature, that inequality does not help set the baseline.
[28] Rawls 1999a, pp. 251–258.

one that promotes improvements for all persons over time, such that each person is entitled to enough resources to sustain herself and her family at present and to partake in social and economic growth. By partaking in growth, persons will enjoy an ever-increasing number of potential life plans and projects to pursue. This does not mean that a just society as a whole must have a shared growth target or explicitly aim at more growth; rather, its institutional rules must be structured so as to grow the bundle of resources to which one has a primary right. Collectively aiming at growth is not required in order to have growth-promoting institutional rules.[29]

Improvement must be *sustainable* in that the forms of growth and civilizational development are ones that our best natural and social science suggest can be maintained over time. I grant that there is widespread disagreement about which forms of economic development are sustainable, and that the term "sustainability" is often used by people who are pessimistic about our capacity for development. But I use the term capaciously to refer to what our best social science suggests we're capable of. Thus, parties choose rights schemes according to a generic principle of sustainable improvements, and the ideas of sustainability and improvements can be specified in the choice scenario or in the structure of political decision-making set by a publicly justified constitution.

The principle of sustainable improvements considerably alters the landscape of publicly justified rights schemes. Public reason liberals usually ignore the moral benefits of economic growth, seemingly preferring to follow Rawls, J. M. Keynes, and J. S. Mill in decrying excessive focus on growth.[30] But if we care about maximizing each person's bundle of income, wealth, and capital, then we should care about maximizing the bundle over time, and this requires that political, legal, and economic institutions be structured so as to promote the sustainable growth of resources. This suggests that policies that stymie economic growth are prima facie suspect.[31]

Perhaps this is too strong. Couldn't some moderately idealized agents, knowing their comprehensive doctrine, opt for a steady-state economy,

---

[29] Aiming at growth might be required in order to *maximize* growth in each person's bundle of resources, but high-growth societies only have growth as a public policy aim, not as a social aim generally.

[30] On the continuity between their views, see Tomasi 2012, pp. 32–37.

[31] Though economic growth alone does not guarantee that the bundle of resources available to the poor will grow at a morally adequate rate. For some social democratic proposals for ensuring that growth promotes progress for the poor, see Kenworthy 2013.

arguing that economic growth brings social change and interconnectedness that can undermine various social goods?[32] While a few agents will have such concerns, it does not seem to me sufficient to veto the pursuit of sustainable growth. First, this complaint would not suffice to show that we shouldn't maximize bundles of resources at a *particular* time. Zero-growth or low-growth members of the public cannot veto their society being presently rich rather than poor even if they think the costs of prosperity are too great. It simply imposes too much of a cost on other citizens to be a reciprocal complaint. This suggests that their complaint would also fail to undermine their society becoming richer *over* time. Second, primary rights of association can be also be fairly strong, strong enough to allow these groups to protect themselves from what they believe to be the deleterious effects of growth. Freedom of association is one way to provide a zero-growth or low-growth group with a kind of exemption from what they regard as the costs of economic growth. Third, many who seem to prefer zero growth are in fact concerned about an *ethos* of growth, where persons are obsessed with their economic welfare. But satisfying the principle of sustainable improvements need not imply that a growth ethos takes hold, and even if it did so, if people freely adopt the ethos, the zero-growth and low-growth parties can no more legitimately complain than they could legitimately complain about the adoption of any other ethos. Finally, in many cases zero-growth or low-growth groups will prefer more resources for themselves on the grounds that they can use them to achieve their other ends, such as charitable work, or structuring separatist institutions. Even monasteries typically don't turn money down; they use it to take care of the elderly, heal the sick, expand their farms and other businesses, and so on.

We can summarize the process of rights selection as follows. From the baseline of choice in the legal state of nature, moderately idealized members of the public propose schemes of primary rights based on their diverse reasons drawn from their conceptions of the good and of justice.[33] They will eliminate from consideration any schemes that do not meet the conditions of primary rights advanced in sections 1 and 2, such as unequal or nonauthoritative rights. They will also reject schemes that fail to secure increasing access to resources like income, wealth, and capital. Members of the public will even have defeaters for particular substantive

---

[32] I thank Adam Gjesdal and Jeff Carroll for raising this objection.

[33] The parties are not self-consciously committed to establishing moral peace, nor do they choose in order to preserve moral peace. The choosers are used as a model for determining the rights that will preserve moral peace. I thank Julian Müller for pressing me to clarify this point.

rights schemes, further restricting the eligible set of such primary rights; I will discuss the selection of substantive rights in chapter 7.

Members of the public will almost certainly converge on a nonempty, plural set of schemes of primary rights. They will prefer a scheme of primary rights to none given their varied and diverse ends because rights protect the social space for each person to live her own life according to her own evaluative commitments. For remember the alternative—effectively living in a state of war with others, forgoing the social and relational value of moral peace between persons, and failing to show due respect to others within a system of trust. Given the great costs of such a state of affairs, at least some rights should satisfy the outlined conditions. Parties will probably recognize more than one scheme as eligible; since members of the public are moderately idealized and diverse, they will not agree to jointly rank a single scheme of primary rights above all other undefeated options. But given the cost of not recognizing any primary rights as authoritative, some rights will be acknowledged, though there may be no consensus on which scheme of primary rights is best.

4. Rights and Trust

One way to understand the argument of this chapter is that legal systems can only maintain a system of trust if they recognize and protect publicly justified primary rights. For no unequal or inadequate legal arrangements can be publicly justified to moderately idealized members of the public choosing rights behind a thin veil of ignorance. The thin veil helps us to identify the schemes of primary rights that are reasonable, moral bargains between diverse persons, such that each person can, on full consideration of her reasons for action, endorse any of these eligible rights schemes as providing her with sufficient moral reason to act. In this way, publicly justified rights schemes give persons adequate moral motivation to respect their rights, as well as a legal order that protects those rights. This in turn incentivizes trustworthy behavior, which, again, is required to sustain a system of trust in the right way and produce moral peace between diverse persons. Publicly justified primary rights thereby help establish that a politics that protects these rights is not war.

Insofar as rights protection is seen as a primary source of political fairness, recent empirical work on trust and fairness provides support for a connection between rights and trust. For instance, Jong-sung You argues that "the fairness of political and legal institutions affects people's incentives for trust and trustworthiness and that individuals' perceptions of fairness of their society directly affect their trust in other people."[34] Many social trust researchers think that economic inequality reduces social trust and trustworthiness. You argues that it does so by leading persons to think that their political and economic institutions are unfair. And You's empirical work shows that "individuals' perceptions of fairness are significantly correlated with social trust." I would argue that public respect for rights is a primary driver of trust in legal and political institutions, and that it correlates with social trust because people feel as though they can socially trust others on the grounds that each person is treated fairly and equally. We need more evidence to definitively tie generalized trust to fairness and fairness to publicly recognized rights claims, which the sequel to this book addresses in more detail.

Primary rights do not provide a complete explanation of how to establish moral peace. They are invariably vague and so require legal codification, interpretation, application, and harmonization. For that reason, we need an account of the rules that allow us to change moral and legal rules—*constitutional rules*.

---

[34] You 2012, p. 702.

CHAPTER 6 | Constitutional Choice

A CONSTITUTIONAL RULE IS a highest order rule of lawmaking that governs the recognition, alteration, creation, and repeal of laws and policies. I now argue that constitutional rules are publicly justified if three conditions are met. They must first identify, codify, protect, and elaborate a system of primary rights. Constitutional rules must also manage errors in the imposition of law, minimizing both the passage of unjustified law and the failure to pass publicly justified law. Finally, constitutional rules must be self-stabilizing in the sense that they can maintain themselves in existence against both external shocks from self-interested agents and provide assurance among those usually disposed to comply with constitutional rules. Chapter 6 is devoted to the second and third stages of constitutional choice. The primary aim of the chapter is to determine how to publicly justify law-altering institutions, specifically legislatures, or lawmaking bodies. In this way, we assign institutions and officials publicly justified power-rights, rights that allow rights holders to create duties and liberties in others; institutions and officials have power-rights associated with their ability to change the law.

For a variety of reasons I review below, I am dissatisfied with traditional Rawlsian approaches to constitutional choice, and I have found it useful to synthesize public reason approaches to constitutional choice with *public choice* approaches to constitutional choice as developed in the work of Buchanan and Tullock. Accordingly, in this chapter I develop a synthesis of public reason and public choice approaches to the selection of constitutional rules. I develop my synthesis of public reason and public choice approaches to constitutional choice in sections 1–3.

I am also dissatisfied with traditional Rawlsian approaches to understanding and establishing stability for the right reasons, for distinct reasons I review below. In particular, I have found it necessary to distinguish between types of stability and to examine how they relate to one another. I introduce the kinds of stability we want constitutional rules to exhibit in sections 4–7.

1. Constitutional Rules and Individuating Laws

Primary rights are general and vague. Constitutions must therefore do more than protect them; they must also identify institutions and practices that codify these rights, extend them to new situations, and harmonize them in cases of conflict. Further, constitutions must govern the laws that execute the productive functions of the state, laws whose content does not usually affect primary rights. Consequently, we must appeal to additional sources of information beyond the factors justifying primary rights in deciding how to select the remaining, eligible constitutional rules. I propose that this information be drawn from the empirical and normative evaluation of particular laws and legislative acts. Recall the argument in chapters 3 and 4 that public reason liberals should individuate the objects of public justification at the level of specific moral and legal rules. Laws are one of the proper units of justification.[1] We can publicly justify the remaining eligible constitutional rules by how effectively they generate publicly justified law and how effectively they block, reform, or repeal unacceptable laws. We can use social science to evaluate particular laws and then make more generic judgments to evaluate constitutional rules that normally produce these laws.

My approach may seem backward. Many may prefer to justify laws by first justifying constitutional rules, while I claim that we justify constitutional rules by appealing to the laws we expect the rules to produce under normal conditions. Why approach it this way? For one thing, moderately idealized agents cannot rationally evaluate the justifiability of constitutional rules and principles of justice in the abstract because they cannot determine the effects of institutionalizing general rules. This is simply because we cannot say with much specificity how those institutional rules will function.[2] For example, we cannot reasonably evaluate judicial review without evaluating the laws and policies that the courts have affected. If we review the impact of judicial review by looking at particular cases,

---

[1] Quong 2011, pp. 273–287 and Gaus 2011, pp. 490–497 argue for fine-grained individuation of proposals.
[2] As argued in Buchanan and Brennan 1985, p. 30. This inability to determine the effect of constitutional rules is Buchanan's "veil of uncertainty."

we can come to a richer and better informed, though far from definitive, judgment. If we evaluate institutional structures in terms of the laws they produce, then, with any luck, we can develop a cumulative case for a particular constitutional rule by looking at its history. We can also appeal to social scientific models in order to organize and interpret that history. Let us hope this is enough to formulate an eligible set of constitutional rules not defeated in the first stage of constitutional choice.

Recall that justice pluralism ensures that we cannot agree to institutionalize substantive principles of justice. Even with enough information, there will still be considerable disagreement at the level of principles, so great that we may be stuck with an unmanageable number of eligible constitutional rules with no way to decide between them. Justifying at the level of particular laws helps to solve this problem. While people will also disagree about which laws are publicly justified, it is easier to evaluate laws and their effects than constitutional rules.

Coarse-grained objects of justification, such as constitutional rules and principles of justice, also allow too many regimes and laws to be publicly justified. If we justify at the level of constitutions, any regime type or constitution that members of the public regard as better than no constitution and that is not Pareto-dominated by another alternative will be eligible for public justification. Given the importance of having *some* constitutional order, members may be prepared to endorse illiberal constitutions. Fine-grained individuation helps us to restrict the set of potentially justified laws to options that better fit with our sense of the eligible options for public justification.

We focus on the public justification of moral rules because they're the kind of social practice that can be internalized by most moral agents. Moral life is not based on generic moral principles like Rawls's difference principle, but on local rules governing local behavior. Based on an analogy with moral rules, we should stick to legal rules as the right level of evaluation simply because of our limitations in internalizing principles rather than specific rules.

The trust foundation helps to motivate individuation at the level of laws, just as it helped to motivate individuation at the level of moral rules in Part I of the book. Trust is vested in officials and generic systems of rules like constitutions, but persons will evaluate whether the objects of their trust are trustworthy by trying to detect violations of public trust. The main way in which violations will be detected is through the violation of specific legal rules. We can assess an official as untrustworthy and incompetent by looking at a legal and policy issue they mishandled, and we can assess a constitution as illegitimate if we can cite particular laws or acts that are regarded as constitutional but are in fact morally unjustified, like a constitution that permits slavery. So if our concern is to explain how social trust among diverse persons can be rational, we should individuate at the level of moral *and legal* rules, and not more complex and coarse-grained units of legal coercion.

Note that individuating units of coercion at the level of specific laws is not the same as individuating coercion at the level of the normal size and complexity of legislative bills. Legislative bills themselves are often better described as large sets of laws, or changes to laws, and so should be judged in a cumulative fashion based on whether their constituent parts are publicly justified. Constitutional rules must therefore be evaluated not merely by the legislative acts that tend to be ratified under such rules, but in terms of the particular parts of legislative acts. This raises the question of how to individuate laws within legislative acts. We should appeal to a causal individuation criterion, where laws count as individuated when moderately idealized members of the public determine that two different legal rules have little or no causal impact on one another's efficacy.[3]

If we individuate coercion at the level of specific legal rules, then working out the second stage of constitutional choice becomes clear. Parties should judge constitutional rules by the *relative frequencies* with which they generate publicly justified law and allow for the reform or repeal of defeated law. A type-1 error is produced by the passage of a defeated law or the failure to reform or repeal that law—a false positive. A type-2 error is the failure to pass publicly justified law—a false negative. The second stage of constitutional choice is to minimize the *weighted sum* of type-1 and type-2 errors it produces over the course of its normal operation.

We can follow Buchanan and Tullock's K-rule analysis for choosing constitutional rules to include not merely the internal costs of decision-making within a legislative body, but the external costs of *both* enduring publicly defeated law and failing to enjoy a regime comprised of publicly justified law. We can aggregate these three cost curves and select the proportion of persons required to pass a law at the minima of the three curves.

Constitutional rules involve much more than settling on a number of decision-makers, however, so the K-rule analysis is only one piece of the puzzle. A fuller picture of the relevant components will be required in

---

[3] I develop a *functional independence* individuation criterion in the sequel to this book.

order to fully evaluate the public justification of a constitutional rule. But we must begin the articulation of the approach somewhere, so it seems appropriate to focus on constitutional rules that specify the proportion of voters or officials required to pass a law or choose an official.[4]

2. The Contribution of Public Choice to Public Reason

What we might call *public choice contractarianism*, the normative theory of contractual justification advanced by Buchanan and Tullock, has three features that commend themselves to the public reason liberal. Buchanan's contract (i) does not depend on agreement on principles of justice, (ii) provides a much more detailed account of the stages and types of constitutional choice, and (iii) due to its greater realism, offers a much broader source of information for determining which constitutional rules can be publicly justified.[5]

Starting with (i), Buchanan's contract never attempted to use principles of justice to substantially limit constitutional choice. Instead, his contract *begins* with the selection of constitutional rules via a unanimity or consensus standard, where everyone must agree to a set of constitutional rules to make them legitimate. Buchanan's contract is thereby insulated from the threat of pluralism about justice.

Regarding (ii), public choice offers a detailed account of constitutional and legislative choice. Buchanan offers two useful distinctions toward this end. First, while Rawls distinguishes between the constitutional stage and legislative stage of institutionalizing a conception of justice, Buchanan postulates a more complex and subtle relationship between constitutional and "post-constitutional" choice.[6] Buchanan develops an account of constitutional choice through the integration of two cost curves, one that tracks the external cost of a decision-making rule and one that tracks the internal cost of that rule. The external cost is understood as the cost an individual pays due to a single rule imposed by other votes.[7] The internal cost is understood as the cost of decision-making itself.[8] The aggregate cost curve

---

[4] The next three sections draw heavily on Vallier 2018a.
[5] A fourth feature of Buchanan's theory of constitutional choice is that it does not assume full compliance with principles of justice. Buchanan also has developed accounts about how to ensure compliance that I will deploy in the next book.
[6] Buchanan 1975, p. 33.
[7] Buchanan and Tullock 1962, pp. 63–68.
[8] Ibid., pp. 68–69.

gives us a method of selecting voting rules based on an assessment of their net external and internal costs.

Second, Buchanan distinguishes between the *protective* and *productive* functions of the state in constitutional choice.[9] Public reason liberals recognize that the state should protect rights and produce public goods, of course.[10] In fact, Rawls's two principles of justice reflect the distinction, as the first principle protects a set of basic liberties and the second organizes the production and distribution wealth. But Buchanan's distinction emphasizes these two types of rational justification at the constitutional and postconstitutional stages of political choice. By adopting his distinction, we can identify a distinct public justification for each function to help specify the details of the constitutional choice process.

Finally, concerning (iii), Buchanan's contract allows us to select constitutional rules by appealing to information concerning patterns of noncompliance among officials and citizens.[11] Buchanan thereby provides two types of information to the public reason liberal, both information about how to design a constitution to produce generally just and effective laws, and information on the functioning of noncompliant institutional actors.[12]

Importantly, public reason liberals and public choice contractarians disagree about which information is relevant to constitutional choice. Rawlsians object to including information on noncompliance in *ideal* theory, rather than nonideal theory. Critically, Rawls extends his assumption of compliance to his second stage of constitutional choice. He criticizes Buchanan and Tullock for making the process of constitutional choice too realistic and nonmoral in character.[13]

I believe that problems of noncompliance are relevant to Rawlsian *ideal* theory, for even ideal theory assumes only conditional compliance with the principles of justice. Noncompliance also enters Rawlsian ideal theory in Rawls's discussion of the strains of commitment; justice cannot be so demanding that it undermines a person's ability to pursue her conception of the good.[14] Second, in *Political Liberalism*, stability for the right reasons depends on persons with reasonable comprehensive doctrines regarding themselves, arguably contingently, as having reason to comply

---

[9] Buchanan 1975, pp. 68–70.

[10] Rawls 1999a, pp. 52–56 and pp. 235–239 respectively.

[11] One could try to pack this information into the knowledge of social science that Rawls gives the parties to the original position. See ibid., p. 119.

[12] Ibid., pp. 171–176 details the structure of the four-stage sequence.

[13] Rawls 1999b, p. 74 n. 1. Also see Rawls 1999a, p. 61, n. 9 and p. 173 n. 2.

[14] Rawls 1999a, pp. 153–154.

with constitutional essentials and matters of basic justice. Third, because persons are required to comply with a conception of justice only when they believe others will do likewise, they might accidentally develop the mistaken belief that this condition obtains, and so choose not to comply. Finally, justice pluralism only exacerbates these problems, as people may find reason not to comply with their institutions when they fail to embody an adequate conception of justice. Both citizens and officials can be non-compliant, and in different respects.

Once we see that the original position idealization no longer identifies a single political conception of justice as most just, much of the rationale for ideal theory restrictions break down. The point of assuming strict compliance was to show how a conception of justice could be self-stabilizing under favorable conditions. But given disagreement about justice, we cannot expect a society to converge on a single conception even in ideal theory.

Further, while I think it makes sense to choose principles of justice assuming strict compliance, it is far less plausible to choose constitutional essentials with this strong and unrealistic assumption. Perhaps justice should not be tainted by real-world failures on the part of citizens and officials. But a constitution should be structured by accounting for the weaknesses of real-world individuals.

For numerous reasons, then, constitutional choice should relax the assumption of strict compliance.[15]

Even if the reader is unconvinced that Rawlsians should take on the revisions I propose, surely *my* approach to constitutional choice is enriched and improved by appealing to the formal and empirical work in the public choice research program. Public choice helps formulate a systematic method of identifying publicly justified constitutional rules, which are necessary for sustaining social, legal, and political trust among real diverse persons. So the value added of public choice for my project is to address justice pluralism, provide more social scientific information about how constitutions function, and to develop a model of constitutional choice that takes noncompliance among citizens and political officials seriously. We will see that this is especially important in addressing the potential for destabilization in the second half of this chapter.

Public choice contractarianism requires a number of modifications before we can use it.[16] For now, it is enough to point out that public reason

---

[15] This is so insofar as the distinction between strict compliance and partial compliance remains theoretically useful in my case, and I'm not sure that it does.
[16] I discuss these alterations in detail in Vallier 2018a.

liberalism replaces the idea of consent in public choice contractarianism with the intelligible reasons standard and replaces Buchanan's conception of costs with the idea of sufficient reasons.

3. Constitutional Decision Rules in Public Reason

The Buchananite attempt to minimize the internal and external cost of decision-making must be recast as an attempt to identify rules that citizens have *most reason* to endorse given their values and commitments, including the internal and external preference-cost of various decision-making rules (since the costs one faces bear on the reasons one has). I have argued above that the public reason liberal should judge constitutional rules by the relative frequencies with which they generate publicly justified law and allow for the reform or repeal of defeated law. We shall therefore understand the external cost of a decision rule as the weighted sum of type-1 and type-2 errors it produces over the course of its normal operation for a given period.[17] The rules with the lowest external costs are those that produce the lowest weighted sum of type-1 and type-2 errors, and other rules can be ranked in accordance with the sum of errors they produce.

Preference costs still help choose between decision rules, but they only affect the balance of reasons each person has to accept or reject a decision rule. Preference costs are relevant to determining our reasons to act, but public reason liberalism denies that preference costs are the only factor relevant to fixing what we have reason to do.

The balance of type-1 and type-2 errors is not a simple quantity. To come up with a balance, we need some trade-off rate between the two types of error. We must also distinguish between better and worse errors of each type. Some type-1 errors are bound to be much worse than others. If a constitutional rule typically produces laws that place enormous costs on a particularly vulnerable subgroup within a society, then this type-1 error, a false positive, a law treated as justified that is in fact defeated, is much worse than the consistent generation of laws that prove to be mildly annoying to the same subgroup. So total external costs must be understood as a complex function of different sorts of type-1 and type-2 errors. Determining the shape of this *error function* will occupy us further below.

---

[17] The idea of a "weighted sum" contains considerable complexity that I address in the next section.

Assume for the remainder of the section that we can identify a total error function that expresses some adequately weighted sum of type-1 and type-2 errors, and can thereby rank constitutional rules in terms of their external costs. If so, we should be able to use public choice theory to select decision rules as a rational bargain between parties. I suggest that we employ the K-rule analysis that Buchanan and Tullock popularized.[18] Let's briefly review the approach they developed in *The Calculus of Consent*.

For Buchanan and Tullock, the cost of a decision rule is derived from integrating the internal and external costs of decision-making. The internal costs are the rising costs of deliberating and forming coalitions as we increase the proportion of the population that must support the policy, approaching the limit case of unanimity.[19] The external cost is understood in terms of the costs imposed on an individual for legislation passed by other coalitions. These costs fall as we reach a large number of individuals, particularly as we approach unanimity, as the only collective actions that will be taken are ones all regard as better than nothing. As more people are required to pass a bill, external costs fall.[20] The two cost curves are aggregated as shown in figure 6.1.

In this analysis, the D-curve represents internal costs, which increase as the number of individuals required to take collective action increases at a low but increasing rate. The C-curve represents the external costs, which decrease as we move from 0 to 100. The C + D curve, represented in figure 6.1, aggregates the two cost curves into one, and point K is where aggregate costs are minimized. The K-rule prescribes the decision rule at the minimum in the C + D curve. Some economists think K, when applied to voting rules, is a simple majority rule, others supermajoritarian.

In my model, the internal costs resemble the standard public choice model, as there should be a monotonic relation between preferences and reasons with respect to the difficulties organizing coalitions of voters.[21] The external costs are the reliability with which voting rules will output publicly justified legislation and block, revise, or repeal defeated legislation—the degree to which they minimize the balance of type-1 and type-2 errors. The external costs are described by the error function. The external cost curve, though, must be split[22] to represent an individual member of the

---

[18] Buchanan and Tullock 1962, p. 76.

[19] Ibid., pp. 65–67.

[20] Ibid., pp. 60–65 covers an argument that external costs are not negative.

[21] To simplify, I assume the primary considerations involved with internal costs are strategic challenges that people prefer to avoid when they can.

[22] Buchanan and Tullock's cost curves already include the value of getting "justified" legislation passed, but I split up achieving this value into avoiding false positives and avoiding false negatives.

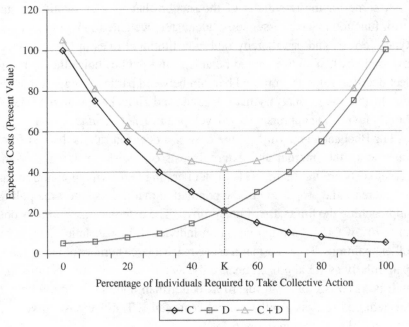

FIGURE 6.1 Buchanan and Tullock's K-Rule Analysis

public's two broad priorities: blocking unjustified legislation—avoiding type-1 errors—and passing justified legislation—avoiding type-2 errors.[23] To simplify, let's assume that each voter's reasons include only those focused on her personal projects and moral principles, not views about others and their projects and principles.

Given these two priorities, I draw two curves, one for publicly justified legislation and the other for defeated legislation. Here I assume a simple error function: an equal weighting of type-1 and type-2 errors, with no quality weights. Further, I leave aside, for purposes of illustration, the effect voting rules have on the ability of voting bodies to alter false positives and false negatives after some law has been passed. At this stage, I am simply illustrating the general model of constitutional choice.

In figure 6.2, the x-axis represents the number of voters required to pass or repeal a law, understood as the percentage of members of the public that have a say in the legislative process (or that at least have a representative

---

[23] Publicly justified legislation is not costless. There is still a cost to being coerced, but with publicly justified legislation, the individual holds that the law has net benefits. So even the rule for passing publicly justified legislation must include the costs of coercion, which will interfere further with the capacity of a decision rule to generate coercive law. I set this complication aside, as it needlessly complicates the model.

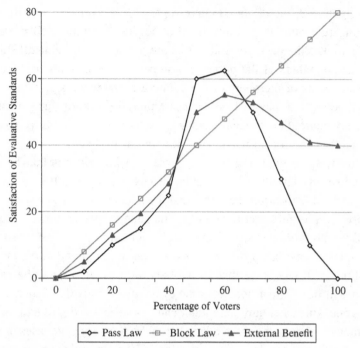

FIGURE 6.2 External Benefit Curves

that has a say). At 1%, only 1% of members of the public are required to pass a law, whereas at 100%, 100% of members of the public are required to pass law. The y-axis represents benefits to the evaluative standards of members of the public, the degree to which members of the public get laws and liberties that advance their values and commitments. Increases along the y-axis represent social states of affairs where members of the public are more able to pursue their ideals. In this way, the curve tracks the strength of the balance of each person's intelligible reasons that favor the legal outputs of the constitutional rule whose public justifiability we are assessing. Thus, we can describe the y-axis as representing the *satisfaction of evaluative standards* based on each person's balance of intelligible reasons. Greater values mean that the relevant arrangement is one that each person has more intelligible reason to endorse, and so one that benefits each person. We can represent these *external benefit* functions as square and diamond curves.[24]

_____

[24] Representing the minimization of type-1 and type-2 errors as maximizing benefits allows for clearer representation than representing the minimization as the minimization of costs.

In figure 6.2, the diamond curve represents the reliability with which a voting rule outputs publicly justified legislation: how well it enables and facilitates the passage of laws that are publicly justified to all suitably idealized members of the public. I assume that the benefits to the evaluative standards of members of the public are low when a small minority of individuals can pass a law because a plurality rule of this sort allows for many contradictory legal changes. As soon as one minority passes a law, another can repeal it. We run into similar problems as we approach unanimity, since requiring that all agree to a law ensures that holdouts can defeat any law they like, making it next to impossible to pass publicly justified legislation. I assume that the benefits increase at some point in between plurality and unanimity. The square curve represents the reliability with which a voting rule blocks publicly unjustified legislation. The square curve has a different shape than the diamond curve because unanimity will guarantee that no publicly unjustified law will be passed, which will be of great benefit to the evaluative standards of members of the public. But when any individual can pass a law, we will end up with enormous amounts of defeated legislation. So the curve increases in value as the number of required voters increases.[25] The triangle curve combines the two functions into the error function, much as Buchanan and Tullock do in their K-rule analysis. Again, take the simplicity of the error function as a mere illustration.

We can now aggregate the external cost curves with the internal cost curve. Here the two curves receive equal weight; other weights will often be appropriate.

The square curve in figure 6.3 represents internal costs, the costs of collectively organizing a clear vote in a decision-making body. These costs are understood in terms of setbacks to the evaluative standards of members that are produced by the organizational costs of voting. The costs are high far below majority rule because, again, voters can pass and repeal legislation with extremely small minorities, so organizing to produce good law is difficult. The same is true at unanimity, when any holdout can spoil the vote. I assume that the curve rises as we approach a plurality rule, as organization will be relatively easy and the possibility of contradictory coalitions is reduced.[26] The curve then falls quickly as we approach unanimity, due to the increasing costs of convincing holdouts.

---

[25] Members of the public get benefits from unjustified legislation, but I will also leave these costs aside to simplify the model.

[26] One famous result of Buchanan and Tullock's work, however, is that contradictory coalitions can form even with majority rule.

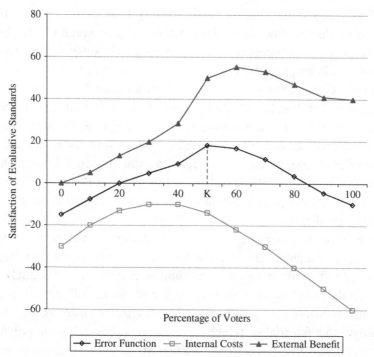

FIGURE 6.3 The Error Function

I then introduce the external benefit function from figure 6.2, again as the triangle curve. Diamonds mark the aggregate curve, which is the error function.[27] The K-rule analysis tells us to select the decision rule that maximizes the benefits to the evaluative standards of members of the public, which in this case lies at 50% of voters required to pass or repeal a law. I do not mean to commit myself to simple majority rules; these numbers serve merely to illustrate my broader point.

To refine the model, recall Buchanan's distinction between the protective and productive functions of the state.[28] The protective function protects rights, whereas the productive functions promote the production of public goods. In my theory, the protective function of the state is to protect primary rights, whereas the productive function promotes the production of goods undersupplied by the moral and legal orders. I carve up the selection of voting rules by indexing them to the protective and productive functions of the state.

---

[27] In figure 6.3, I weighted the internal and external costs equally, but this too is a simplifying assumption, as is the weighting choice in figure 6.2.
[28] Buchanan 1975, p. 68.

Here's why. While citizens can reasonably disagree about conceptions of justice, they will be able to secure agreement on certain basic rights, rights of the fundamental sort that Rawls and other contractarians identify as belonging to each person and protecting their fundamental interests. Constitutional rules that fail to adequately protect primary rights will therefore be ineligible or defeated. In light of this limitation on the selection of constitutional rules, we will want to ensure, above all, that constitutional rules adequately protect primary rights, even if these rules have significant flaws regarding other issues. I distinguish the protective function of the state from the productive, then, to give proper priority to the adequate protection of rights in the process of selecting constitutional rules.

It is, therefore, more important for the state to protect primary rights than to produce public goods. If the state fails to protect rights, it is deeply unjust and illegitimate, and its constitutional rules cannot be publicly justified. If the state fails to produce collective goods, but still protects rights, it is merely derelict and incompetent. To illustrate, compare the protection of a right to a fair trial with highway maintenance. A failure to provide a fair trial makes the state less just and legitimate, but a failure to maintain highways makes the state less competent and responsible. As a result of the greater relative importance of protecting rights, we should assign more weight to selecting a protective rule. And in cases of conflict between the protective and the productive functions, we will want to weight the protective function more heavily.

Let us distinguish, then, between four functions of a publicly justified constitutional order. The constitution must

(1) Enable the passage of legislation protecting and specifying basic rights;
(2) Allow for the review, reform, and repeal of legislation that unjustifiably specifies and fails to protect basic rights;
(3) Develop and pass publicly justified legislation concerning the financing and production of public goods; and,
(4) Review, reform and repeal legislation that unjustifiably finances and produces public goods.

These functions yield two eligible sets of constitutional decisions rules, the first is a ranking of undefeated, undominated constitutional rules that govern the two protective functions of the state, whereas the second is a ranking of undefeated, undominated constitutional rules that govern the productive functions of the state.[29] The eligible set of either type of constitutional rule may have more than one member.

We have to be mindful of a challenge to formulating the weights of type-1 and type-2 errors in individual error functions. This problem is similar to the familiar problem of generating a social welfare function. Given that constitutional choice is sensitive to evaluative pluralism, it must allow different members of the public to endorse different balances of type-1 and type-2 errors in formulating their individual rankings of constitutional rules. Some persons may be most concerned about unjustified coercion, whereas other persons may be more concerned about the failure to pass certain publicly justified laws. This means that different members of the public will have different error functions that specify the costliness of a rule in terms of that person's balance of type-1 and type-2 errors. If we wish to construct a social ranking of constitutional rules, a ranking that applies to society as a whole, however, we may need a *social* error function that is generated by aggregating individual error functions.

The reason to aggregate is that a failure to aggregate will invariably privilege one person's error function over the functions affirmed by other citizens. This means that constitutional rules will be more sensitive to the reasons of some rather than others, which might violate a range of primary rights, including procedural rights to equal influence. While there is something to this worry, it need not delay us, because a commitment to public justification does not require that undefeated constitutional rules be socially ranked *at all*. In other words, once we are faced with a series of constitutional rules that do not violate primary rights, such that having any constitutional rule in the set is better than none, any of these constitutional rules should be capable of adequately conforming the legal and moral orders to what is publicly justified for each person.

Instead, we can settle on ranking the remaining eligible constitutional rules in accord with a much weaker Pareto criterion, where a rule is removed from the eligible set if members of the public all regard the rule as inferior to at least one alternative. This rule will further refine the eligible sets. The goal of members of the public then is to select a constitutional rule from these eligible sets to govern their legal and moral order.

That said, if one wishes to refine the model by aggregating individual error functions into a social error function, this might be done. Members

---

[29] Here I understand an undominated rule as one that at least some members of the public rank as superior to other rules in the eligible set. There is no rule that is Pareto superior to it among members of the public as a whole.

of the public will surely reasonably disagree about the best aggregation rule. But Brian Kogelmann has recently argued that the fact that members of the public cannot agree on a social choice rule does not mean that aggregation is forbidden among members of the public. This is because the dynamics of social choice in a large public imply that different social choice rules will tend to produce similar, perhaps even identical, rankings. If Kogelmann is correct, then all attractive aggregation rules will yield the same ranking of constitutional decision rules, so even if members of the public disagree about social choice rules, their disagreement should not greatly alter the optimal eligible set of constitutional rules.[30]

4. Stability

The last step in selecting constitutional rules involves determining whether otherwise eligible constitutional rules can be *stable for the right reasons*— whether they can be self-stabilizing for moral reasons, rather than by compliance with nonmoral practical reasons alone. We have already discussed this form of stability in developing the idea of a moral rule in chapter 1. Moral rules are internalized social norms backed by the threat of characteristically moral punishment. The stability of moral rules derives in part from the motivation of the person's moral reasons that result from internalization and the fear of appropriate negative reactive attitudes that would be expressed if that person were to violate the moral rule. But in this chapter we are concerned with the stability of constitutional rules in relation to how they preserve publicly justified moral and legal rules. Call this the *moral stability*[31] of constitutional rules.[32]

The moral stability of constitutional rules has two parts. First, constitutional rules must be stable because *officials* comply with them directly. If a constitutional rule specifies that Congress may make no law abridging free speech, then that constitutional rule is stable insofar as legislators do

---

[30] Kogelmann calls this the "convergence solution." See Kogelmann 2017a, p. 6. For his defense of the convergence of social choice rules, see pp. 12–19. If Kogelmann is correct, it rehabilitates the project of constructing a related social error function in Gaus 2008.

[31] From here forward, I will use the terms "moral stability" and "stability" interchangeably.

[32] Watson and Hartley 2018 object that convergence views like mine cannot establish stability for the right reasons in large part because points of convergence are contingent. Diverse reasons can shift and change and so leave the stability of constitutional essentials up to excessive risk. I have two replies. First, shared reasons can change too; if our comprehensive doctrines change, or society shifts from one political conception of justice to another, shared reasons might be similarly unstable. Second, the ability to use diverse reasons in discussion can help to produce stability through costly signaling. On this second point, see Kogelmann and Stich 2016.

not attempt or ultimately fail to pass laws abridging free speech. If officials do not comply with constitutional rules, then since constitutional rules are themselves social norms, the norms will collapse and the constitution, or at least the ignored part of the constitution, will become mere sentences on a sheet of paper.

Second, constitutional rules must be stable because *citizens* comply with the laws produced and permitted by those rules. Constitutional rules are stabilized by citizens who take themselves to have reason to comply with the laws they produce. Since the constitutional rule is a rule governing the imposition, revision, and repeal of laws, the constitutional rule can only count as effectively stable when its outputs are obeyed.

The constitutional rules meet a kind of publicity condition in virtue of being publicly recognized, though my model does not require that the reasons persons endorse constitutional rules themselves be publicly recognized or easily detected by all members of the public. Instead, trust is based on each person's perception that others have sufficient reason of their own to endorse the public constitutional rule. So stability only requires a modest form of publicity. Common knowledge of which constitutional rules are justified can be established on this basis, if common knowledge is required. I doubt stability requires a common knowledge condition because trust requires only that each person know what the public rules are, whether she has adequate moral reason to endorse the public rule, and whether she can tell that others probably have adequate moral reason of their own to endorse the public rule, reasons she may not know.

Since my model evaluates constitutional rules under normal conditions, we must also consider the threat noncompliant agents pose to stability. Noncompliant persons are those who lack an effective motivation to act morally or justly, or even to respond to cooperation with cooperation. To address the threat such persons pose, my conception of stability involves stabilization under conditions of noncompliance, an assumption found in the contractarian theory common among public choice economists like Buchanan. An appropriate model of constitutional choice should treat noncompliance as an endogenous variable: some constitutional rules will encourage more compliance than others.[33] If so, we should model constitutional choice by assuming that some real-world agents (not the contracting parties) are prepared to defect under a variety of conditions. So an important kind of stability obtains when compliant agents can successfully repel

---

[33] Schmidtz 2011, p. 778.

noncompliant agents, preventing noncompliant agents from getting a foothold in controlling constitutional rules for their own ends.

Some have criticized public reason accounts of stability, especially Rawls's, as redundant.[34] A constitutional regime will be stable for the right reasons just because it is publicly justified, since citizens will comply with the regime in virtue of being reasonable. So once we've identified a publicly justified regime, then it will be stable for the right reasons—morally stable—by definition. If that's right, the third stage of my model of constitutional choice might be redundant as well.

Consider two replies to this complaint. First, note that stability is determined in part based on whether citizens believe that other citizens will cooperate. Even with proper moral motivation, if citizens are convinced that others are not properly motivated, they will lack sufficient practical reason to comply with legal and constitutional rules. Public justification does not require persons to make themselves vulnerable to negative political outcomes that result when they cooperate and others defect. Cooperators are not morally required to cooperate with defectors. So stability is not redundant because even eligible constitutional rules might fail the stability test if a society lacks social mechanisms that provide assurance to cooperatively disposed persons. We will see below that providing assurance is complicated by social dynamics that can undermine stability in unexpected circumstances and in unanticipated ways. So the achievement of stability is even less redundant on my view than on the orthodox Rawlsian position.

A second reason that stability is not redundant is that we want a society of reciprocal cooperators to be resistant to various kinds of internal and external shocks. A collapse in assurance due to "cheap talk" can be understood as an internal shock or dynamic which the agents can generate themselves without the entry of new agent strategies or changes in the social parameters governing that society.[35] An external shock is a significant change in social conditions due to changes outside reciprocal cooperators, such as a collapse in their environment's carrying capacity, perhaps due to famine or war, or invasion by uncooperative agents who pursue their own gain at the expense of others whenever they can get away with it. So we cannot assume that stability is guaranteed by public justification because internal and external system shocks can undermine stability even if its constitutional rules are publicly justified.

---

[34] Habermas 1995; Barry 1995, pp. 901–902; Quong 2011, pp. 166–170.
[35] Farrell and Rabin 1996.

5. Constitutional Stability Defined and Disaggregated

Based on the foregoing discussion, define a constitutional rule as morally stable if and only if

(i) Officials acquire and fulfill their roles as specified by the constitution.
(ii) Regular operation of the rule produces publicly justified laws.
(iii) Citizens generally comply with the laws produced by the rule.[36]
(iv) Violations of the rule and the laws it produces are discouraged by moral and/or legal pressure.

Constitutional rules do not typically issue direct commands to citizens *qua citizens*; rather, the rules specify the roles of officials, including requirements, prohibitions, and permissions, along with their associated normative powers and rights of enforcement. The Third Amendment to the US Constitution forbids Congress from forcibly quartering troops in the homes of citizens. So the rule does not directly apply coercion to everyone. It forbids legislative and executive powers from passing laws that permit or require troop quartering. A constitutional provision for collecting government revenue is similar. It does not directly impose upon citizens, but it gives Congress the power to do so.

Let us now expand upon the four conditions of stability. First, and most importantly, officials must acquire and fulfill their roles regarding a constitutional rule in accordance with it or with other constitutional rules. Officials have to acquire and fulfill their rule-specified role. Second, the constitutional rule should typically produce publicly justified legal rules. If it tends to produce defeated rules, people will lack sufficient reason to comply with those rules and so many will defect. And by disobeying the laws generated by the constitutional rule, the rule is destabilized since it consists in a procedure that attempts to successfully impose laws on citizens (or prohibit laws from being imposed). Third, while morally stable constitutional rules can withstand some defection, they cannot survive if violations are considerable and regular. So a constitutional rule can only be stable if citizens comply with its legal outputs.

Fourth, moral and legal pressure must be used to enforce the constitutional rule in many cases. Sometimes a constitutional rule is so obviously

---

[36] At least the publicly justified rules. Stability might involve *disobeying unjustified* laws.

good and moral that few officials or citizens will violate it. But citizens and officials will be tempted to disobey constitutional rules that impose costs upon them. And if too many people are allowed to disobey a constitutional rule and the laws it produces, the rule will destabilize. So we need punishment to enforce many constitutional rules. Punishment need not be legal in nature; it might be merely moral. But there must be some pressure applied to violators for the constitutional rule to be fully stable.[37]

Destabilization can occur due to two types of factors—*internal* dynamics and *external* shocks. The primary internal dynamic that can lead to instability is a collapse in assurance between agents.[38] This can easily happen in large N-person systems, given how frequently we misinterpret speech or behavior, and so acquire doubts about how committed other agents are to cooperating with some rule (a constitutional rule, or more likely, a law produced by the rule). Assurance failures could result in violations of any of the four stability conditions. If officials become suspicious of the motives of other officials, they might violate constitutional rules; a prime illustration is the contemporary use of the filibuster in the US Senate, which makes it more difficult to pass laws that even a significant majority of legislators (not to mention citizens) would like and probably regard as justified. Failures of assurance could affect the error rate of the constitutional rule, given that it could be commandeered by less cooperative agents. And in many cases, failures of assurance will lead to defection even from publicly justified laws. In that case, moral and legal pressure might be insufficient to keep the constitutional rule stable, given that mass violations are hard to police and deter.

If we want to understand how stability is maintained despite the threat of internal destabilization, we need to identify assurance mechanisms. This is not easy. John Thrasher and I have argued that the use of public reasons to assure others that one is committed to shared political institutions is subject to instabilities even among reasonable agents.[39] In our view, the main method by which assurance is provided is public compliance with moral, legal, and constitutional rules. Stability derives less from what we say than from what most people are publicly observed to do. Stability is also driven

---

[37] As noted in chapter 4, ideally these legal penalties will be backed by internalized social norms (publicly justified moral rules), such that the penalties will be effective.

[38] Another internal dynamic could arise from an overly demanding system of norms that would lead persons to defect due to the strains of commitment.

[39] Thrasher and Vallier 2015. Kogelmann offers a distinct argument for the same conclusion. See Kogelmann 2018.

by the same factors that keep a social norm in place—both empirical and normative expectations on behalf of most members of society.

Second, a constitutional rule can be destabilized if it can be easily disrupted by *external* shocks. External shocks include, among other things, invasion by uncooperative and purely self-interested agents. The kind of external shock to a constitutional rule most relevant for our public choice-inspired approach to constitutional choice is the accumulation of rent-seeking agents, agents that manipulate constitutional rules to benefit themselves at the expense of others.[40] We can focus on constitutional rules governing taxation and the distribution of revenue as the most obvious sites for rent-seeking.[41] In those cases, legislators frequently abuse their roles by misappropriating funds, violating stability condition (i). Rules can also be used to produce publicly unjustified legislation, violating condition (ii). There may even be considerable defection by legislators, special interest groups, lobbyists, and the like. Sufficient corruption can also increase citizen defection since people observe others escaping punishment or detection despite their rent-seeking activities, which violates condition (iii). Since these people escape punishment, adequate moral or legal pressure is not applied to them, violating condition (iv).

Here I only provide an account of the stability of constitutional rules. My account of the stability of legal rules is that they are analogous to social norms, whose stability is maintained by empirical and normative expectations that are sometimes reinforced by punishing violators. But Thrasher and I have argued that in a free, liberal, *open society* we may not want laws to be too stable, since we want to allow them to change in order to improve our legal order.[42] So we argue in favor of moral stability of constitutional rules, but develop an ideal of *robustness* for laws, where legal conditions tend to stabilize, but when challenged can establish a new set of rules in an equilibrium condition. So the legal order, when challenged, does not return to its previous state, but will return to *some* equilibrium as a result. This is an important feature of constitutional stability since constitutional rules are supposed to establish new legal frameworks, and so we want legal frameworks to be stable, but not so stable that they cannot be easily altered, and so we should want our legal rules to be *robust* for the right reasons, rather than stable for the right reasons. Robustness can be seen at

---

[40] For several articles on the nature of rent-seeking, see Tullock 2005. For a classic discussion of agglomeration of rent-seeking groups, see Olson 1984.

[41] Mueller 2003, pp. 333–335.

[42] Thrasher and Vallier 2018a.

work in conditions (ii) and (iv) of constitutional stability. The public justifiability of laws can change as those governed by it change, and so we will want constitutional rules to shift the sorts of laws they produce in response to changes in citizens and their justificatory reasons. Accordingly, moral and legal pressure used to enforce constitutional rules should aim to keep the same rules in equilibrium, but the moral and legal pressure used to enforce legal rules should allow for more variability despite seeking to generate some new legal equilibrium in the future.

6. Durability, Immunity, and Balance

Durability is the ability to resist internal dynamics, whereas *immunity* is the ability to resist external shocks. These are *first-order* forms of stability, as they are concerned with the capacity of a system to maintain a high level of cooperation and social trust in the face of threats. But there is a third factor that determines whether a constitutional rule is stable, which is the level of *variance* in the system in response to internal dynamics and external shocks. I understand the variance of an internal dynamic in terms of the level of variation in a system's level of social trust within which legal rules will be followed, whereas variance in an external shock relates to how predictably and regularly a system copes with an external cause of mass defection. We can understand this form of stability, which I call *balance*, as *second-order stability*, or the stability of measures of stability.

These three types of stability—durability, immunity, and balance—are new to the literature, but I believe they will prove helpful in developing an attractive account of moral stability. For example, my conception of durability ties stability to the idea of social trust, which I used to ground public justification in chapters 1 and 2. Durability will be understood as the capacity of a polity, and constitutional rules, to preserve a high degree of social trust among persons through the imposition of law. Immunity refers to the ability of a system to survive invasion by merely self-interested agents like rent-seekers, and so to maintain social trust among cooperative agents. Balance just refers to a society's variance in its social trust level.

In general, given the importance of assurance and the idea of social trust discussed below, I understand cooperative behavior as *trustworthy* behavior, where persons comply with expectations set by social rules within that society. This means that they will forgo pursuing gains from defection not merely because they might be caught, but because they are independently morally motivated to cooperate. Most officials refuse to take bribes not merely because they trust that others will not corrupt the system but because they are independently motivated not to take bribes.

As noted in chapter 2, we can understand defection as a kind of *opportunism*, which is "acting to promote one's welfare by taking advantage of a trust extended by an individual, group, or society as a whole."[43] Trust is based on the expectation that everyone complies with the publicly justified constitutional rules present in that society. Opportunistic behavior is usually untrustworthy behavior. When moral and legal rules are publicly justified, persons lack sufficient moral reason to engage in opportunistic behavior, since the moral rules they break are ones that they've internalized, such that violations of the rule generate guilt. Guilt alone cannot prevent all cases of opportunism, but it can discourage violations to a significant enough degree to sustain compliance with moral rules in private, and so to sustain social trust generally.

In other work, I have created a computational model that measures and relates all three forms of stability.[44] My main finding is that durability, balance, and immunity are functionally distinct even though they interact. The model's key input values result in distinctive dynamics having to do with the average level of social trust (durability), the variance in social trust (balance), and the capacity of cooperative agents to survive invasion by noncooperative agents (immunity). I find no strong interaction between durability and balance, but I hypothesize that in a more complex model, a relatively unbalanced order will prove less durable than a balanced order. One of my central results is that low levels of immunity quickly undermine a system's durability, such that high immunity becomes a critical necessary precondition to maintain high level of social trust, that is, to have a durable order with low opportunism.[45] What these results suggest is that an order that is stable for the right reasons must be durable, balanced, and immune for the right reasons.

The model has another important implication. Even setting immunity aside, distinguishing durability and balance reveals that we may not be

[43] Rose 2014, p. 21.

[44] Vallier 2017a. I draw on the agent-based modeling approach in Muldoon, Borgida, and Cuffaro 2012. For an explanation of my model and some of my data files, see http://www.kevinvallier.com/stability.

[45] Chung 2017 has shown analytically that even a very small number of rational agents can undermine stability among reasonable agents, so long as agents cannot identify whether one another are playing rational or reasonable strategies. My first response is that Chung's model does not apply to officials because identifying who is playing a cooperative strategy isn't too hard most of the time. I also think that cooperation among citizens can be achieved through legal penalties for defection (in contrast to officials, who can often avoid legal penalties).

able to establish stability via a single social mechanism. Consequently, the arguments made on behalf of various assurance mechanisms in a well-ordered society are threatened. For example, some political liberals have argued that complying with the requirements of public reason can help citizens of a well-ordered society assure one another that they are committed to one conception, or a small set of political conceptions, of justice.[46] The point of assurance is to generate a political order that is stable for the right reasons. But if the ideal of political stability is deeply ambiguous, it is no longer clear what such an assurance mechanism accomplishes.

7. Constitutional Durability and Immunity

A constitutional rule should be durable, balanced, and immune for the right reasons. However, given our definition of constitutional stability, we can go further and index the different forms of stability to the four different conditions for constitutional stability. I will not integrate balance into my account of constitutional stability, however, because including it overly complicates the analysis. That's because balance is partly a function of other forms of stability. Fortunately, my main line of argument in the book does not require appealing to balance, though it would be enriched by such an appeal.

The first condition, which requires that officials comply with their constitutionally specified roles, is most naturally the subject of *immunity*. We want to prevent those disposed to defect from constitutional rules from benefitting themselves or their constituents at the expense of the public as a whole. There will be trust and assurance problems among officials, where they cannot tell, for instance, whether other officials are sincere, but typically legislative bodies are small enough that the assurance problems that arise in mass society, such as trusting strangers, is less important.

The second condition requires that the constitutional rule normally produce publicly justified laws and undermine defeated laws. If a constitutional rule has high immunity, it will be more effective in these ways. This is because noncompliant officials will tend to pass laws that cannot be publicly justified more often than officials who comply with their constitutional duties. A common example is when legislators abuse budgetary rules by passing rent-seeking legislation, since those hurt by rent-seeking will typically have defeaters for the legislation. In this context, we are

---

[46] Weithman 2010.

not as concerned with durability because we are more worried about persistently corrupt or rent-seeking officials destabilizing the rule, as well as ideologues that seek to impose defeated legislation on citizens.

Given that most citizens comply with most laws, and that most people are conditional cooperators in most social contexts, immunity becomes less important with respect to the stability of rules among the citizenry. So the third condition, which requires that citizens regularly comply with publicly justified laws, should be more focused on the provision of citizen assurance than preventing defection by generally noncompliant or exploitative citizens. Most citizens will only defect from laws when they find that others aren't obeying them; in cases of widespread defection, the conditions for motivating trustworthiness and so for justified social trust break down. This means that durability is the relevant notion of stability in this case. Citizens exhibit durability when they tend to comply with the laws imposed by a constitutional rule. Without durability, citizens will defect from the laws, and as defection accumulates, the constitutional rule, while still on the books, may destabilize and dissolve.

The fourth condition involves the enforcement of both constitutional rules and the laws they produce. Violations must be punished by formal and informal pressure. When officials violate publicly justified constitutional rules, they should be subject to punishment, and when citizens violate the law, they should be subject to the same. Punishment should usually be both legal and moral, though in many cases, we might restrict punishment to legal mechanisms due to concerns about moral punishment being too informal, erratic, and unfair. Immunity applies to the punishment of officials since a system that lacks immunity will experience a breakdown in appropriate punishment. The presence of defectors and the system's limited ability to force them to comply undermine immunity. Punishment is also required to sustain high levels of durability. My model does not include punishment, but punishment, rightly applied, should generate higher levels of durability and immunity.[47]

Given that different notions of stability are relevant to different components of a morally peaceful polity, I suggest that we generalize in the following way. *A constitutional rule is stable if and only if it is adequately*

---

[47] Punishment, we know, is a powerful mechanism for enforcing compliance; the problem is that it can stabilize almost any norm, justified or not. Boyd and Richerson 2005 discuss the power of punishment; Gaus 2011 draws on their work in employing punishment as a stabilizing mechanism. Abbink et al. 2017 find that punishment can often reinforce bad social norms, and this raises a need to develop an agent-based model of stability that contains both appropriate and inappropriate punishment. Also see Barrett and Gaus 2018.

(i) immune against abuse by political officials and (ii) durable among citizens subject to the rule in virtue producing similarly durable laws.

I have said little about the mechanisms that generate immunity and durability because it takes enough work just to show that we should distinguish between different concepts of stability. Outlining the role of different concepts of stability in the third part of my model of constitutional choice is significant enough that details about assurance and compliance mechanisms can wait until future work. I have also said little about the connection between constitutional rules and the empirical evidence on the connection between real-world social trust and political trust and trust in officials. I will address these issues further in the sequel to this book.

We have a model of political public reason that proceeds in three stages: the selection of primary rights, economization on legislative error, and determining whether constitutional rules exhibit the requisite degrees of immunity and durability. We can now step back and look at the big picture of public justification. A morally peaceful polity, by establishing a publicly justified legal system, helps to complete the order of publicly justified moral rules, and so helps to realize moral peace between persons by sustaining a system of trust. And a publicly justified legal system is established by means of a constitution that is publicly justified according to my three-stage model. *Politics is not war when it proceeds in accord with such a constitution.*

CHAPTER 7 | Liberalism Justified

WE CAN NOW USE my three-layer model of public justification to vindicate liberal institutions.

A liberal order protects a range of extensive, equal liberties, from freedom of speech, press, and religion, to voting rights and a right to a fair trial. Here I argue that only liberal constitutional rights can be publicly justified; nonliberal schemes of rights should be defeated. If I am correct, only liberal constitutional rights can sustain a system of social trust and treat persons with adequate respect. Only liberalism can keep moral peace.

Recall the restrictions on the scheme of primary rights from chapter 5. These are rights all people with a rational conception of the good and justice would want for themselves and would be prepared to extend to others on the same terms. Such rights are chosen from a baseline of the legal state of nature and appeal to a Pareto criterion to rule out dominated rights schemes. Primary rights are equal, authoritative, and broadly compossible. They include both negative rights to liberties and choices, as well as positive rights to the secure possession of a bundle of resources, specifically income, wealth, and capital. The chosen rights schema will expand those resources over the long term in accord with the principle of sustainable improvements.

Primary rights merit legal and constitutional recognition and protection when such safeguards are necessary to both protect and stabilize certain liberty-rights and claim-rights in the legal state of nature and in legal systems. Thus, while there are many moral liberties and claims in the legal state of nature, not all rise to the level of primary rights because social morality can largely handle the enforcement of some moral rights, such as our claim-right that our friends not lie to us. So we focus on the subset of moral rights that members of the public believe require legal protection.

To discover an eligible scheme of primary rights, I appeal to a thin veil of ignorance where people propose schemes of primary rights in light of their various ideals and doctrines, but which others can defeat by appealing to their own ideals and doctrines. The parties are merely deprived of their knowledge of their relative social standing and the power and influence of their points of view. The thin veil of ignorance tracks eligible rights schemes because people behind such a thin veil will recognize that they may not be in a privileged position in their society. Because the vast majority of adherents to comprehensive doctrines and moral ideals will prefer to be protected in living out their doctrines and ideals rather than betting on being the political hegemon, they will choose extensive, equal rights. Since these groups will want to be able to authoritatively demand that others not violate these rights in order to prohibit violations and sustain social trust, they will choose rights schemas that are authoritative for everyone, and that others can hold against them. Primary rights will include rights to resources because persons will want them regardless of their social group and regardless of the relative position of their social group.

This line of reasoning is within the capacity of moderately idealized agents. While they reason in diverse ways and sometimes make mistakes, the need to recognize and establish various rights practices should be fairly obvious to them. Most people can see the importance of establishing and protecting an extensive scheme of equal rights. And most can recognize that it is better to be a member of a rights-protected minority group than an unprotected group. So while different groups will propose different schemes, they should be required by their own reasoning to endorse a scheme of primary rights even if they regard those rights as suboptimal from their own moral point of view. Furthermore, moderately idealized agents will be able to recognize the need to protect primary rights with legal and constitutional rules if they are prepared to sacrifice hegemony in order to secure primary rights for themselves. While they will surely disagree about which legal and constitutional rules are best, they should be able to jointly populate an eligible set of such rules.

For similar reasons, we can see why moderately idealized agents, despite disagreeing about so much, will be able to agree on at least some specific kinds of primary rights. All moderately idealized members of the public can value social goods other than establishing a scheme of rights that is optimal from their own point of view. They will see the great value that arises from an ongoing system of social trust and the moral peace that results. Since the benefits of cooperation are so great, moderately idealized members of the public will prefer a suboptimal, but authoritative and trust-reinforcing, rights scheme to a legal state of nature with no protected primary rights. Constitutional and legal rules should be eligible on similar grounds, since if primary rights can be publicly justified despite being suboptimal for some, then rights-protecting legal and constitutional rules should be eligible. So my approach to public reason should not be vulnerable to the anarchy objection. This is clear enough once we focus on the opportunity costs of forgoing an authoritative rights scheme.

I must also speak to the question of the order of justification, or the order in which we justify rights. An order of justification specifies the order in which issues are "settled" and this "settlement provides a background for further justification."[1] The fact that some rights claims are settled does not mean we can never revisit them. Rather, we can take them to be fixed for the purpose of assessing other rights claims. Contractarian theories frequently have an account of the order in which rights are justified, whether they make this explicit or not. On my contract view, the order of justification is determined by which rights (i) secure the most essential protections for pursuing one's conception of the good or justice, along with the necessary resources for making use of those protections, (ii) secure the largest amount of protections[2] and resources, and (iii) are the subject of the greatest agreement by the largest number of members of the public and are most highly ranked by them. So we justify rights in order, starting from those that best realize (i)–(iii), and ending with those that have the smallest role in realizing (i)–(iii). Based on this framework, the order of justification begins with rights of agency, proceeds to associational and jurisdictional rights, then adopts procedural rights, and ends with international rights.

To see what such an approach would look like, let us now identify several classes of primary constitutional rights that can be publicly justified. I discuss rights of agency in section 1, associational rights in section 2, jurisdictional rights in section 3, procedural rights in section 4, and

---

[1] Gaus 2011, p. 275.

[2] Readers familiar with Rawls may greet the proposal that we maximize protections with skepticism based on Hart's famous criticism of Rawls's first principle of justice as found in the original version of *A Theory of Justice*, which required that persons have the most extensive possible scheme of liberties compatible with a similar liberty for others. Hart 1973, esp. pp. 543–547. However, my parties know much more than Rawls's and so have greater bases for making the sorts of trade-offs between liberties and protections that Hart thinks Rawlsian parties cannot make. Second, I allow multiple feasible sets of rights with different trade-offs between the protections they secure. To vindicate the argument of this book, we need to find only *one* eligible scheme of primary rights and show that this scheme is recognizably liberal. My view is not threatened by the possibility of multiple eligible schemes, as long as they are recognizably liberal.

international rights in section 5. I focus in particular on the jurisdictional right of private property since readers will find it controversial. Section 6 explains how primary rights form a conception of social justice. Section 7 explains how a constitution should recognize and protect these rights.

1. Rights of Agency

Fundamental rights of agency protect the formation of coherent agent psychologies and the minimal capacity of persons to extend their projects and plans into the external world. Since a person must exercise her agency in order to pursue any conception of the good or justice, everyone will want some substantive, weighty rights of agency.[3] And given how important agency is even to nonliberals, they will sacrifice their authority to control others so as to secure authoritative protection for themselves. So rights of agency secure the most essential protections and resources and to a great degree; moreover, such rights will be subject to unanimous agreement by all moderately idealized members of the public and given strong, if not lexical, priority over other rights.

Rights of agency come in two varieties—negative and positive. The most fundamental right of agency is freedom of thought, a negative right. No one may interfere with how a person thinks or reasons, since any other rational activity depends on this capacity. Parties will also adopt a negative right against coercive interference with one's pursuit of justice and the good because authoritative prohibitions on coercion and interference protect agency from control or harm by private parties or the state.

Negative rights of agency also include a right against harm. Harm is a terribly complicated moral concept, and there is little space to say much about it here; to simplify, then, we can follow Joel Feinberg's classic understanding of harm as a substantive setback to a person's welfare interests and ulterior interests.[4] Feinberg distinguishes between welfare interests, like the protection of one's health and bodily integrity, one's emotional stability, financial security, and so on, and ulterior interests, like a person's ability to pursue her fundamental goals and aspirations.[5] Harm can be understood as a setback to either sort of interest. Given that my account of public reason involves justification to each person on her own terms, we

---

[3] Gaus 2011, pp. 337–357 discusses rights of agency, as I understand them here.
[4] Feinberg 1987 contains the classic discussion. For a discussion of welfare interests, see p. 112.
For discussion and analysis of Feinberg's view, among others, see Gaus 1999, pp. 136–159.
[5] Feinberg 1987, p. 37.

should also understand harm intersubjectively, as a substantive setback to what a *moderately idealized member of the public regards* as her welfare interests and ulterior interests. Persons have a primary right against what members of the public regard as a setback to their interests.[6]

For similar reasons, a right against legal coercion is a right of agency, given that legal coercion usually imposes at least a prima facie restriction on the agency of persons and typically imposes a risk of significant harm to one's interests, including one's bodily integrity. So if members of the public will adopt an authoritative moral right against harm, they will also adopt an authoritative moral right against coercion. This does not mean that coercion can never be justified, however, just that legal coercion is assumed to be illegitimate unless the legal coercion can be publicly justified to the person coerced. This right against legal coercion is also grounded in my arguments in previous chapters in favor of a presumption against coercion and the need to publicly justify law.

The choice of equal, authoritative rights of agency implies that persons have a long list of primary rights, including the right to life and bodily integrity, freedom of thought, freedom of speech, and the formation of intimate relations with others through marriage or other contractual arrangements. Persons will have a primary right to own personal property, including clothes, keepsakes, and a home. They also possess the primary right to freedom of occupation, such that the state may not forcibly determine what their job will be. Restricting freedom of occupation threatens more fundamental primary rights.

These primary rights, taken together, imply further primary rights that public reason liberals seldom recognize. The combination of the right of freedom of occupation and the right to own personal property implies a right to self-employment. Freedom of occupation is insufficiently robust if persons only have the right to work for someone else and not for themselves. Further, the right to own personal property extends to one's home, and so arguably the right to use one's home for some commercial purposes. But if persons have a right to self-employment and the right to use their homes for commercial purposes, we have the foundations for a right to own *private capital*, since capital goods just are goods that produce consumption or investment goods. If persons have a right to own and operate their home business, and they have a right to self-employment, then they at least have the right to use their home as capital. And if this

---

[6] Members of the public might recognize the harm or at least recognize that the person putatively harmed is harmed in her own eyes.

is so, then there is a strong case that persons have the right to acquire private capital outside of the home. The right to private capital is further strengthened by the fact that primary rights must help to secure, among other things, capital goods.

The fundamental negative rights of agency do not require capitalism understood as complete private property in the means of production and voluntary exchange. Government should restrict the property rights claims characteristic of libertarianism. But the rights of agency do imply that socialism, understood as the planned economy and the public ownership of the means of production, violates the fundamental rights of agency. Since most versions of classical socialism are defined by an abrogation of rights to own and operate private capital, these classical versions of socialism cannot be publicly justified. I will expand on the ineligibility of socialism below.

Positive rights of agency are rights to meaningful access to resources required for an agent to freely develop and exercise her agency. These resources include income, wealth, and capital because those resources can be used to purchase food, healthcare, housing, clothing, and education. As noted in chapter 5, these welfare rights are not necessarily rights to state provision of these goods. Instead, they are rights to have social institutions organized such that these goods are available and adequate in supply. This means that if free market orders are as productive as their proponents believe, these orders can respect welfare rights by producing cheap, abundant products and supplying voluntary charity, perhaps with a basic social minimum guaranteed by the state.

Given the negative rights of agency, there are strong reasons to favor noncoercive, voluntary means of respecting welfare rights. It is best to kill two birds with one stone—the protection of both negative and positive rights of agency. Therefore, in seeking to secure positive rights, we should first remove any coercive restrictions preventing people from securing resources and exercising their agency. To illustrate, suppose we have a choice between lowering the cost of healthcare through a single-payer system, which creates a health insurance monopsony and associated queuing, or allowing health insurance competition via health insurance exchanges subsidized by government. We have strong reason to favor the latter system of provision because it is less coercive. Companies can enter the market for health insurance provision, and consumers have more choices. In this way, the market-friendly policy respects a positive right to healthcare, along with a negative right to choose one's own health insurance or to go into the healthcare insurance business.

Primary rights to assistance, while publicly justified, can be qualified by the presence of citizens who believe that such rights are sensitive to facts about what persons deserve. Many people believe, and may believe even if moderately idealized, that the able-bodied poor are, by and large, responsible for their poverty. If so, then poor persons do not automatically merit coercively financed assistance from those who have concerns about their deservingness. To take an extreme case, if middle-class John gives all his money to his church to live a life of poverty, many will believe that he does not have a right to assistance since he freely donated his income and wealth. The same would be true of people who freely engage in various forms of gambling or drug use, as opposed to gamblers or drug addicts whose agency is compromised. This means that there are at least some poor people who are undeserving, and reasonable conservative members of the public will have sufficient reason to reject redistribution that goes to those they reasonably regard as undeserving. However, in practice, it is not clear how restrictive this defeater reason will be given that determining who is deserving and undeserving is frequently difficult, and often impossible.

Again, basically everyone will agree to the vast majority of rights of agency, even those who would violate these rights to secure political hegemony, since these groups will usually not be prepared to risk being a morally and legally unprotected minority. This means that agency rights should be publicly justified to nonliberal members of the public, as long as they are sufficiently committed to establishing and maintaining a system of social trust that treats all as free and equal. While we need not insist that reasonable nonliberals sacrifice greatly to sustain a system of social trust, they must be prepared to give some ground in assigning authority to rights schemes that are suboptimal from their own point of view. They will not prefer a legal state of nature where their liberties and claims to live out nonliberal projects and plans are not recognized or constitutionally protected. And even if nonliberals would prefer to use unjustified force to establish political hegemony when they have the power to do so, the thin veil of ignorance deprives them of their knowledge of their degree of political power relative to other groups. Nonliberals should be prepared to embrace liberal rights regimes for this reason.

My reply may not work for libertarians who oppose positive welfare rights, since many libertarians gladly cede welfare rights for themselves. One might think, therefore, that libertarians have defeaters for welfare rights. However, libertarians lack defeaters for welfare rights based on the right to private property in external objects because the extensiveness of the right to private property will be determined in part by the reasons of social democratic members of the public. Libertarians will insist that government use coercion to protect property rights, but since this coercion must be publicly justified, and it presumably cannot be publicly justified to social democratic members of the public, the coercion required to prohibit the enforcement of welfare rights is defeated. Welfare rights get their grip in libertarians, then, because they cannot insist on state coercion to protect their property from at least relatively mild forms of redistribution. And their commitment to social trust and cooperation should lead libertarians to ascribe moral and political authority to a property regime with at least some welfare rights established through the redistribution of external goods and services.[7]

2. Associational Rights

We now branch out from rights of individual persons to the rights of associations, such as families, churches, service organizations, and unions. Associational rights typically involve interactions between persons, rather than protecting the body and mind of each individual person. This is why they come a bit later in the order of justification, since members need freedom of thought and a right of bodily integrity more. That said, associational life deeply shapes each person's life, including her conception of the good and justice, so associational rights will be fundamental primary rights, found early in the order of justification.

Given how many conceptions of the good and justice require membership in social organizations, the chosen rights of freedom of association are bound to be strong. Most people, and perhaps all moderately idealized persons, will so value their right to form associations like families and churches that they will happily extend the same right to others.[8] Even the most authoritarian religious and ideological organizations prefer a state of affairs where they and others are free to form their own organization to a state of affairs where neither has that right. And since the equality constraint on primary rights rules out special privileges for dominant groups,

---

[7] Though not goods and services that can *only* be financed by bodily interference. But there will still be a right to social services like healthcare that do require coercing the physical provision of healthcare services, and libertarians can regard such a limited right to healthcare as suboptimal, but still authoritative.

[8] Kogelmann 2017b argues that jurisdictional arrangements are one way to address justice pluralism from within a Rawlsian perspective.

members of the public must choose between equal protections or universal nonprotection. Given this choice, they will again opt for equal protection.

Associations, like individuals, are normatively prior to the legislative order, which provides a further basis for a right of association. Associations are not creatures of the legislative state, but rather can function in its absence. Families, churches, service organizations, and unions would exist in the absence of modern states given that they serve critical needs. Further, we know that such organizations in fact existed prior to modern nation-states, for example in the medieval period in Europe, where few political organizations had the powers of the modern state but associations proliferated. This means that, while social rules comprise these institutions, the priority of moral rules and nonstate legal rules strongly protects the autonomy of these associations against state power.

Given the priority of social morality and the centrality of prepolitical organizations like the family, religious institutions, labor unions, and universities, a public legal system cannot be publicly justified in violating the freedom of persons to form associations, to choose their own rules of operation, or to discipline or remove people from those associations. Many for-profit institutions are on a par with nonprofit institutions, such that some commercial enterprises will enjoy extensive protections against coercive interference. I pursue this argument in detail in the sequel to this book.

3. Jurisdictional Rights

Once agency and associational rights are secure, members of the public will select rights of jurisdiction. Jurisdictions are spheres of social control where an individual or group has the sole authority to authoritatively determine what occurs within that social space.[9]

Jurisdictional rights must be distinguished from agency rights because they involve protections that are not strictly speaking required for a person to exercise her agency. They might include the right to private property in a commercial enterprise, but if the state restricted this right, few people would regard their basic agency as frustrated or violated. Rights of agency are critical to the safety of mind and body, to a person's fundamental coherence as a doer and planner, jurisdictional rights less so. Jurisdictional rights also have a unique grounding in the fact that evaluative pluralism

---

[9] Mack 2000; Gaus 2011, pp. 370–374.

prevents persons from making publicly justified collective decisions on a variety of matters. Following Gaus, we can say that jurisdictional rights function as devices for resolving collective conflicts among diverse members of the public. One problem for liberal socialism—the combination of liberal democracy and a planned economy—is that people will not be able to agree on a central plan. A market order avoids this disagreement by allowing different people to develop and live out their own economic plans. Jurisdictional rights operate similarly: they protect social space for persons to make decisions for themselves that cannot be settled collectively.

To illustrate, consider the ownership of land. Owning land is no mere liberty-right. The landowner also has a de facto claim-right against private parties or government from trespassing on her land without a strong justification. Strictly speaking, ownership is not required for a person to exercise her agency over land. But given that diverse persons will have trouble agreeing on how to use common property, private property in land can address evaluative pluralism about land use by giving each individual a parcel she can use to make her own choices.

Gaus has argued that two of the most fundamental jurisdictional rights are the right to privacy and the right to private property.[10] The case for the right to privacy is relatively straightforward. Moderately idealized agents will endorse a moral immunity against certain forms of monitoring, searches, and seizures. Not only must private parties refrain from engaging in some forms of monitoring, searching, and seizing, but governments lack the normative authority to authorize government officials to engage in the same activities.[11] The right to privacy is grounded not only in the protection of agency but in the fact that members of the public cannot collectively answer questions about what a person may do in the privacy of her own home, such as whether the use of pornography is morally appropriate. Given evaluative pluralism, people will not share many of the same ends, and they will not place equal importance on the ends that they share. As a result, they will not be able to secure collective agreement on how to conduct their private lives.

A related argument grounds the right to private property. Private property not only allows us to protect our fundamental agency and to extend it into the world via complex life plans, it allows people to individually or locally resolve disputes that cannot be resolved collectively. Private

---

[10] Gaus 2011, pp. 374–386.
[11] Ibid., pp. 382–384.

property, for instance, solves the collective decision problem posed by extensive government operation of the economy, as markets allow people to live their own lives according to their own evaluative standards.

In contrast to the right to privacy, however, the right to private property generates passionate disagreement. The extent of the right to private property animated the global contest between capitalism and socialism in the twentieth century, and was accordingly the subject of intense dispute, much of which was probably reasonable and the result of sincere evaluative pluralism. Given criterion (iii) in establishing the order of justification, which holds that rights find their place in the order of justification depending on how many members of the public can agree on establishing the right, the right of private property comes later in the order of justification than agency rights or associational rights.

Fortunately, we needn't settle the question of the extensiveness of the right of private property as a whole. We can make progress by dividing the right into components. For instance, the right to private property in one's home and yard is nowhere near as controversial as the right to the productive use of property. A right to own property to be used for nonprofit purposes is also relatively uncontroversial. Few reasonable socialists would grant a federal legislative body the right to bulldoze a church against the will of its members, at least not without sufficient compensation. Further, consider Rawlsian property-owning democrats who hold that large inequalities of capital and wealth should be broken up and redistributed to those who lack capital. They probably wouldn't give the government the power to take over or directly regulate their places of employment—colleges and universities. Congress lacks the moral power to shut down Harvard. The same goes for historical sites, cemeteries, and the like. I will expand on this point further in the sequel to this book.

The central disagreement about private property rights between political ideologies in most liberal democracies concerns whether the jurisdictional right of private property includes the use of property for commercial purposes.[12] Controversy surrounds a primary right to acquire and control private capital for profit.[13]

---

[12] People already have a limited *agency* right to own some private capital, but that right is sharply limited to owning capital required to exercise one's agency. A jurisdictional right promises to be more extensive.

[13] Few dispute that governments are permitted to establish the constitutional or legal right to own and acquire private capital. The question is whether the right is primary, that is, whether it *morally* limits government interference.

To begin assessing whether persons have a jurisdictional right to own and operate private capital, let us note that every developed liberal democracy protects extensive private property rights in capital.[14] While controversial among philosophers, the right is not controversial in any developed, free society. This suggests that few reflective people would even claim to have defeaters for such a right. The public justification for this broadly capitalist arrangement involves appreciating the difficulty in drawing any principled distinction between uncontroversial liberal rights to personal property and freedom of occupation on the one hand and rights to own and operate productive property on the other. We can surely own our homes, and it seems natural to think that we should be permitted to use our homes to run a small business, say for piano lessons, counseling, massage, dog breeding, etc.

Granted, the right to one's home is limited. Property is widely regarded as legitimately subject to taxation and zoning regulations, such that the government can prohibit building a place of residence in a particular area (though excessively strict zoning laws are sufficiently intrusive to be defeated in many social orders). Further, homeowners can be prevented from imposing negative externalities on their neighbors. So running a rock concert in one's backyard at night can be limited because it greatly disrupts others' lives.

That said, despite these limitations, rights to operate a massage parlor, host piano lessons, or babysit, which are uses of productive capital, are on a par with one's right to safety and protection in one's personal possessions, one's home, and one's church. Government should keep its hands off church bake sales, making wine for sale in monasteries, running lemonade stands, and mowing the neighbor's lawn.

We can further refine the question before us to concern whether people have a primary right to own and operate productive capital *beyond their home*. But we have already seen reason to think that moderately idealized members of the public will embrace this primary right—the considerations that justify the primary right to own and use a home apply to public commercial enterprises. All liberal orders agree that, by and large, people must have the freedom to choose their occupation, at least between employers. They also agree that people must have the freedom to go into business for themselves. For those on the left who worry about the treatment of workers under capitalism, the idea that the government can wholly abrogate the

---

[14] Gaus 2011, pp. 511–521.

right to start one's own business should be deeply morally suspect.[15] Owning capital is critical for starting worker-owned businesses and for many of the rights that Rawlsians assign to unions. Without a primary right to own capital, governments could legitimately prohibit the unionization of workers in a single firm—syndicates. If Reba's home is not suitable for business, or if she wants to work outside of her home because she is more productive that way, she should have the primary right to contract with others to rent a space or to buy a building where they can run their business together. Again, free societies recognize these rights; and they raise little controversy among reasonable persons.

In this way, we can identify a weakness in the egalitarian liberal commitment to "economic exceptionalism," where economic liberties are treated differently than other liberal rights.[16] I have argued that the right to own and operate productive resources is similar in character to rights that liberals find much less controversial. Egalitarian liberals push back primarily when a business becomes large enough to have major economic effects on large groups of people. These effects include the ability to hire and fire a large number of wage-laborers, to impact the direction of markets, to impose large negative externalities on society, and to influence the political process. Based on this observation, it seems to me the issue that animates the indignation of people on the left is not the right to own productive property, but rather the right of persons to form large private firms that can control the livelihood and freedoms of their workers and adversely affect the public in a way that is unchecked by legitimate legal and political institutions.

This seems to be a reasonable disagreement. Consequently, I think we should reject a strong primary right to own and operate large commercial enterprises to the same degree that persons have in freelance labor or running a small business, especially a business out of one's home. True, being able to create and run a large, successful firm can be part of someone's conception of the good. It can even be part of living out one's conception of justice, such as creating an environmentally conscious manufacturing firm. But if the right to own and operate large commercial enterprises involves enormous latitude in the treatment of workers, a strong primary right to operate a firm could be used to excessively or unjustifiably restrict the right of workers to press for better

---

[15] Though government will of course have some say about how these new business owners should treat the workers they hire. I thank Lucy Randall for this point.
[16] Tomasi 2012, p. 42.

working conditions. But workers have a strong right of freedom of association with one another, such that large commercial enterprises may lack primary rights to restrict, or at least heavily restrict, organizing and resistance. In this way the primary right to unionize will generate conflicts between capital and labor, and an extensive right to own productive capital would tip the balance of reasonable objections in favor of capital and against labor in a way that many people have sufficient reason to reject. Large commercial enterprises may therefore be permissibly regulated to protect primary rights, again including the primary associational rights of workers to form a union.

That said, legitimate owners of large commercial enterprises have a primary right against expropriation by government, despite having limited rights to control and determine the behavior of their employees. Governmental expropriation generally involves a massive amount of redistribution and control, which seriously curtails the ability of persons to live out their life plans. I would also argue that *workers* have a right against government nationalization. If Congress nationalized Google, it would violate the primary rights of Google's shareholders *and* Google's employees. And while it is possible that employees will seek out nationalization to protect their primary rights, few employees in free societies are socialists in this sense, and so the coercion required for nationalization may not be publicly justified for them. Further, unions are prepolitical associations in the sense that they would exist in the legal state of nature, much as medieval guilds existed prior to the formation of strong nation-states. Consequently, unions set limits on government law and legislation much as families and churches do. So if unions have sufficient reasons to oppose nationalization, then those reasons will figure into a defeater for nationalization.

We should also be careful to craft economic liberties so that the interests of capital and labor are better aligned. Classical Marxists see this conflict as ineliminable short of socialist revolution, but their concerns are widely regarded as exaggerated. If workers have the primary right to unionize, if governments can regulate business activity on behalf of the common good and encourage competition within those industries, the government has quite a bit of power to protect its citizens from dangerous corporate activity. No government needs the right to seize the means of production to protect the primary rights of its citizens, but every modern government will violate the primary rights of citizens if it nationalizes industries. Classical state socialism cannot be publicly justified.

Questions remain about the status of economic rights and liberties, particularly with respect to freedom of contract and the right to keep a portion of one's wealth and income. I must also address questions about how a morally peaceful order regulates economic inequalities. I will discuss both issues much further in the sequel to this book.

4. Procedural Rights

We now turn to the procedural rights of citizens, both with respect to *legal* procedures and with respect to *political decision-making*. Legal procedural rights include the right to a fair trial, the right to a public defender, the right against self-incrimination, and so on. Political procedural rights include the right to vote, the right to financially contribute to campaigns, the right to run for office, and the right to engage in public deliberation.

While aspects of these rights are controversial, procedural rights are deeply entrenched in every free society, and with good reason. Anyone with a conception of the good and a conception of justice will want to be treated fairly by a legal system that could destroy their lives, and in some cases, kill them. Moderately idealized persons will want this right sufficiently badly that they would gladly extend the same right to others on reciprocal terms.

Political rights can be justified on similar grounds, as each reasonable person will want the right to influence the political process, and to be able to have a genuine effect inasmuch as this is possible. In the vast majority of cases, citizens are not able to impact the political process because there are simply too many citizens for any one person to have a major impact. But, collectively, the right to vote has a critical role in preventing governments from engaging in disastrous policies.[17] Democracies have *many* bad policies. But they are typically superior to policies in nondemocracies, such as authoritarian regimes like China. So even if no single person can significantly impact an election through the right to vote, nearly all suitably idealized persons will recognize the easily accessible information on the record of democratic states in reducing violence, fighting relatively few wars, and preventing mass starvation. As Mill noted, the right to vote is the right to control others, and so I would argue that the right to vote should be limited to the right to vote over issues that do not violate primary

---

[17] Democracies are thought to fight few wars against other democracies, and to avoid famines. On the former, see Köchler 2001 and Hensel et al. 2000. On the latter, see Sen 1981 and Rubin 2011.

rights.[18] But democratic rights over other social decisions can be publicly justified.

Further, many citizens see political rights as their only effective means of pursuing justice. Political organizing, for instance, gives meaning to the lives of millions of people in democratic states, and even in nondemocratic states with groups attempting to create a democratic order. So the reasons persons have to pursue justice only strengthen democratic rights. Again, however, democratic rights can be used to control others, and thereby set back their capacity to pursue justice, so this rationale only goes so far.

Libertarians raise a potential challenge to political rights since they often have little interest in participating in politics and voting. Many libertarians would gladly give up their right to vote in exchange for financial compensation or for more economic liberties, given that libertarians are skeptical about the power and goodness of the democratic process. But libertarians, with few exceptions, prefer democratic regimes to real-world authoritarian alternatives. And since progressive and conservative members of the public arguably have sufficient reasons to defeat libertarian regimes, a system with the limited right to vote is the best regime libertarians can insist upon.

But all is not lost for libertarians, for they will want certain *other* political rights, specifically rights of *exit* from a political order, such as the right of secession or the right to a reservation or charter city. If libertarians wish to trade voting rights for rights of exit, then a publicly justified polity may allow such an exchange. Libertarians can also justifiably insist that limited exit rights should supplement democratic rights, such as the forms of exit found in federalist regimes.

5. International Rights

Finally, we turn toward international rights, or rights to engage with other political orders and members of those orders. I set aside questions of war and international peace, as they raise complications beyond the scope of the book. Instead, I will focus on international freedom of movement and trade. I think persons have primary rights to freedom of movement because Reba's ability to exercise her conception of the good and justice depends upon the availability of opportunities to escape institutions that

---

[18] Here Mill speaks of the right that a member of Parliament has over others, but that there can be no weighty, general right to power over others. Mill 1963, p. 326.

significantly undermine her welfare and violate her other primary rights.[19] Immigration restrictions impose incredible harms on immigrants, especially those who wish to move from very poor and poorly governed countries to rich and effectively governed countries, and so it is hard to see how they don't have defeaters for those restrictions.[20] I grant that citizens may have the right to deny immigrants citizenship and some nonessential social services, but they do not have the right to exclude immigrants from entering the country unless those specific immigrants present a clear and present danger to the stability or efficacy of political and economic institutions. I would make the same argument for a primary right to trade with persons internationally. The right to free exchange is vital for the livelihood of many people, and so many limitations on trade will be defeated.

The main counterargument to primary rights of immigration and trade is that some will be made worse off by the free movement of goods, services, and persons, in particular those who will lose their jobs to immigrants or foreign workers. But economists agree more on the benefits of free trade and immigration than almost any other issue.[21] This strongly suggests that the evidence supporting the economic benefits of free trade and free immigration will meet the necessary publicly recognized standards of evidence. Moderately idealized persons will understand and accept these benefits and so endorse these rights because such rights will benefit them all on balance. In response to concerns about displaced workers, moderately idealized persons are much more likely to pursue ways of mitigating these losses other than restricting trade and immigration. Consequently, persons displaced from their jobs by free immigration and free trade may have a primary right to a job-retraining program, financed by taxpayers if necessary.

A hard question arises when we consider the prospect that mass immigration could lead to fundamental changes to a country's moral, religious, and political culture. I allow that a publicly justified polity can place some restriction on immigration to maintain public order and perhaps some degree of cultural continuity. But we must again remember the great harms that immigration restrictions place on immigrants. All immigration restrictions aimed at protecting cultural continuity must be weighed

---

[19] In this way, the primary rights to immigration and trade are on all fours with other primary rights. They have the same justificatory basis. For a powerful, recent argument that rights to immigrate have the same ground as other liberal rights, see Hildalgo and Freiman 2016.
[20] Gaus 2011, pp. 478–479.
[21] On immigration, see Kerr and Kerr 2011. On free trade, the consensus is even greater. See http://www.igmchicago.org/igm-economic-experts-panel/poll-results?SurveyID=SV_0dfr9yjnDcLh17m.

against the interests and freedom of immigrants. In a large, diverse country like the United States, which can accommodate many immigrants without large-scale social change, the government has less latitude to restrict immigration. Immigration restrictions for small countries surrounded by enemies can be justified more easily.

6. Social Justice between Rawls and Hayek

The foregoing list of primary rights constitutes a theory of social justice. Social justice is achieved when these primary rights are systematically recognized and protected for everyone. And remember that primary rights include rights to the resources required to exercise one's other primary rights.

My account of social justice differs from Rawls's justice as fairness in three respects. First, I reject the difference principle, as Rawls admitted many reasonable persons could do.[22] The difference principle should be rejected on the grounds that the case for the difference principle depends on a sectarian conception of equal treatment, where equal treatment must be understood in terms of justifying departures from an equal distribution of primary goods. Many members of the public will be less egalitarian than Rawls, and so will prefer to be governed by a system of primary rights alone rather than be governed by the difference principle.

Some members of the public will also reject fair equality of opportunity. A reasonable person could deny that society is a race to garner positional goods, such that the fact that Reba has more opportunities than John requires no justification to John. The opportunities Reba has could easily improve John's opportunities, and he has no natural entitlement to have as many opportunities as Reba.[23] This makes a principle of *sufficient* opportunity quite plausible, but we have already established a primary positive right of assistance that resembles such a principle.[24]

Finally, conceptions of justice that sustain social trust are limited to cases where the moral order requires reform. Social justice is thereby bound by a prior set of moral rules; political public justification occurs within moral rules.[25]

---

[22] Rawls 2005, p. xlvii.

[23] Schmidtz 2006, pp. 109–114.

[24] For a discussion of sufficientarianism, see Arneson 2013, especially http://plato.stanford.edu/entries/egalitarianism/#Suf.

[25] In this way, I follow Buchanan and Brennan 1985.

In offering an account of social justice, I do not thereby reject Hayek's critique of social justice, since the conception of social justice I adopt does not involve judging the justice of specific economic distributions, but rather determining which rights and rules should govern the moral and political order. Hayek had no problem with this understanding of social justice.[26] In fact, in many ways, my conception of a society governed by constitutional rules that protect basic rights resembles regimes that Hayekians can endorse.

7. Constitutional Choice

We now need an argument that these primary rights merit constitutional protection. Toward this end, we must first show that these primary rights merit legal protection. Recall the criteria for legal protection I advanced in chapters 4 and 5. Legal protections must overcome a presumption against legal coercion; and since primary rights can be publicly justified to basically all reasonable perspectives, protection of these rights can overcome the presumption. They do so because moderately idealized members of the public will recognize that primary rights will not be adequately protected by the moral order alone because we need legal protections that are stable, flexible, and efficient, and whose penalties are more severe than the ostracism of the moral order.

We can next argue that primary rights deserve constitutional protection, meaning that primary rights must be legally recognized as well as protected from alteration or abrogation by those same legal institutions. Members of the public will embrace constitutional protection in order to prevent political officials from violating primary rights. Constitutional protections help for two reasons. First, constitutional protections usually imply further institutional remedies for violations. In the United States, for instance, the Supreme Court, and not just the legislature and the executive, protect the Bill of Rights. Second, constitutionally protecting primary rights provides them with a sacred quality. People see constitutional rules as fundamental to their social and national character, such that violations are greeted not merely with legal penalties and restrictions, but national moral outrage.

Primary rights-protecting constitutional rules will be eligible for public justification. We can therefore try to determine which

---

[26] See Hayek 1978, p. 100. For discussion of the sense in which the Rawlsian project does not conflict with Hayek's hostility to social justice, see Tomasi 2012, pp. 142–150.

constitutional rules can be used to protect primary rights. Toward this end, we should appeal to the other parts of the model of constitutional choice, specifically to minimize legislative error in the protective and productive functions of the state, and to ensure that constitutional rules be durable and immune for the right reasons.

Constitutional rules that undermine a society's ability to prohibit or repeal laws that seriously violate primary rights are defeated. The remaining eligible rules are likely to involve or at least not conflict with restrictions on legislative procedures. The United States protects many primary rights with strong supermajority rules; the First Amendment would have to be repealed in order to make free speech-restricting laws constitutional, and amending the Constitution is incredibly difficult. On my account of constitutional choice, supermajority rules are probably an appropriate method of reducing legislative error because they make passing bad law more difficult. Bicameralism and judicial review may be appropriate for similar reasons.

Constitutional rules also govern the productive function of the state, where primary rights are not typically directly at stake. I will have much more to say about the productive function of the state in the sequel to this book, but primary rights already give us some guidance in structuring the state's productive function. Recall that income, wealth, and capital are resources to which persons have a primary right and that parties behind a thin veil of ignorance will want to maximize their share of income, wealth, and capital over time.[27] This means that the productive function of the state must include progrowth policies and policies that will ensure that everyone has sufficient access to income, wealth, and capital. So that means we have at least two tests for the legitimacy of legislation generated by the productive function of the state: a growth test and a sufficiency test. All productive policies must not unnecessarily stymie economic growth and not undermine universal access to income, wealth, and capital. We will see, beyond this, that there are constraints on productive legislation, such as a cost-benefit analysis I call *policy epistemology*. But for now we only narrow the eligible set of constitutional rules to those that are adequately conducive to both growth and poverty reduction.

The final stage of constitutional choice is the stability condition, which requires that all eligible constitutional rules must be adequately immune

---

[27] This is so even if some members are known to adhere to poverty-friendly values because greater income, wealth, and capital can be voluntarily renounced in order to help the disadvantaged.

against abuse by political officials and durable among citizens subject to the rule and the laws normally produced by the rule.

Concerning immunity, we want constitutional structures that will prevent political officials from acting in accord with their self-interest or sectarian ideology when doing so will tempt them to violate primary rights through imposing unjustified legislation or opposing justified legislation. Fortunately, supermajority rules, bicameralism, an independent executive, and an independent judicial system effectively protect many primary rights by greatly increasing the costs of imposing rights-violating legislation. The bigger threats to immunity come from the productive function of the state, where public policy is more open-ended and less restricted. Productive functions include the capacity to generate complicated legislation within which rent-seeking is easily hidden from the public. So the only adequately immune constitutional rules will include protections against rent-seeking activity. I will discuss some sensible protections in the sequel to this book.

The fact that primary rights are publicly justified helps ensure that constitutional rules protecting primary rights are durable for the right reasons. If people recognize that primary rights are compatible with their personal ideals, doctrines, and values, they will recognize both moral reason to comply with laws that protect those rights and moral reason to oppose and perhaps even disobey laws that violate those same rights. And as long as these rights remain publicly justified, social trust based on these rights should remain high once established. However, some people violate social and legal norms, and without the threat of punishment, the relevant social, legal, and constitutional norms may destabilize and collapse. So a publicly justified polity must coercively protect its primary rights to stabilize them.

8. Liberalism Justified

Liberal order is justified because a constitution that protects liberal rights is uniquely publicly justified according to the procedures set out in chapters 4–6. Recalling chapters 1–3, we can now say that a liberal political constitution completes a free and open moral order by amplifying the capacity of that moral order to sustain social trust for the right reasons. A liberal constitution is therefore essential for creating moral peace between diverse persons and is one where politics is more than mere institutionalized aggression. We can conclude that a politics governed by liberal institutional structures keeps politics from being a perpetual, partisan war.

Epilogue
Liberal Politics Is Not War

THIS BOOK ASKS WHETHER politics under conditions of deep diversity must be institutionalized aggression—war—between opposing groups. As we have seen, a regime of liberal constitutional rights can be publicly justified. It can serve as the basis of social trust and so, over time, form moral peace between persons. In a liberal regime, politics will be a process of public negotiation among persons who profoundly disagree but who are still able to trust one another to act according to their shared moral and political constitutions.

Liberal institutions also preserve respect for persons within a system of trust because persons treat each other according to norms that they each have their own reason to accept. So liberal institutions not only have the teleological value of establishing moral peace, they have the deontological value of treating persons in the right way.

But what of nonliberals? It may seem pointless to argue that nonliberals can live in moral peace with liberals if nonliberals accept liberal institutions, since nonliberals reject liberalism. But while liberal institutions are not ideal for nonliberals, liberal institutions should still be mutually morally acceptable to them all, given that most nonliberals will refuse to ascribe moral authority to hegemonic political institutions controlled by competitor groups.

This is all well and good, but is a principled liberal order within our grasp? After all, if real human beings cannot reasonably hope to achieve such an order, then perhaps politics *will* be war even if it doesn't *have* to be. There is reason to hope, however; liberal democratic orders already exhibit some degree of moral peace. Social trust is all around us. As this book has attempted to show, there is also hope for *more* moral peace than we have now on the grounds that only liberal institutional practices are mutually acceptable and so should prove to be an enduring basis for strengthening moral peace over time.

I should also stress that my arguments appeal to no heroic assumptions about human history or human nature; neither are they especially individualistic or collectivist, religious or secular. I have not assumed that humans are basically good or that they will agree about what is good. I have not even assumed that people will agree upon the right conception of justice or social ontology. I account for morally corrupt and self-interested agents in my model of constitutional choice. I have simply argued that, under realistic assumptions, liberal institutions like ours can establish moral peace between persons. So we already have some moral peace and getting more of it is plausibly within our grasp. Real liberal politics need not be war.

Some readers will remain impressed by the depravity of humanity, our nasty history, and the relations of oppression that continue to generate injustice to this day; they have no hope that we can achieve more than a decent balance of power. But I ask those readers to simply observe the advanced liberal orders that surround us. Their existence, our populist moment notwithstanding, is a challenge to continuing skepticism about the capacity of human beings to establish and maintain morally peaceful social orders.

Many reasonable skeptics need more convincing, however. To answer them, I have written a sequel to this book. *Must Politics Be War?* argues that liberal institutions can be publicly justified and so liberal institutions can *in principle* can establish moral peace between persons. But in my next book, I argue that liberal institutions establish moral peace between persons in liberal democratic practice. There I will use my account of public justification to vindicate several core liberal institutions: freedom of association, the market economy, the welfare state, and democratic governance. I will argue that each of these institutions can be justified as parts of a scheme of primary rights of agency, association, jurisdiction, and procedure. I will also show that liberal regimes have high levels of social trust and that the fact that people see the central features of these regimes as mutually acceptable can rationally sustain the high social trust we observe. So while *Must Politics Be War?* is a generic possibility proof that liberal politics need not be institutionalized aggression, the next book will argue that actual liberal politics helps to complete a system of social trust.

My message in both books is that we should step back from our determination to destroy each other on the political field of battle. If we care about being reconciled to one another, about trusting those who are different from us, then we need not despair. We can find peace by pursuing liberal political and economic arrangements. Nothing prevents us from forming moral relations with one another. Moral peace is within our grasp if we want it. Whether we establish it is up to us.

In cynical moments, I wonder whether we think politics is war because we *want* it to be. Contemporary ideological fights might be a less violent way to satisfy our desire to compete with and defeat our out-groups. Perhaps *ideological* war is a force that gives us meaning.[1] But if the argument of this book is successful, indulging this impulse has great costs. It not only threatens to deprive us of the great goods of social trust, but encourages us to forget that we are all human beings who should recognize one another's great worth.

---

[1] Hedges 2002.

ACKNOWLEDGMENTS

Given that the aim of this book is to argue that politics is not war and that there is a rational basis for people with divergent worldviews to trust one another, it is fitting that writing this book has been in many ways a collaborative effort between persons with diverse viewpoints. The book has taken several forms since I wrote the first draft in 2015, and has been gradually improved with help from dozens of people. So I owe many debts of gratitude.

First and foremost, I thank my wife, Alicia, who made this book possible by being an incredible wife and mother. She has been a constant source of support throughout the writing process and has inspired me more than anyone to look past ideology and see the worth of everyone regardless of their values and views.

I would have never been able to finish a project like this one without my mother's unwaivering encouragement, which she has provided for as long as I can remember. I thank her too.

I am indebted to everyone who worked for or with Oxford University Press in helping me get this book under contract and ready for publication. I am most grateful to my incredible editor, Lucy Randall, who has been consistently helpful and wise. I am grateful to Hannah Doyle, as well as Andrew Lister, Christie Hartley, Bob Talisse, and the anonymous referees for the book, for convincing me to split the original project into two book projects. I thank Jeff Carroll for helping me put together the index of the book. I am grateful to Christopher Andersen's photography and Aira Burkhart's graphic design in composing the book's cover art.

I thank everyone in my department at Bowling Green State University who helped me move the project forward. I am especially grateful to my graduate students, whose input into the project was invaluable, especially

Colin Manning, whose insights reformed the book, Will Lugar, who gave me extensive comments, and Cheyanne Wescott, my research assistant who greatly enhanced my editing process. Other BGSU graduate students helped as well, especially Marcus Schultz-Bergin, Ryan Fischbeck, Ian Irwin, Ami Palmer, Sam Schmitt, Liz McPherson, Mark Herman, Natalie Coté, John Luchon, and Austin McGrath. I am also grateful to my fellow BGSU faculty who helped me most with the project, Christian Coons, Michael Weber, and Brandon Warmke, as well as for conversations with Molly Gardner and Max Hayward. But I am most grateful to our legendary department secretary, Margy DeLuca, for helping with a huge number of small, cumbersome tasks that gave me the headspace to focus on writing. I am also grateful to the Charles Koch Foundation for financial support for time off from summer teaching at BGSU to finish the book.

Several people provided me with extensive comments on much of the manuscript, especially Paul Billingham, Jeff Carroll, Fred D'Agostino, Chris Eberle, Jerry Gaus, Adam Gjesdal, Greg Robson, and Chad Van Schoelandt. Their comments were tremendously helpful.

This book was the subject of two manuscript workshops, one at Brown University in 2016, organized by John Tomasi, and the other at St. Louis University in 2017, organized by Chad Flanders. I am grateful to the commentators at Brown, Charles Larmore, David Estlund, and Julian Müller, as well as the commentators at SLU, Chad Flanders, Katherine Sweet, Jonathan Reibsamen, Twigz McGuire, and James Dominic Rooney. I am also grateful to all the other participants at Brown, Josh Preiss, Shany Mor, Gianna Englert, Kirun Sankaran, and Nick Geiser, and at SLU, Heidi Banos, Daniel Aldruich, Luke Kallberg, Nicholas Zavediuk, and Dan Haybron.

Some of this book is based on articles that I have presented at conferences or gave as talks in England, Canada, Australia, and the United States. I can't hope to name everyone who contributed, but I will try. At Tulane, Chad Van Schoelandt, Bruce Brower, and Eric Mack were extremely helpful, as were Chris Morris, Dan Moller, Eric Pacuit, and Rachel Singpurwalla at Maryland. I had similar help at Purdue from Patrick Kain, Jeff Brower, and a number of others. I'm grateful to audiences at two of the PPE (Philosophy, Politics, and Economics) Society meetings, as well as a number of attendees at the Australasian Association of Philosophy, such as Toby Handfield, Rosa Terlazzo, Jon Herington, and John Thrasher. I'm grateful to Michael Moehler for comments at Virginia Tech, and comments from Jon Inazu and Kit Wellman during a talk at St. Louis University. Audiences at George Mason University, the University of Birmingham, the University of North Carolina at Chapel Hill, and McGill

University were instrumental in improving chapter 6. Ryan Muldoon, Alan Hamlin, and Geoff Brennan were especially helpful in commenting on chapter 6 as well. And I am grateful to Bill Edmundson and Bas van der Vossen for comments on chapter 4. Conversations about public reason with Paul Weithman and Lori Watson also contributed to the structure of the book. I also had helpful discussions with Greg Robson, Fabian Wendt, Jess Flanigan, Javier Hildalgo, Mark Murphy, Nathan Ballantyne, Jeremy Williams, Thomas Sinclair, Jonathan Quong, Fred Miller, Dan Waxman, Ralf Bader, Chris Freiman, and Jason Brennan, as well as Alex Motchoulski, Neera Badhwar, Mike Munger, Geoff Sayre-McCord, and Hartmut Kliemt.

Parts of this book draw on published journal articles. Some of the material in chapter 3 is indebted to "In Defense of Intelligible Reasons in Public Justification." *Philosophical Quarterly* 66, 596–616, 2016 and "Public Reason Is Not Self-Refuting." *American Philosophical Quarterly* 53, 349–363, 2016. Chapter 6 draws on "Social Contracts for Real Moral Agents: A Synthesis of Public Reason and Public Choice Approaches to Constitutional Design." *Constitutional Political Economy*, 29, 115–136, as well as "Three Concepts of Political Stability." *Social Philosophy and Policy* 34, 232–259, 2017.

BIBLIOGRAPHY

Abbink, Klaus, Lata Gangadharan, Toby Handfield, and John Thrasher. 2017. Peer Punishment Promotes Enforcement of Bad Social Norms. *Nature Communications* 8, 1–8.

Adams, N. P. 2018. The Relational Conception of Practical Authority. *Law and Philosophy*, 1–27, http://doi.org/10.1007/s10982-017-9323-3.

Ahn, T. K., Elinor Ostrom, David Schmidt, and James Walker. 2003. Trust in Two-Person Games: Game Structures and Linkages. In *Trust and Reciprocity: Interdisciplinary Lessons for Experimental Research*, edited by Elinor Ostrom and James Walker, 323–351. New York: Russell Sage.

Altschul, Jon. 2014. Epistemic Entitlement. *Internet Encyclopedia of Philosophy*, http://www.iep.utm.edu/ep-en/.

Arneson, Richard. 2013. Egalitarianism. *Stanford Encyclopedia of Philosophy*, http://plato.stanford.edu/entries/egalitarianism.

Badhwar, Neera, and Roderick Long. 2014. Ayn Rand. *Stanford Encyclopedia of Philosophy*, http://plato.stanford.edu/entries/ayn-rand/.

Baier, A. C. 1986. Trust and Antitrust. *Ethics* 96, 231–260.

Baier, Kurt. 1954. The Point of View of Morality. *Australasian Journal of Philosophy* 32, 104–135.

———. 1995. *The Rational and the Moral Order: The Social Roots of Reason and Morality*. Peru, IL: Open Court Publishing.

Barrett, Jacob, and Gerald Gaus. 2018. Laws, Norms, and Public Justification: The Limits of Law as an Instrument of Reform. University of Arizona.

Barry, Brian. 1995. John Rawls and the Search for Stability. *Ethics* 105, 874–915.

Becker, Lawrence. 1996. Trust as Noncognitive Security about Motives. *Ethics* 107, 43–61.

Benn, Stanley. 1988. *A Theory of Freedom*. New York: Cambridge University Press.

Benson, Bruce. 2011. *The Enterprise of Law: Justice without the State*. Oakland: Independent Institute.

Berlin, Isaiah. 1969. *Four Essays on Liberty*. Oxford: Oxford University Press.

Bicchieri, Cristina. 2006. *The Grammar of Society*. New York: Cambridge University Press.

————. 2017. *Norms in the Wild: How to Diagnose, Measure, and Change Social Norms.* New York: Oxford University Press.

Bicchieri, Cristina, Eugen Dimant, and Erte Xiao. 2018. Deviant or Wrong? The Effects of Norm Information on the Efficacy of Punishment. http://www.nottingham.ac.uk/cedex/news/papers/2017-14.aspx.

Bicchieri, Cristina, and Ryan Muldoon. 2011. Social Norms. http://plato.stanford.edu/entries/social-norms/.

Bicchieri, Cristina, Erte Xiao, and Ryan Muldoon. 2011. Trustworthiness Is a Social Norm, but Trusting Is Not. *Politics, Philosophy, and Economics* 10, 170–187.

Billingham, Paul. 2017. Liberal Perfectionism and Quong's Internal Conception of Political Liberalism. *Social Theory and Practice* 43, 79–106.

Bowles, Samuel, and Herbert Gintis. 2011. *A Cooperative Species: Human Reciprocity and Its Evolution.* Princeton: Princeton University Press.

Boyd, Robert, and Peter Richerson. 2005. *The Origin and Evolution of Cultures.* New York: Oxford University Press.

Bradford, Ben, Jonathan Jackson, and Mike Hough. 2017. Trust in Justice. In *The Oxford Handbook of Social and Political Trust*, edited by Eric Uslaner, 1–26. New York: Oxford University Press.

Braithwaite, Valerie, and Margaret Levi, eds. 1998. *Trust and Governance.* New York: Russell Sage.

Brennan, Geoffrey, Lina Eriksson, Robert Goodin, and Nicholas Southwood. 2016. *Explaining Norms.* New York: Oxford University Press.

Brewer, Marilynn. 1999. The Psychology of Prejudice: Ingroup Love or Outgroup Hate? *Journal of Social Issues* 55, 429–444.

Buchanan, James. 1975. *The Limits of Liberty: Between Anarchy and Leviathan.* Chicago: University of Chicago Press.

Buchanan, James, and Gordon Tullock. 1962. *The Calculus of Consent: Logical Foundations of Constitutional Democracy.* Ann Arbor: University of Michigan Press.

Buchanan, James, and Geoffrey Brennan. 1985. *The Reason of Rules: Constitutional Political Economy.* New York: Cambridge University Press.

Campbell, James. 2016. *Polarized: Making Sense of a Divided America.* Princeton: Princeton University Press.

Castelfranchi, Christiano, and Rino Falcone. 2010. *Trust Theory: A Socio-cognitive and Computational Model.* West Sussex: Wiley.

Chung, Hun. 2017. The Instability of John Rawls's "Stability for the Right Reasons." *Episteme*, 1–17, http://doi.org/10.1017/epi.2017.14.

Cocking, Dean, and Jeanette Kennett. 2000. Friendship and Moral Danger. *Journal of Philosophy* 97, 278–296.

Cohen, M. A., and J. Dienhart. 2013. Moral and Amoral Conceptions of Trust, with an Application to Organizational Ethics. *Journal of Business Ethics* 112, 1–13.

Cohen, Marc. 2015. Alternative Conceptions of Generalized Trust (and the Foundations of the Social Order). *Journal of Social Philosophy* 46, 463–478.

Cook, Karen, ed. 2001. *Trust in Society.* New York: Russell Sage.

Cooper, John, ed. 1997. *Plato: Complete Works.* Indianapolis: Hackett.

Curry, Oliver Scott, Matthew Jones Chesters, and Caspar J. van Lissa. 2017. Mapping Morality with a Compass: Testing the Theory of 'Morality as Cooperation' with a New Questionnaire. *Open Science Framework.* http://osf.io/w5ad8/.

D'Agostino, Fred. 2013. The Orders of Public Reason. *Analytic Philosophy* 54, 129–155.

Darwall, Stephen. 2006. *The Second-Person Standpoint: Morality, Respect, and Accountability*. New York: Harvard University Press.

Dasgupta, Partha, and Ismail Serageldin, eds. 2000. *Social Capital: A Multifaceted Perspective*. Washington, DC: World Bank.

Delhey, Jan, Kenneth Newton, and Christian Welzel. 2011. How General Is Trust in "Most People"? Solving the Radius of Trust Problem. *American Sociological Review* 76, 786–807.

Dinesen, Peter Thisted, and Kim Mannemar Sønderskov. 2017. Ethnic Diversity and Social Trust: A Critical Review of the Literature and Suggestions for a Research Agenda. In *The Oxford Handbook of Social and Political Trust*, edited by Eric Uslaner, 1–35. New York: Oxford University Press.

Dorsey, Dale. 2017. Idealization and the Heart of Subjectivism. *Noûs* 51, 196–217.

Dunn, John. 1984. The Concept of "Trust" in the Politics of John Locke. In *Philosophy in History: Essays on the Historiography of Philosophy*, edited by Richard Rorty, J. B. Schneewind, and Quentin Skinner, 279–301. New York: Cambridge University Press.

Ebels-Duggan, Kyla. 2008. Against Beneficence: A Normative Account of Love. *Ethics* 119, 142–170.

———. 2010. The Beginning of Community: Politics in the Face of Disagreement. *Philosophical Quarterly* 60, 50–71.

Eberle, Christopher. 2002. *Religious Conviction in Liberal Politics*. New York: Cambridge University Press.

Edmundson, William. 2004. State of the Art: The Duty to Obey the Law. *Legal Theory* 10, 215–259.

Ehrenberg, Kenneth. 2011. Joseph Raz's Theory of Authority. *Philosophy Compass* 6, 884–894.

Enoch, David. 2013. The Disorder of Public Reason. *Ethics* 124, 141–176.

———. 2015. Against Public Reason. In *Oxford Studies in Political Philosophy*, vol. 1, edited by David Sobel, Peter Vallentyne, and Steven Wall, 112–144. New York: Oxford.

———. 2017. Political Philosophy and Epistemology. In *Oxford Studies in Political Philosophy*, vol. 3, edited by David Sobel, Peter Vallentyne, and Steven Wall, 132–163. New York: Oxford.

Fahmy, Melissa Seymour. 2010. Kantian Practical Love. *Pacific Philosophical Quarterly* 91, 313–331.

Farrell, Joseph, and Matthew Rabin. 1996. Cheap Talk. *Journal of Economic Perspectives* 10, 103–118.

Feinberg, Joel. 1987. *Harm to Others: The Moral Limits of the Criminal Law*. Vol. 1. New York: Oxford University Press.

Fessler, Daniel M. T., H. Clark Barrett, Martin Kanovsky, Stephen Stich, Colin Holbrook, Joseph Henrich, Alexander H. Bolyanatz, et al. 2015. Moral Parochialism and Contextual Contingency across Seven Societies. *Proceedings of the Royal Society B*. http://dx.doi.org/10.1098/rspb.2015.0907.

Fiala, Andrew. 2014. Pacifism. *Stanford Encyclopedia of Philosophy*, http://plato.stanford.edu/entries/pacifism/.

Foucault, Michel. 1997. *Society Must Be Defended*. Edited by Mauro Bertani and Alessandro Fontana. Translated by David Macey. New York: Picador.

Fowler, Timothy, and Zofia Stemplowska. 2015. The Asymmetry Objection Rides Again: On the Nature and Significance of Justificatory Disagreement. *Journal of Applied Philosophy* 32, 133–146.

Francis. 2015. Laudato Si' [Encyclical Letter on Our Common Home]. http://w2.vatican.va/content/francesco/en/encyclicals/documents/papa-francesco_20150524_enciclica-laudato-si.html.

Freeman, Samuel. 2014. Original Position. http://plato.stanford.edu/archives/fall2014/entries/original-position/.

Fukuyama, Francis. 1995. *Trust: The Social Virtues and the Creation of Prosperity.* New York: Free Press.

———. 1999. *The Great Disruption: Human Nature and the Reconstitution of Social Order.* London: Profile.

Fuller, Lon. 1969. *The Morality of Law.* Rev. ed. New Haven: Yale University Press.

Gaus, Gerald. 1990. *Value and Justification: The Foundations of Liberal Theory.* Cambridge: Cambridge University Press.

———. 1996. *Justificatory Liberalism: An Essay on Epistemology and Political Theory.* New York: Oxford University Press.

———. 1999. *Social Philosophy.* Armonk, NY: M.E. Sharpe.

———. 2000. *Political Concepts and Political Theories.* Boulder, CO: Westview.

———. 2008. The (Severe) Limits of Deliberative Democracy as the Basis for Political Choice. *Theoria* 117, 26–53.

———. 2011. *The Order of Public Reason.* New York: Cambridge University Press.

———. 2013. Moral Constitutions. *Harvard Review of Philosophy* 19, 4–22.

———. 2014. The Good, the Bad, and the Ugly: Three Agent-Type Challenges to the Order of Public Reason. *Philosophical Studies* 170, 563–577.

———. 2016. *The Tyranny of the Ideal.* Princeton: Princeton University Press.

———. 2018. Respect for Persons and Public Justification. In *Respect for Persons*, edited by Richard Dean and Oliver Sensen, 1–22. New York: Oxford University Press.

Gaus, Gerald, and Chad Van Schoelandt. 2017. Consensus on What? Convergence for What? Four Models of Political Liberalism. *Ethics* 128, 145–172.

Gauthier, David. 1986. *Morals by Agreement.* New York: Oxford University Press.

Glaeser, Edward, David Laibson, and Bruce Sacerdote. 2002. The Economic Approach to Social Capital. *Economic Journal* 112, 437–458.

Goldman, Alvin, and Thomas Blanchard. 2015. Social Epistemology. http://plato.stanford.edu/entries/epistemology-social/ - PeeDis.

Green, T. H. 1895. *Lectures on the Principles of Political Obligation.* New York: Longmans, Green and Co.

———. 2011. On the Different Senses of "Freedom" as Applied to Will and to the Moral Progress of Man. In *Works of Thomas Hill Green*, vol, 2, *Philosophical Works*, edited by R.L. Nettleship, 307–333. Cambridge: Cambridge University Press.

Grootaert, Christiaan, Deepa Narayan, Veronica Nyhan Jones, and Michael Woolcock. 2004. Measuring Social Capital: An Integrated Questionnaire. World Bank Working Papers.

Grootaert, Christiaan, and Thierry van Bastelaer. 2001. Understanding and Measuring Social Capital: A Synthesis of Findings and Recommendations from the Social Capital Initiative. World Bank Working Papers.

Habermas, Jurgen. 1995. Reconciliation through the Public Use of Reason: Remarks on John Rawls's *Political Liberalism. Journal of Philosophy* 92, 109–131.

Haji, Ishtiyaque. 1998. *Moral Appraisability: Puzzles, Proposals, and Perplexities.* New York: Oxford University Press.

Hall, Robert, and Charles Jones. 1999. Why Do Some Countries Produce So Much More Output Per Worker Than Others? *Quarterly Journal of Economics* 114, 83–116.

Hardin, Russell. 2004. *Trust and Trustworthiness.* New York: Russell Sage Foundation.

Harding, Matthew. 2011. Responding to Trust. *Ratio Juris* 24, 75–87.

Hart, H. L. A. 1961. *The Concept of Law.* Oxford: Clarendon Press.

———. 1973. Rawls on Liberty and Its Priority. *University of Chicago Law Review* 40, 534–555.

Hasnas, John. 2013. Is There a Moral Duty to Obey the Law? *Social Philosophy and Policy* 30, 450–479.

Hayek, F. A. 1952. *The Sensory Order: An Inquiry into the Foundations of Theoretical Psychology.* Chicago: University of Chicago Press.

———. 1973. *Law Legislation and Liberty.* Vol. 1: *Rules and Order.* Chicago: University of Chicago Press.

———. 1978. *Law, Legislation and Liberty.* Vol. 2: *The Mirage of Social Justice.* Chicago: University of Chicago Press.

———. 1979. *The Counter-revolution of Science: Studies on the Abuse of Reason.* 2nd ed. Indianapolis: Liberty Fund.

———. 2007. *The Road to Serfdom.* Definitive ed. Edited by Bruce Caldwell. London: Routledge.

Hedges, Chris. 2002. *War Is a Force That Gives Us Meaning.* New York: PublicAffairs.

Helliwell, John, Shun Wang, and Jinwen Xu. 2014. How Durable Are Social Norms? Immigrant Trust and Generosity in 132 Countries. NBER Working Paper No. 19855.

Hensel, Paul, Gary Goertz, and Paul Diehl. 2000. The Democratic Peace and Rivalries. *Journal of Politics* 62, 1173–1188.

Hetherington, Marc. 2005. *Why Trust Matters.* Princeton: Princeton University Press.

Hetherington, Marc, and Thomas Rudolph. 2015. *Why Washington Won't Work: Polarization, Political Trust, and the Governing Crisis.* Chicago: University of Chicago Press.

Hewstone, Miles, Mark Rubin, and Hazel Willis. 2002. Intergroup Bias. *Annual Review of Psychology* 53, 575–604.

Hidalgo, Javier, and Christopher Freiman. 2016. Liberalism or Immigration Restrictions, but Not Both. *Journal of Ethics and Social Philosophy* 10, 1–22.

Hieronymi, Pamela. 2008. The Reasons of Trust. *Australasian Journal of Philosophy* 86, 213–236.

Hjerppe, Reino. 1998. Social Capital and Economic Growth. Government Institute for Economic Research (VATT).

Hobbes, Thomas. 1994. *Leviathan.* Edited by Edwin Curley. Indianapolis: Hackett.

Holton, Richard. 1994. Deciding to Trust, Coming to Believe. *Australasian Journal of Philosophy* 72, 63–76.

Hosner, Larue. 1995. Trust: The Connecting Link between Organizational Theory and Philosophical Ethics. *Academy of Management Review* 20, 379–403.

Huemer, Michael. 2013. *The Problem of Political Authority: An Examination of the Right to Coerce and the Duty to Obey*. New York: Palgrave Macmillan.

Jankauskas, Vidmantas, and Janina Seputiene. 2007. The Relationship between Social Capital, Governance and Economic Performance in Europe. *Business: Theory and Practice* 8, 131–138.

Jennings, M Kent, and Laura Stoker. 2004. Social Trust and Civic Engagement across Time and Generations. *Acta Politica* 39, 342–379.

Jones, Karen. 1996. Trust as an Affective Attitude. *Ethics* 107, 4–25.

———. 2012. Trustworthiness. *Ethics* 123, 61–85.

Kahneman, Daniel. 2011. *Thinking: Fast and Slow*. New York: Farrar, Straus and Giroux.

Kant, Immanuel. [1797] 2009. *The Metaphysics of Morals*. Edited and translated by Mary Gregor. New York: Cambridge University Press.

Kappel, Klemens. 2017. Fact-Dependent Policy Disagreements and Political Legitimacy. *Ethical Theory and Moral Practice* 20, 313–331.

Kennedy, Jessica, and Maurice Schweitzer. 2017. Holding People Responsible for Ethical Violations: The Surprising Benefits of Accusing Others. *Academy of Management Proceedings* 1, 11258.

Kenworthy, Lane. 2013. *Progress for the Poor*. New York: Oxford University Press.

Keren, Arnon. 2014. Trust and Belief: A Preemptive Reasons Account. *Synthese* 191, 2593–2615.

Kerr, Sari Pekkala, and William R. Kerr. 2011. Economic Impacts of Immigration: A Survey. NBER Working Paper No. 16736.

Köchler, Hans. 2001. *Democracy and the International Rule of Law: Propositions for an Alternative World Order*. New York: Springer.

Kogelmann, Brian. 2017a. Aggregating out of Indeterminacy: Social Choice Theory to the Rescue. *Politics, Philosophy and Economics* 16, 1–23.

———. 2017b. Justice, Diversity, and the Well-Ordered Society. *Philosophical Quarterly* 67, 663–684.

———. 2018. Public Reason's Chaos Theorem, *Episteme*, 1–20, http://doi.org/10.1017/epi.2017.37.

Kogelmann, Brian, and Stephen G. W. Stich. 2016. When Public Reason Fails Us: Convergence Discourse as Blood Oath. *American Political Science Review* 110, 717–730.

Kohn, Marek. 2009. *Trust: Self-Interest and the Common Good*. New York: Oxford University Press.

Kolodny, Niko. 2003. Love as Valuing a Relationship. *Philosophical Review* 112, 135–189.

Kramer, Roderick. 2017. Ingroup-Outgroup Trust: Barriers, Benefits, and Bridges. In *The Oxford Handbook of Social and Political Trust*, edited by Eric Uslaner, 1–25. New York: Oxford University Press.

Kronenburg, Clemens, Isolde Heintze, and Guido Mehlkop. 2010. The Interplay of Moral Norms and Instrumental Incentives in Crime Causation. *Criminology* 48, 259–294.

Lahno, Bernd. 2001. On the Emotional Character of Trust. *Ethical Theory and Moral Practice* 4, 171–189.

Larmore, Charles. 2008. *The Autonomy of Morality*. New York: Cambridge University Press.

Leeson, Peter. 2014. *Anarchy Unbound: Why Self-Governance Works Better Than You Think*. New York: Cambridge University Press.

Leland, R. J., and Han van Wietmarschen. 2017. Political Liberalism and Political Community. *Journal of Moral Philosophy* 14, 142–167.

Lister, Andrew. 2010. Public Justification and the Limits of State Action. *Politics, Philosophy and Economics* 9, 151–175.

———. 2013. *Public Reason and Political Community*. New York: Bloomsbury Academic.

Locke, John. [1690] 1988. *Two Treatises of Government*. Cambridge: Cambridge University Press.

———. 1997. *Locke: Political Essays*. Edited by Mark Goldie. Cambridge: Cambridge University Press.

Lomasky, Loren. 1987. *Persons, Rights, and the Moral Community*. New York: Oxford University Press.

Mack, Eric. 2000. In Defense of the Jurisdiction Theory of Rights. *Journal of Ethics* 4, 71–98.

Mason, Elinor. 2015. Moral Ignorance and Blameworthiness. *Philosophical Studies* 172, 3037–3057.

McCabe, David. 2010. *Modus Vivendi Liberalism: Theory and Practice*. New York: Cambridge University Press.

McLeod, Carolyn. 2000. Our Attitude towards the Motivation of Those We Trust. *Southern Journal of Philosophy* 38, 465–479.

———. 2015. Trust. *Stanford Encyclopedia of Philosophy*, http://plato.stanford.edu/entries/trust/.

Messick, David, and Roderick Kramer. 2001. Trust as a Form of Shallow Morality. In *Trust in Society*, edited by Karen Cook, 89–117. New York: Russell Sage Foundation.

Mill, John Stuart. 1963. *Collected Works of John Stuart Mill*. Edited by J. M. Robson. Vol. 21. Toronto: University of Toronto Press.

Mueller, Dennis. 2003. *Public Choice III*. New York: Cambridge University Press.

Muldoon, Ryan. 2016. Exploring Tradeoffs in Accommodating Moral Diversity. *Philosophical Studies* 174, 1871–1883.

———. 2017. *Diversity and the Social Contract*. New York: Routledge.

Muldoon, Ryan, Michael Borgida, and Michael Cuffaro. 2012. The Conditions of Tolerance. *Politics, Philosophy, and Economics* 11, 322–344.

Muldoon, Ryan and Kevin Vallier. 2019. Public Reason Paradigms. Unpublished.

Mullin, Amy. 2005. Trust, Social Norms, and Motherhood. *Journal of Social Philosophy* 36, 316–330.

Murphy, Mark. 2006. *Philosophy of Law: The Fundamentals*. Oxford: Wiley-Blackwell.

Nannestad, Peter. 2008. What Have We Learned about Generalized Trust, If Anything? *Annual Review of Political Science* 11, 413–436.

Narveson, Jan. 2001. *The Libertarian Idea*. Peterborough, Ontario: Broadview Press.

Nickel, Philip. 2007. Trust and Obligation-Ascription. *Ethical Theory and Moral Practice* 10, 309–319.

Norris, Pippa. 2017. The Conceptual Framework of Political Support. In *Handbook of Political Trust*, edited by Sonja Zmerli and Tom W.G. van der Meer, 19–32. Northampton: Edward Elgar.

North, Douglass. 1990. *Institutions, Institutional Change, and Economic Performance*. New York: Cambridge University Press.

Nozick, Robert. 1969. Coercion. In *Philosophy, Science, and Method: Essays in Honor of Ernest Nagel*, edited by Sidney Morgenbesser, Patrick Suppes, and Morton White, 440–472. New York: St. Martin's Press.

Nunner-Winkler, Gertrude, and Beate Sodian. 1988. Children's Understanding of Moral Emotions. *Child Development* 59, 1323–1338.

Nussbaum, Martha. 2001. *Women and Human Development: The Capabilities Approach*. Cambridge: Cambridge University Press.

O'Neil, Collin. 2012. Lying, Trust, and Gratitude. *Philosophy and Public Affairs* 40, 301–333.

Olson, Mancur. 1984. *The Rise and Decline of Nations: Economic Growth, Stagflation, and Social Rigidities*. New Haven: Yale University Press.

Ostrom, Elinor. 1990. *Governing the Commons: The Evolution of Institutions for Collective Action*. Cambridge: Cambridge University Press.

Ostrom, Elinor, and James Walker, eds. 2003. *Trust and Reciprocity: Interdisciplinary Lessons from Experimental Research*. New York: Russell Sage Foundation.

Pappas, George. 2005. Internalist vs. Externalist Conceptions of Epistemic Justification. http://plato.stanford.edu/entries/justep-intext/ - 3.

Pinker, Steven. 2011. *The Better Angels of Our Nature: Why Violence Has Declined*. New York: Viking.

Pollock, John. 2006. *Thinking about Acting*. New York: Oxford University Press.

Popper, Karl. 2013. *The Open Society and Its Enemies*. Vol. 1. Princeton: Princeton University Press.

Preston-Roedder, Ryan. 2017. Civic Trust. *Philosopher's Imprint* 17, 1–23.

Putnam, Robert. 1994. *Making Democracy Work: Civic Traditions in Modern Italy*. Princeton: Princeton University Press.

Quintelier, Katinka, and Daniel Fessler. 2015. Confounds in Moral/Conventional Studies. *Philosophical Explorations* 18, 58–67.

Quong, Jonathan. 2011. *Liberalism without Perfection*. New York: Oxford University Press.

———. 2012. Liberalism without Perfection: Replies to Gaus, Colburn, Chan, and Bocchiola. *Philosophy and Public Issues* 2, 51–79.

Rawls, John. 1980. Kantian Constructivism in Moral Theory. *Journal of Philosophy* 77, 515–572.

———. 1999a. *A Theory of Justice*. New York: Oxford University Press.

———. 1999b. *Collected Papers*. Edited by Samuel Freeman. Cambridge: Harvard University Press.

———. 2001. *Justice as Fairness: A Restatement*. Edited by Erin Kelly. New Delhi: Universal Law Publishing.

———. 2002. *The Law of Peoples with "The Idea of Public Reason Revisited"*. Cambridge: Harvard University Press.

———. 2005. *Political Liberalism*. 2nd ed. New York: Columbia University Press.

Raz, Joseph. 1970. *The Concept of a Legal System*. New York: Oxford University Press.

———. 1986. *The Morality of Freedom*. Oxford: Oxford University Press.

———. [1975] 1990. *Practical Reason and Norms*. Princeton: Princeton University Press.

———. 2006. The Problem of Authority: Revisiting the Service Conception. *Minnesota Law Review* 90, 1003–1044.

———. 2009. *The Authority of Law: Essays on Law and Morality*. New York: Oxford University Press.

Reeskens, Tim, and Marc Hooghe. 2008. Cross-Cultural Measurement Equivalence of Generalized Trust from the European Social Survey (2002 and 2004). *Social Indicators Research* 85, 515–532.

Rescorla, Michael. 2015. Convention. http://plato.stanford.edu/entries/convention/.

Robeyns, Ingrid. 2016. The Capability Approach. plato.stanford.edu/entries/capability-approach/.

Robichaud, Philip, and Jan Wieland, eds. 2017. *Responsibility: The Epistemic Condition*. New York: Oxford University Press.

Robinson, Paul. 2000. Why Does the Criminal Law Care What the Layperson Thinks Is Just? Coercive versus Normative Crime Control. *Virginia Law Review* 86, 1839–1869.

Rosati, Connie. 1995. Persons, Perspectives, and Full Information Accounts of the Good. *Ethics* 105, 296–325.

Rose, David. 2014. *The Moral Foundation of Economic Behavior*. New York: Oxford University Press.

Rothstein, Bo. 2011. *The Quality of Government: Corruption, Social Trust, and Inequality in International Perspective*. Chicago: University of Chicago Press.

Rothstein, Bo, and Dietlind Stolle. 2002. How Political Institutions Create and Destroy Social Capital: An Institutional Theory of Generalized Trust. Paper presented to the American Political Science Conference, Boston.

———. 2008. The State and Social Capital: An Institutional Theory of Generalized Trust. *Comparative Politics* 40, 441–459.

Rousseau, Jean-Jacques. 1997. *Rousseau: "The Social Contract" and Other Later Political Writings*. Edited by Victor Gourevitch. New York: Cambridge University Press.

Rubin, Olivier. 2011. *Democracy and Famine*. London: Routledge.

Rudy-Hiller, Fernando. 2017. A Capacitarian Account of Culpable Ignorance. *Pacific Philosophical Quarterly* 98, 398–426.

Sabatini, Fabio. 2007. The Role of Social Capital in Economic Development. AICCON Cultura Cooperazione.

Sapienza, Paola, Anna Toldra-Simats, and Luigi Zingales. 2013. Understanding Trust. *Economic Journal* 123, 1313–1332.

Schmidtz, David. 2006. *The Elements of Justice*. New York: Cambridge University Press.

———. 2011. Nonideal Theory: What It Is and What It Needs to Be. *Ethics* 121, 772–796.

Scott, James C. 1999. *Seeing Like a State: How Certain Schemes to Improve the Human Condition Have Failed*. New Haven: Yale University Press.

———. 2009. *The Art of Not Being Governed*. New Haven: Yale University Press.

Sen, Amartya. 1980. Equality of What? In *The Tanner Lecture on Human Values*, 197–220. Cambridge: Cambridge University Press.

———. 1981. *Poverty and Famines*. New York: Oxford University Press.

Shapiro, Scott. 2004. Authority. In *The Oxford Handbook of Jurisprudence and Philosophy of Law*, edited by Jules Coleman and Scott Shapiro, 382–439. New York: Oxford.

Sher, George. 2009. *Who Knew? Responsibility without Awareness*. New York: Oxford University Press.

Shoemaker, David. 2011. Psychopathy, Responsibility, and the Moral/Conventional Distinction. *Southern Journal of Philosophy* 49 (Special Supplement), 99–124.

———. 2015. *Responsibility from the Margins*. Oxford: Oxford University Press.

Simmons, A. John. 1981. *Moral Principles and Political Obligations*. Princeton: Princeton University Press.

———. 1993. *On the Edge of Anarchy*. Princeton: Princeton University Press.

———. 1999. Justification and Legitimacy. *Ethics* 109, 739–771.

Simpson, Thomas. 2018. Trust, Belief, and the Second-Personal. *Australasian Journal of Philosophy*, 1–13, http://doi.org/10.1080/00048402.2017.1382545.

Smith, Adam. 1981. *An Inquiry into the Nature and Causes of the Wealth of Nations*. 2 vols. Edited by R. H. and A. S. Skinner Campbell. Indianapolis: Liberty Fund.

Steiner, Hillel. 1977. The Structure of a Set of Compossible Rights. *Journal of Philosophy* 74, 767–775.

Strawson, P. F. 1974. *Freedom and Resentment and Other Essays*. New York: Routledge.

Stringham, Edward. 2015. *Private Governance: Creating Order in Economic and Social Life*. New York: Oxford University Press.

Stump, Eleonore. 2012. *Wandering in Darkness: Narrative and the Problem of Suffering*. New York: Oxford University Press.

Tajfel, Henri, ed. 2010. *Social Identity and Intergroup Relations*. New York: Cambridge University Press.

Taylor, Anthony. 2018. Public Justification and the Reactive Attitudes. *Politics, Philosophy and Economics* 17, 97–113.

Taylor, Gabriele. 1985. *Pride, Shame, and Guilt: Emotions of Self-Assessment*. Oxford: Clarendon Press.

Thrasher, John, and Kevin Vallier. 2015. The Fragility of Consensus: Public Reason, Diversity, and Stability. *European Journal of Philosophy* 23, 933–954.

———. 2018. Political Stability in the Open Society. *American Journal of Political Science* 62, 398–409.

Tomasi, John. 2012. *Free-Market Fairness*. Princeton: Princeton University Press.

Tullock, Gordon. 2005. *The Rent Seeking Society*. Vol. 5 of *Selected Works of Gordon Tullock*. Indianapolis: Liberty Fund.

Tyler, Tom. 2006. *Why People Obey the Law*. Princeton: Princeton University Press.

Tyndal, Jason. 2016. Moderate Idealization and Information Acquisition Responsibilities. *Res Publica* 22, 445–462.

Uslaner, Eric. 2002. *The Moral Foundations of Trust*. New York: Cambridge University Press.

Vallier, Kevin. 2014. *Liberal Politics and Public Faith: Beyond Separation*. New York: Routledge.

———. 2015. On Distinguishing Publicly Justified Polities from Modus Vivendi Regimes. *Social Theory and Practice* 41, 207–229.

———. 2016a. In Defense of Intelligible Reasons in Public Justification. *Philosophical Quarterly* 66, 596–616.

———. 2016b. The Moral Basis of Religious Exemptions. *Law and Philosophy* 35, 1–28.

———. 2016c. Public Reason Is Not Self-Refuting. *American Philosophical Quarterly* 53, 349–363.

———. 2017a. Three Concepts of Political Stability. *Social Philosophy and Policy* 34, 232–259.

———. 2017b. On Jonathan Quong's Sectarian Political Liberalism. *Criminal Law and Philosophy* 11, 175–194.

———. 2018a. Social Contracts for Real Moral Agents: A Synthesis of Public Reason and Public Choice Approaches to Constitutional Design. *Constitutional Political Economy* 29, 115–136.

———. 2018b. Public Justification. *Stanford Encyclopedia of Philosophy*, http://plato. stanford.edu/entries/justification-public/.

———. 2019a. Political Liberalism and the Radical Consequences of Justice Pluralism. *Journal of Social Philosophy*, forthcoming.

———. 2019b. In Defense of Idealization in Public Reason. *Erkenntnis*, forthcoming.

Van Schoelandt, Chad. 2015. Justification, Coercion, and the Place of Public Reason. *Philosophical Studies* 172, 1031–1050.

Velleman, David. 1999. Love as a Moral Emotion. *Ethics* 109, 338–374.

Walker, Margaret Urban. 2006. *Moral Repair: Reconstructing Moral Relations after Wrongdoing*. Cambridge: Cambridge University Press.

Wall, Steven. 1998. *Liberalism, Perfectionism and Restraint*. New York: Cambridge University Press.

———. 2002. Is Public Justification Self-Defeating? *American Philosophical Quarterly* 39, 385–399.

———. 2013. Public Reason and Moral Authoritarianism. *Philosophical Quarterly* 63, 160–169.

Wanderer, Jeremy, and Leo Townsend. 2013. Is It Rational to Trust? *Philosophy Compass* 8, 1–14.

Watson, Gary. 1996. Two Faces of Responsibility. *Philosophical Topics* 24, 227–248.

Watson, Lori, and Christie Hartley. 2018. *Equal Citizenship and Public Reason: A Feminist Political Liberalism*. New York: Oxford University Press.

Weithman, Paul. 2010. *Why Political Liberalism? On John Rawls's Political Turn*. New York: Oxford University Press.

———. 2017. Autonomy and Disagreement about Justice in Political Liberalism. *Ethics* 128, 95–122.

Wendt, Fabian. 2018. Rescuing Public Justification from Public Reason Liberalism. In *Oxford Studies in Political Philosophy*, vol, 5, edited by David Sobel, Peter Vallentyne and Steven Wall, 1–23. New York: Oxford University Press.

Whiteley, Paul. 2002. Economic Growth and Social Capital. *Political Studies* 48, 443–466.

Wilson, Rick. 2017. Trust Experiments, Trust Games, and Surveys. In *The Oxford Handbook of Social and Political Trust*, edited by Rick Wilson, 1–32. New York: Oxford University Press.

Wolff, Robert Paul. 1970. *In Defense of Anarchism*. New York: Harper and Row.

Wolterstorff, Nicholas. 2010. *Practices of Belief*, Vol. 2: *Selected Essays*. New York: Cambridge University Press.

———. 2012. *Understanding Liberal Democracy*. Oxford: Oxford University Press.

You, Jong-sung. 2012. Social Trust: Fairness Matters More Than Homogeneity. *Political Psychology* 33, 701–721.

Zimmerman, Michael. 1988. *An Essay on Moral Responsibility*. Totowa, NJ: Rowman & Littlefield.

Zmerli, Sonja, and Ken Newton. 2008. Social Trust and Attitudes toward Democracy. *Public Opinion Quarterly* 72, 706–724.

INDEX

accountability, 7n, 9, 49, 63–66, 69–73, 77–79, 83, 88–90, 97–101, 112–113, 117–118, 129, 134, 142–145
  argument from, 9, 49, 66, 69–73, 77, 79, 88, 100, 118, 144–145
adjudicative institutions, 128–131
agent-based model, 13, 195n, 197n
aggregate cost, 176–177, 181, 184–187
anarchy objection, 114–115, 120, 201
appropriate resentment, 84
assurance, 44, 95n, 173, 190–198
asymmetry, 120–123
authority, 5, 84, 107, 112, 128, 131–132, 147, 150, 153–155
  authoritative claim-rights, 133, 138, 159–161
  authoritative moral demands, 84–85, 161
  moral, 84, 88, 96, 146, 154, 220
  practical, 153–154, 161
  service conception of, 153

balance, 194–196
Bicchieri, Cristina, 10n, 30–34, 35n, 62n, 65, 113, 133n, 143
blame, 9–10, 21, 26, 30–35, 62–66, 70, 71n, 80, 94–95, 101, 114, 117, 132–133
Buchanan, James and Gordon Tullock, 12, 173, 176–178, 181–184

candidates for internalization, 107
civic friendship, 47–48
coercion, 85–87, 121–123, 127–142, 161–162, 176, 203, 206
  legal, 11, 129–142, 150, 155, 162, 176, 203, 217
  political, 85, 133
  presumption against legal, 139–142, 162, 203, 217
cognition criterion, 98–100
common knowledge, 149, 189
compatibility relation, 78–80, 89, 97, 100, 116–119
constitutions, 82, 174–175, 179, 220
  constitutional choice, 12, 173–198, 217–218, 221
  constitutional essentials, 179, 188n
  constitutional protection, 217–219
  moral, 8, 11–13, 150–172
  political, 8, 11, 156–161, 220–221
convergence, 88–90, 96, 116, 188n
cultural change, 39, 161, 215

democracy, 1, 52–53, 208
dignity, 17–18, 29, 55
distribuendum of justice, 163–164
diversity, 19, 23, 91, 97, 111, 119, 220
durability, 194–198
duties of inquiry, 101
duty to obey the law, 11, 131, 145–151

Ebels-Duggan, Kyla, 47n, 55–56
economic justice, 3, 170, 211–217
Edmundson, William, 146–148
eligible set, 110–117, 152n, 156–157,
    165–168, 171, 175, 186–188,
    200–201, 218
  optimal, 110–115, 156–157, 168, 188,
    200–201
  of proposals, 110–117
  socially, 110–112, 187
Enoch, David, 2n, 22n, 89n-90n, 103–106,
    114–115, 121n
epistemic condition, 70–71, 98, 100
epistemic entitlement, 21, 93, 151
equality, 48, 87–88, 160, 168, 206, 216
error function, 180–187
evaluative pluralism, 19–24, 45–47, 89,
    101, 110–112, 121, 137, 141, 157,
    187, 207–209
exemption, 115n, 145, 170
external cost, 176–185, 192n
external shocks, 173, 190–194

false negative, 176, 180–183n, 187
false positive, 176, 180–183n, 187
Feinberg, Joel, 202
freedom of association, 5, 115, 161, 170,
    206–207, 212, 221
freedom-as-self-rule, 162
Freeman, Samuel, 164–165
friendship, 8, 17, 47–48, 54–58, 62, 75
functional independence individuation
    criterion, 176

game theory, 53, 95
Gaus, Gerald, 3n, 5–10, 32–35, 47n, 48,
    54n, 57n, 58n, 61n, 63–66, 70n, 71n,
    75, 82n, 85–88, 92n, 94–95, 99n,
    104, 108n, 110n, 111–112, 119n,
    121n, 130n, 134n, 136n, 137n, 139n,
    140n, 142n, 162n, 174n, 197n, 201n,
    202n, 207n, 208, 210n, 215n
goal, 20, 25–28, 35–37, 142
Green, T.H., 138, 162n
guilt, 59–60, 64–65, 74, 84, 108,
    128, 195

Hardin, Russell, 24n-25n, 27, 40, 52
harm, 25, 34, 59, 66, 137, 202–203, 215
Hasnas, John, 131, 146n
Hayek, F.A., 20, 21n, 101–102, 119, 131,
    216–217
heuristics, 98–99, 166

ideal theory, 7, 178–179
idealization, 10–11, 69–71, 92–93, 97–106,
    109, 115–122, 159, 179
  epistemic dimension of, 99–100
  information dimension of
    epistemic, 99–100
  rationality dimension of epistemic, 99
ideology, 219, 223
illusion of culpable dissent, 19, 24, 45–46
immunity, 194–198, 219
individuation, 81–82, 157, 174n-176
ineffective, 66, 134–135, 139–141
institutions, 2–8, 11–13, 45–46, 49–53,
    61, 78, 80, 96–97, 102, 110, 123,
    128–135, 142–146, 156, 161–164,
    169–174, 179, 192, 199, 204, 207,
    211, 214–217, 220–221
intelligibility, 11, 88–92, 96–97
internal cost, 176–185
internal dynamics, 188–190, 194–195
internalization, 107–109, 128, 150n, 154
internalized, 33, 103, 109, 116, 128, 175,
    188, 192n, 195

justice, 3, 6, 12, 22, 57, 74, 81, 94,
    98–99, 111, 156–160, 162–163,
    165–167, 170, 174–175, 177–179,
    186, 188n, 196, 201–202, 206, 211,
    213–217, 221
  pluralism, 6n, 22, 94, 111, 157, 175,
    177, 179, 206n
  principles of, 81, 99, 157–158, 163,
    166, 174–175, 177–179
justification, 4–11, 41–43, 47–123, 127,
    131, 136–147, 152–162, 174–178,
    187, 190, 194, 198–202, 206–210,
    216–217, 221
  legal, 11, 48–49, 127, 131, 136, 139–147,
    152–158

personal, 116
principle of public, 4, 8–9, 11, 47n, 73,
    81–82, 152
public, 4–11, 19, 47–49, 61–62, 66–123,
    127, 131n, 139–147, 152–158, 162,
    174–178, 187, 190, 194, 198–202,
    206–210, 216–217, 221
testing conception of public, 119–120

K-rule analysis, 176, 181–185
Kant, Immanuel, 54–55
knowability constraint, 154
Kogelmann, Brian, 188, 192n, 206n
Kolodny, Niko, 55

Larmore Charles, 48, 58n
laws, 127–139, 145–157, 174–198, 210,
    218–219
legal constitution, 152–155
legal efficiency, 134–137
legal obligation, 131–132, 145–155
legal protection, 159–160, 199, 217–219
legal state of nature, 11, 132–137,
    140–142, 148, 158–159, 168–170,
    199–201, 205, 212
legal systems, 12, 123, 127, 131–155,
    159, 165, 171
liberalism, 199
liberty, 85–89, 114, 117, 127, 130–133,
    139, 142, 158–162, 201, 208
    legal, 139
    moral, 85–89, 114, 127, 139, 142n, 161
    negative, 87–88
    positive, 88
Lomasky, Loren, 111, 156n, 159n
Love, 8, 17, 47, 54–62, 75–76

McCabe, David, 107–108
members of the public, 11–12, 36, 43, 59,
    69n, 72, 89, 91–98, 103, 105, 107,
    110–116, 119–123, 132, 136–149,
    156–160, 163–171, 175–176,
    182–189, 199–210, 214–217
members of the system of trust, 8, 10–11,
    49, 56–61, 68–69, 72–75, 88, 103,
    105, 120, 131–132, 139–144

models, 98–99, 120, 166, 175
moderately idealized, 11, 69, 80, 99–107,
    116–118, 136–137, 140–144, 156,
    161, 163, 166, 168–171, 174, 176,
    200–210, 213, 215, 217
modus vivendi, 43, 107–109
modus vivendi liberalism, 107
moral demands, 83–88, 96, 106–107, 135
moral ignorance, 101
moral peace, 2–8, 13, 19, 43–47, 61,
    75–87, 105, 107–109, 118, 122–123,
    137–138, 155–156, 158, 170, 172,
    198–200, 219–222
moral responsibility, 8, 10, 70, 98–100
Muldoon, Ryan, 23n, 31n, 47n, 62n,
    97n, 195n
Murphy, Mark, 134

non-ideal theory, 7, 178
norms, 8, 10, 28–35, 63–67, 128–130,
    133, 136
    formal, 129
    informal, 129–130
    moral, 34–39
    social, 8, 10, 28–35, 38–39, 59, 63–65,
        67, 70–71, 75, 82–83, 89, 113,
        128–130, 134, 136, 188–189

objects of justification, 174–175
    coarse-grained, 175–176
    fine-grained, 174–175
obligations, 27, 31, 33, 35, 37, 43, 49,
    73–74, 81, 84–85, 132, 139, 145–155
    political, 131–132, 147
open society, 3, 13, 24, 193
opportunism, 58–59, 108, 195
    first-degree, 59
ostracism, 32, 34, 85–86, 98, 108,
    130–133, 144

Pareto criterion, 110–111, 168, 187, 199
participant stance, 26–27, 29–30n,
    41n, 140
partisanship, 1
perspective, 3–6, 23, 56, 65, 83–84, 89, 92,
    100, 102, 120, 149n, 164, 206n, 217

polarization, 1–2
policy epistemology, 218
preference costs, 180–181
primary goods, 12, 159n, 163, 168, 216
principle of sustainable improvements, 168–170, 199
private capital, 203–204, 209–211
productive functions, 174, 185–187, 218–219
protective functions, 178, 185–186, 218
public choice, 12, 173, 175–183, 189, 193
contractarianism, 12, 177–180
public reason liberalism, 5–6, 42n, 77, 111, 121, 131n, 154n, 158, 180
publicity condition, 33, 81, 189
punishment, 30, 34–37, 63–66, 74, 80, 85, 95, 98–99, 114, 122, 130, 134–136, 144, 149, 188, 192–193, 197, 219

Quong, Jonathan, 22, 81n, 96, 157–158, 174n, 190n

Rawls, John, 5–8, 12, 20–22, 43, 55, 77, 81n, 85n, 94–101, 107n, 110–11, 119, 121n, 136n, 137n, 155n, 156n, 157–160, 163–169, 173, 177–179, 186, 190, 201n, 206n, 209, 211, 216, 217n
Raz, Joseph, 10, 128–132, 146, 153–155
reactive attitudes, 10, 26, 35, 63–65, 80, 85, 94, 100n, 109, 188
reasonable disagreement, 5–6, 20, 23, 71, 157, 209–211
reasonable pluralism, 5, 23, 121
reasonableness, 20n, 68, 94–96
reasons, 3–5, 9–12, 20–22, 26–31, 36–43, 55–83, 87–122, 127–128, 132, 134, 138–154, 157–158, 162, 166–167, 170–173, 178–183, 187–196, 200–206, 212–214, 217–219
diversity criterion of justificatory, 91, 97
first-personal, 78–79
intelligible, 10, 68, 80, 91–92, 97, 103, 107, 109–119, 132, 145, 148, 151, 154, 166–167, 180, 183

intelligible reasons requirement, 91, 97, 154
justificatory, 80, 88–98, 109–114, 117, 154, 194
moral criterion of justificatory, 91, 97–98
practical, 22, 79, 91, 116, 128, 153–154, 166, 188, 190
public, 5–13, 22, 43, 47–49, 61n, 74–78, 79–122, 140, 155, 173–174, 177–183, 190, 192, 198, 201
second-personal, 79
reciprocity, 33–34, 57
reflexivity requirement, 121–122
relative frequencies, 176, 180
reliance, 25–26, 64–65
rent-seeking, 193, 196–197, 219
respect, 1–4, 6, 8–11, 17–19, 21–26, 30–31, 37–41, 48–49, 57, 62–63, 66–68, 71–77, 83, 85, 102–104, 140, 143–145, 151–153, 171–172, 220
for persons, 9–11, 48, 62, 71, 74, 76–77, 118, 143–145, 220
rights, 3, 5, 12–13, 220–221
of agency, 201–206
associational, 201, 206–209, 212
claim-right to make moral demands, 84–85
claims, 135–138, 158–161, 172, 201, 204
constitutional, 3, 5, 199, 201, 220
economic, 3, 13, 213
international, 166, 201–202, 214–215
jurisdictional, 201–210
liberal, 3, 61, 111, 198–221
liberty-right to coerce, 85, 132–133
power-, 161–163, 173
primary, 12, 120, 147, 156–174, 186–187, 198–206, 210–221
procedural, 165, 187, 201, 213
property, 95, 164, 203–211
welfare, 162–163, 204–206
robustness, 193–194
rules, 4, 11–12, 33–34, 36, 81, 216
legal, 11, 127–155
moral, 10, 31–46, 81–94, 107–120, 216
social, 2–4, 6, 32–35

self-defeat objection, 120–122
self-interested agents, 173, 193–194, 221
Simmons, A. John, 45n, 131n, 146n
social capital, 8, 49–52
social choice, 110–111, 188
social error function, 187–188
social justice, 202, 216–217
social ontology pluralism, 213
social scientific models, 175
stability, 5, 12–13, 52, 107–108, 136,
     147, 173–174, 178, 188–202,
     215, 218
   first-order forms of, 194–196
   moral, 188–198
   political, 196
   second-order forms of, 194–196
state of nature, 11, 43–45, 88
   legal, 11, 132–142, 148, 158–159,
     168–170, 199–201, 205, 212
static, 134
strains of commitment, 178, 192n
Strawson, P.F., 10, 26, 34, 41n, 65
strict compliance, 7, 179

tracing, 101
trust, 2–13, 17–19, 24–31, 35–46,
     47–54, 56–78, 79–81, 83–90,
     102–103, 105–109, 118–122, 127,
     139–145, 157–161, 171–172,
     175–176, 194–201, 205–206, 216,
     219–222
   deontological value of social, 48, 75–78,
     140, 220
   incentives for, 66, 172
   justified social, 2, 4–13, 18–19, 40–46,
     56–58, 61, 72–81, 85–96, 102–122,
     127, 138–144, 195–199, 219–221

legal, 142–145
personal social, 36–39
political, 52–53, 179, 198
social, 2–13, 17–31, 35–46, 47–78, 79,
     85, 89–90, 102–109, 114–115, 118,
     127, 139–140, 157, 172, 194–195,
     197–198, 199–200, 205–206, 216,
     219–222
system of social, 6–11, 48–88, 103n,
     118, 120–121, 127, 138–144,
     157–161, 194–200, 205, 220–221
teleological value of social, 9, 48–49,
     59–61, 73–78, 140, 220
trustworthiness, 4, 9, 19, 30–31, 39–49,
     58–80, 88–89, 102–107, 117–122,
     139–143, 172, 197
   argument from, 9, 49, 66–78, 79–80,
     117–118, 132, 142–143
   social, 41–49, 66–78
trustworthy. See trustworthiness
type-1 error. See false positive
type-2 error. See false negative

unanimity standard, 177, 181, 184
uncertain, 134, 174n

variance, 136, 194–195
veil of ignorance, 98n, 165, 166
   thin veil of ignorance, 158, 160, 166,
     171, 200, 205, 218
Velleman, David, 54–55
veto power, 112–115
viewpoint prejudice, 18, 23–24

Watson, Lori and Christie Hartley, 7,
     90, 188n
Wolterstorff, Nicholas, 93n, 103–104, 106